Bob Atwood's
ALASKA

Copyright 2003
Marilaine Publishing, Inc.
2000 Atwood Drive
Anchorage, AK 99517

ISBN 0-9740036-1-1

Cover photo courtesy of the Atwood personal files.

Bob Atwood's
ALASKA

By
Bob Atwood

Acknowledgments

Many people assisted Bob Atwood in writing the story of his life in Alaska and many others assisted in the preparation of the book for publication.

With the understanding that some of these contributors are not receiving the recognition they deserve, it is nonetheless important to salute a few special individuals for the part they played in bringing this work to completion:

- John Strohmeyer, who held the Atwood Chair of Journalism at the University of Alaska Anchorage from 1987-1989, was extremely involved with Bob Atwood in the editing and research that kept the author motivated during his work on the book. Strohmeyer, former vice president and editor of the Bethlehem (Pa.) Globe-Times, won a Pulitzer Prize for editorial writing in 1972.

- Gloria McCutcheon readily made available most of the photographs that appear in this book. The photographs are from the files of her late husband, Steve McCutcheon, whose camera artistry captured the beauty of Alaska in every part of the state, and whose magic lens recorded Alaskans at work and play for more than half a century.

- U.S. Sen. Ted Stevens, a friend of the Atwood family since before statehood became a reality, was a colleague of Bob Atwood in the pursuit of a countless number of Alaska issues on the national scene. His forward to this book recalls special memories of times he shared with his old friend in happy days gone by.

- Paul Martone and Marie McConkey of AT Publishing Co., whose skill and expertise in design, editing and production blended to make this book possible.

- Robert Reeves, counsel and general manager of Elaine Atwood's business affairs, who served as the coordinator for the publication of this book.

- Ron Dalby, who was the former managing editor of Alaska magazine and is currently the managing editor of Alaska Quality Publishing.

- William J. Tobin, who worked with Bob Atwood as his right-hand man at The Anchorage Times for nearly 30 years. His forward to this book pays tribute to one he believes earned the right to be called the father of Alaska statehood.

- Ken Catalino, prize-winning Anchorage Times editorial cartoonist for many years until the newspaper ceased publication, who graciously granted permission to reprint on the back cover his depiction of Bob Atwood reaching the Pearly Gates. Catalino's work is now distributed by Creators Syndicate.

Contents

Acknowledgements		iv
Prologue	by Ted Stevens, United States Senate	vii
Forward	by William J. Tobin	ix
Chapter One	"Worthless Alaska"	1
Chapter Two	Initiation	15
Chapter Three	Frontier Life	27
Chapter Four	Era of Neglect Ends	39
Chapter Five	WWar	57
Chapter Six	Post War Turmoil	73
Chapter Seven	Air Age	83
Chapter eight	Black Gold	99
Chapter Nine	Statehood	113
Chapter Ten	White House Visit	129
Chapter Eleven	Victory at Last	139
Chapter Twelve	Earthquake	155
Chapter Thirteen	Recovery and Redication	177
Chapter Fourteen	Filthy Rich	195
Chapter Fifteen	Capital Move	215
Chapter Sixteen	Battle Heats Up	225
Chapter Seventeen	Victory Without Reward	237
Chapter Eighteen	Newspaper War	247
Chapter Nineteen	Between Us	261
Epilogue		275

vi | BOB ATWOOD'S ALASKA

Prologue

As I contemplate Bob Atwood's Alaska," my immediate reaction is to utter a silent prayer to the Almighty for Bob being in Alaska at the time he was really needed.

No one worked harder to achieve statehood for Alaska. Bob worked even harder after the 49th star was placed on our flag to assure that Alaska achieved the goals he set. His vision for Alaska was as broad and deep as the state itself. He traveled to every area of the territory searching for potential uses of its vast resources, and for people who shared his vision and were willing to join his crusade to enhance the future of our new state.

With his wife Evangeline at his side, an historian in her own right, he became a beacon of culture in Alaska's institutions of higher learning and the creation of centers for world affairs and all forms of the arts.

Congressional approval of Alaska statehood, a major milepost on the long trail toward providing full rights of citizenship for Alaskans, consumed much of Bob Atwood's time and energy. As chairman of the Alaska Statehood Committee, Bob worked with his fiend and fellow publisher Fed A. Seaton, the Secretary of the Interior, and a host of other, to convince Congress to fulfill President Dwight D. Eisenhower's request to admit Alaska into our union.

It was my privilege, as an assistant to Secretary Seaton, to be with Bob when he and Seaton met in Washington, D.C., Alaska and elsewhere innumerable times. These two outgoing, experienced newsmen, both were editors and publishers, shared a dream — a dream that they could help create a new and more vibrant United Sates by enlarging it to include two offshore areas as new states.

Seaton made but one speech as a U.S. Senator. It extolled the virtues of admitting Alaska and Hawaii to statehood. Both Bob Atwood and Seaton believed in responsible development of Alaska's resources, in protecting the great beauty of the northland, and in taking strong measures to attract new generations of Americans to Alaska.

As publisher of Alaska's largest daily newspaper, Atwood captured the voices of Alaskans in the quest for statehood. Beginning as early as 1949, he penned more that 250 editorials, urging his readers to join the fight.

"Everyone can help win Senate vote," he wrote on June 10, 1958. This editorial launched an intensive letter-writing campaign, for Atwood said, "Now is the time for Alaskans to write their friends in old hometowns urging that they write their senators and suggesting some points they might make."

"We're In" announced the Times headline on June 30, 1958, reporting the fact that Alaska's statehood bill, previously passed by the House of representatives, had passed the Senate without an amendment. This meant the Alaska bill went directly to President Eisenhower for signature.

Singularly humble about his massive contribution to the statehood cause, Bob Atwood then would work even harder to meet the goals he envisioned for Alaska. This book is the story of his decades-long commitment to assure that Alaskans would enjoy all benefits and privileges of citizenship in our nation.

He joined several friends in leasing land on Alaska's Kenai Peninsula for oil and gas exploration, assigning the leases to the Richfield Oil Company. Following successful completion of the "wildcat" well, he pursued his friend Fred Seaton to urge revocation of public land order 82, which had withdrawn Alaska's Arctic from all-non-military uses to further the conduct of World War II. That revocation enabled Alaska's Gov. Walter J. Hickel to select state lands in the Arctic where later discoveries of vast oil and gas deposits were made at Prudhoe Bay.

Bob understood Alaska's strategic location and became a friend and advisor to a long succession of Alaska-based military commanders. He ensured that men and women serving in Alaska were made welcome and part of the Alaska society. Thousands of them stayed, became Alaskans, built homes and schools and made small towns like Anchorage and Fairbanks into cities.

That was the genius of Atwood's vision: he worked with people to instill in them the passion he had for this vast North Country. He loved getting out in deep snow with his snow machine with those who love Alaska's winters.

My vision of Bob on his snow machine with my youngest sone Ben behind him, and me on my machine with our black Labrador sitting behind me, gliding across acres and acres of snow, exploring moose tracks, setting up a barbecue on his snow machine to cook hamburgers in the quiet Arctic meadow, brings back many memories of Bob Atwood, my friend and mentor.

Bob's daughter Marilyn worked with Sec. Seaton and me on statehood; her sister Elaine, totally dedicated to her dad, worked at his side; and Evangeline was the premier hostess for our new state of Alaska.

Generations change our system. Elections bring different measures designed to achieve goals we all espouse. But nothing will change the impact one man can have on our nation and a substantial portion of our population if that man is a loyal American, a patriot and an entrepreneur who cares about his fellow citizens and his employees; a family man who instills in his children his vision and his love for his profession; a man of his word who is not afraid of making enemies as he crusades to fulfill his vision.

Bob Atwood was such a man. His vision was a new America with 50 states.

It is my hope that readers of "Bob Atwood's Alaska" will learn the real meaning of being an Alaskan. One of my favorite alaska sayings is, "If you ever come to Alaska, you will never get all the way home!"

To be an Alaskan is to share a sate of mind, not a political philosophy, not a dream of gold or riches, but a true commitment to a brotherhood and sisterhood of humans who value freedom, friendship and family above anything else.

My thanks to my great friend and editor, Elaine. You have made Bob really proud by sticking with this project.

— Ted Stevens
United States Senate

Forward

The legacy that Bob Atwood left to Alaskans is one rich with accomplishments that span virtually every aspect of life in the 49th State.

Atwood was not just the editor and publisher of what was the most influential newspaper in the territory and the state for more than half a century. He was all of that, of course. But he was much more. From the day he arrived on June 15, 1935, he was a visionary who knew from the outset that Anchorage's destiny was to be a city of international stature.

As a 28-year-old newcomer to Alaska, Atwood embraced his new home with vigor and passion. Until his death on Jan. 10, 1997, his love affair with Anchorage never flagged. And the city never lacked his nourishing help as it grew from a little town on the edge of the wilderness to the great metropolitan area it is today.

It is not altogether an exaggeration to say that Alaska became a state on Jan. 3, 1959, because of Bob Atwood. There were other great Alaskans who fought the statehood battle — Ernest Gruening, Bob Bartlett, C.W. Snedden, William A. Egan, Walter J. Hickel, and Ted Stevens among them — and they deserve much credit, also. But it was Atwood who led the charge, in powerful editorials that rallied Alaskans to the cause of statehood and whose personal salesmanship gained support from countless members of Congress and from his fellow editors across the land.

As chairman of the Alaska Statehood Commission, Atwood successfully gathered Alaskans from throughout the territory to help overcome the arguments constantly raised by opponents in Washington, D.C., and throughout the country: Alaska was too distant. It was too cold. It had no economy. It could never sustain its own government. Statehood would destabilize the political makeup of the Congress. Its population was too small. On and on the anti-statehood arguments went.

But Atwood, editor and publisher of The Anchorage Times, knew otherwise.

He knew the territory was rich in natural resources and was convinced its people possessed a pioneer spirit strong enough to overcome whatever difficulties might arise.

Through Atwood's leadership, the oil industry was encouraged to invest in Alaska — and huge discoveries at Swanson River on the Kenai Peninsula in 1958 and at Prudhoe Bay on the North Slope in 1968 proved him right.

An early and enduring supporter of the military, Atwood championed Anchorage's strategic global position and was instrumental in convincing leaders of the armed services of the importance of building and maintaining major Air Force and Army installations in Alaska.

Like most Alaskans, Atwood had a love affair with aviation — and of the early bush pilots who built commercial flight operations in the territory.

Before statehood, he was the prime mover in winning approval for construction of Anchorage International Airport, and was the man behind the scenes in obtaining the necessary congressional funding to get it built. In the process, he earned for Anchorage its claim to be the Air Crossroads of the World.

Born Robert Bruce Atwood in Chicago, Ill., on March 31, 1907, the future Alaskan graduated from New Trier High School in Winnetka, Ill., and went on to Clark University in Worcester, Mass., from which he graduated in 1929.

During his last two college years, he worked as a reporter for the Worcester Telegram. After graduation, he became a reporter for the Illinois State Journal in Springfield, Ill., and it was there he met his wife-to-be, Evangeline, an Alaska-born social worker and the daughter of early territorial missionaries. Her father, E.A. Rasmuson, later became one of Alaska's most successful bankers.

They were married on April 2, 1932, and three years later Atwood had the opportunity to buy The Anchorage Daily Times, as it was called back then. It was a newspaper that traced its roots to the founding of the city in 1915.

Atwood was able to make an easy deal to buy the paper, because the primary stockholder at the time was his father-in-law, who was more interested in banking than he was in running a small-town daily newspaper.

The Times and Anchorage prospered under Atwood's dynamic leadership. But at the age of 82, after more than 50 years as a publisher, Atwood sold the paper in December 1989 and retired from active journalism. The newspaper, after its 92-year history of service, finally ceased publication on June 3, 1992.

The Times ' place in Alaska history is secure, however. As, too, is that of its long-time editor and publisher, Bob Atwood. Alaskans will remember him for many things — but statehood will be his most enduring achievement.

— William J. Tobin

Bob and Evangeline Atwood on their wedding day. April 2, 1932.

— CHAPTER ONE —

"Worthless Alaska"

"Experience is sometimes an expensive teacher and this is true of this country's expenditures in a country where the thermometer itself freezes and where darkness obtains six months each year. Americans never can be persuaded to migrate there unless supernatural power changes nature itself..."Rep. Allen T. Treadway of Massachusetts in an interview with the New York Times in 1926 on why he was opposing further appropriations for "worthless Alaska."

ॐ

My wife, Evangeline, and I, both in our 20s, arrived at Anchorage, Alaska, June 15, 1935, after a six-week sea voyage that had started in Boston. It was nine years after Rep. Treadway's denouncement of the territory as worthless. Nothing had changed, but exciting changes were on the horizon.

Most Americans thought of Alaska as a vast wasteland, somewhere in the far north, not sure where, at the very top of the continent. The common image of the territory was that is was dark six months each year, was eternally frigid, and only Eskimos knew how to survive its harsh living conditions. The land, having been stripped of its gold during the '98 stampedes, was worthless.

Anchorage was a frontier town of 2,200 people. It fit pretty well into the worthless mold, as noted by the soothsayer Treadway. It did not have a paved street. The town depended on one payroll to support it, and every building seemed of temporary construction. A rundown jailhouse housed the marshal and a tool room for the potato patch tilled in the adjacent yard by the prisoners.

There was only one street with a concrete sidewalk. Other streets, if they had more than mud paths for walkways, had wooden sidewalks. The main street was Fourth Avenue and the heart of downtown was at Fourth Avenue and E Street. The entire business district was on that one street. And the business district was predominantly Mom-and-Pop stores in one-story wood-frame buildings.

Despite the fact that it was a dusty and sometimes muddy low-grade gravel street, Fourth Avenue was the pride and joy of local residents because it was extra wide and ran east and west straight as an arrow with the beautiful Chugach Mountains visible beyond the wilderness at the east end and beyond the west end was an arm of the majestic Pacific ocean, the forever white Alaska mountain range and also the world's most beautiful sunsets. No other town in Alaska had anything to equal that.

From my perspective as a young reporter who made $35 a week at the Worcester, Mass., Telegram-Gazette, the move here was exciting. It meant a chance to run my own newspaper and be the boss. Having never run a business I didn't know whether I would make money or not.

With the whole country wallowing in the Great Depression, the Anchorage Daily Times, circulation 650, was in difficult times. A little band of businessmen started it in 1915 because they thought their town should have a newspaper. They didn't know how to run it and weren't happy with it. Quite a few advertisers supported it with little block ads, not because they thought it would spur business but just to do their share in keeping it alive. Their banker, E.A. Rasmuson, who was Evangeline's father, told them he had a son-in-law in the newspaper business and asked if they wanted to sell to him and let him run it. Rasmuson had come to Alaska as a missionary and ended up president of the bank that became Alaska's largest, the National Bank of Alaska.

"The paper in Anchorage is available, do you want it?" he wrote to us in Massachusetts, the home state of the great Congressman Treadway who thought Alaska was worthless.

I turned for advice to my geographer uncle, Wallace W. Atwood, president of Clark University in Worcester. Between 1908 and 1912 he had spent his summers in Alaska with field parties of the U.S. Geological Survey. He wrote reports on the geological structures he found in various areas, one of which was the townsite of Anchorage when it was yet untouched wilderness. He knew Alaska and knew it wasn't worthless.

My uncle talked about the terrain, climate and topography, noting that Anchorage had good access to the sea. Transportation facilities for overland travel by road or railroad and ocean-going operations would be feasible. The city was strategically located in Alaska and was surrounded by land and sea rich in resources. Like a good physiographer should, he even recalled that most of the townsite consisted of glacial moraine and would be an excellent base to build a big city on.

"If any place in Alaska is going to grow, Anchorage will," he said. "If I were 20 years younger, I'd go."

That was good enough for me.

Newspaper reporters generally have little credit at banks. But I had married a banker's daughter. It was while talking about moving to Anchorage that I discovered that a newspaper reporter who marries a banker's daughter has credit. I bought the paper for $10,000, not a dime of it my own money. I came to Alaska deeper in debt than I had ever been. Evangeline's father made sure that she was installed as majority owner, but I, at age 28, became publisher of a daily newspaper.

The day our train arrived in Anchorage was exciting for me, but it would have been even more exciting had I known what I know now. Little did I suspect that those people at the depot were going to be my friends and neighbors for the next 60 years or that we would divide up as adversaries or partners on the public issues involved in building our town into the metropolis of Alaska, and winning full-fledged membership in the United States of America for our neglected corner of the world.

Mr. Rasmuson introduced Evangeline and me, the son-in-law, to a dozen or more of his friends while our luggage was being found and loaded into George Mumford's car.

Unlike other newly arrived cheechakos, I had friends taking care of me now that I was in a strange, distant land. And I didn't have to worry about making a niche for myself to earn a living in my new locale. I was guaranteed a niche because I was buying the local newspaper and was to be the owner, manager, editor or whatever other title I chose.

While most other arriving passengers went to a restaurant for lunch, Evangeline and I, with her father, were taken on a quick sortie the length of Fourth Avenue. It was an overview of the one-street business district. Sightseeing ended at the First Presbyterian Church manse where Rev. and Mrs. E.L. Winterberger had lunch ready for us. And there it was that we learned our new hometown had one movie house, one radio station, four churches (Presbyterian, Episcopalian, Christian Science and Catholic), one elementary and one high school. There were a few pool halls. The Elks had a bowling alley. The Finnish Club had a sauna. And not much else in way of community facilities.

After lunch we settled down in an apartment in the Anchorage Hotel. Mr. Rasmuson was generous with his time, introducing me to key people in the business community and in every introduction it was noted as part of my identification that I was "Evangeline's husband."

Train day and the excitement that came with it usually meant a quiet evening in Anchorage. But then, all evenings were quiet unless the Elks Club held a Purple Bubble Ball that everyone turned out for. Anchorage was such a tiny town that it had no fine restaurants or nightclubs. Eating places were mostly lunch counters with the fry cook before you. There were frequently some booths along one wall for sit-down groups. The tables had oil cloth covers and the seats were plain wood.

Consequently, entertaining was always in the home. The local ladies responded to the needs of the day magnificently by developing a technique for serving extraordinarily delicious dinners to their guests at card tables in the tiny rooms of the frame houses of those early days. The common entertainment after dinner in the home was playing bridge.

We had saved enough to get to Alaska but when we arrived we found the town had only two houses available for sale. We paid $1,700 for a cottage that had been built by the Alaska Engineering Commission in 1915.

Our new neighbors said we were lucky because it was one of the few in town with an Iron Fireman, the highest tech of the time. That was a device that fed the coal into the furnace. But I had to pull out the clinkers and the ashes and haul them away.

I had arrived 15 days before the annual meeting of the newspaper's directors, at which the stock transfers would be recorded and I would be elected editor, manager and president. I spent those 15 days working as a printer in the newspaper shop. I had learned the printer's craft while managing the college press at Clark University.

The Times had five employees—three printers, a bookkeeper and one editorial person. The shop, located at the ground floor of the Independent Order of Odd Fellows lodge building on Fourth Avenue, seemed adequate to handle a weekly but hardly a daily newspaper. Having worked on progressive papers in Worcester and Springfield, Ill., I found the editorial operation a mess by comparison.

Charlie Settlemeier, the editor and business manager, had come to town from gold camps in interior Alaska and Canada. He probably qualified as a "tramp editor" since he just drifted into town. His type roamed the country working for a while at one paper and moving on when the travel itch recurred. Such journeymen lived by their wits but rarely stayed in one place long enough to worry about standards.

Charlie simply filled the paper with wire stories. In those days we relied on the Army Signal Corps to transmit in Morse code the Associated Press reports, which provided the bulk of the paper's news. The AP stories came in from Seattle in a language we called telegraphese—no articles, no prepositions, and lots of abbreviations. Words cost a penny and a half apiece. Charlie would pencil in missing words and send the stuff out to be set by the printers. I noticed that sometimes the printers couldn't read his handwriting. So they would doctor the copy and set their own version in type.

The Times always consisted of eight pages, but the printers didn't know what page anything went on. The last thing before leaving for the day, Charlie would write four banner headlines to be stacked at the top of the front page, but he wouldn't designate the type. So the printers picked out what they thought looked and fit best. Then they would hunt for the stories that were supposed to go with the banners. Sometimes they never found them, and a story would end up inside while the headline for it screamed alone on page one.

Settlemeier, knowing it would be only a matter of time before I took over, stayed around for a few months and then disappeared. Someone said he headed for a mining town in Canada. Shortly after, early 1936, I put my name in the masthead as editor and publisher.

I introduced the staff to page layouts which I learned early in my career. Then I taught the printers how to match headlines with copy by assigning each the same catchline or slug. I rewrote all those AP cryptic stories in newspaper style and added background from my file of the New York Times. The New York paper came in the mail three weeks late, but even the old copies were a great resource for backgrounding stories. I reduced the four banners to one streamer a day on top of page one, and specified the type size.

Then I did something about local news. I covered city council and school board meetings in the evening. I wrote an editorial every night before going to bed, and always kept my eyes and ears open to pick up personal items about people. We printed hotel registrations, hospital lists, births, deaths and marriages. I reversed the old practice of putting only national news on page one. When we had a good local story, we led the paper with it.

I carried this to such an extreme that one day we had a big black banner line story saying the school board had fired the janitor. It was big news because he had been janitor for so many years that he had what we call today "seniority." The story was the subject of conversation all day and by nightfall townspeople had another job for him. He had a large family to support.

People began to read about events that they had only heard rumors about before—bush pilot crashes, ice jams that threatened the power supply at Eklutna dam, and perils encountered by the steamers serving Alaska from Seattle. Formerly, the townspeople were told only that the arrival of the SS Northwestern would be delayed. Now we informed them the ship had to wait for high tide to back off a sand bar near Ketchikan or had lost time undergoing emergency repairs because of the battering it took from a storm on the way to Kodiak.

I was fascinated by bush pilots. They were the intrepid young men who flew their one-engine planes over the roadless wilderness to interior villages, which were scattered like islands over a sea of tundra. When they came home I found them a source for the latest news. I met them at the airport like the reporters of yore stood on the New York docks when Atlantic liners arrived, to interview passengers for the latest news from Europe.

Those pilots were pioneering airways in the sky which would be useful to the U.S. Air Force when World War II came, and subsequently would become an important part of the global network of today's intercontinental routes over the pole and between continents.

Soon after taking charge, I found that my newspaper was operating under false colors in that it had claimed, the previous October 1, that the circulation was 812. We were printing only 650. My corporate directors told me we didn't dare go below 800 because we would lose what little national advertising we had, and we couldn't get more subscribers because "everybody is getting the paper now."

Fortunately, by October first our circulation was well over 800. The only major change I had made was to emphasize local news by printing more of it and displaying it prominently.

Continued growth started to strain our flat bed press, which had to be fed by hand, sheet by sheet. Adding people to the staff was a problem. Every time I needed talent, I imported people from Outside. We were too poor to pay travel expenses to interview candidates 3,000 miles away. The guys who answered my ads had to use their own money to get here and take a job. It is surprising how many good people came up that way.

Having trained the staff, I found I also had to train the big wheels in town how to deal with a newspaper. Public officials in early Anchorage were not used to having their activities reported nor did they feel obliged to answer questions.

The police chief was a nice fellow named Walter Brewington, but he tried to dissuade us from printing police news. One day, I found out that the chief had arrested a guy and put him in jail, so I wrote the story about it. That night at dinner time, when my wife and I were having guests, the chief appeared at the door. I went out to the front porch and saw he had brought his prisoner with him.

"This man is mad at me because of what you put in the paper," the police chief said. "He is my first enemy in town and it's your fault."

The chief told me off in a loud voice, much to the amusement of my guests. It took a while, but I finally got the chief to accept the fact that an arrest was news. When I came back into the house I got advice from everyone. They knew the chief. They knew the prisoner. And they all, including the police chief, thought themselves better newspaper editors than the editor was.

It was harder to shake the Chamber of Commerce from its frontier mentality. The chamber was run by three oldtimers, Tom C. Price, the town magistrate; Robert S. Bragaw, secretary of the Anchorage Power and Light Co.; and Winfield Ervin Sr., cashier at the First National Bank.

A chamber meeting consisted of a luncheon for three around the oil-cloth napery of the Anchorage Grill, one of the few decent restaurants in town. I surprised them soon after I arrived by showing up with a pad and pencil.

"What are you doing here? " one asked.

"I came to cover the news," I replied.

It never occurred to them that what the chamber did could be news-worthy or that publicity might even be helpful to them. After a few encounters, I realized why. Those three—among the town's most influential power brokers—did not want to disturb the status quo.

Reading the mail was usually the most exciting item on the chamber agenda. When an undertaker in Arkansas inquired as to the need of a new mortuary in town, the chamber leaders would refer the letter to their good member and friend, "Doc" Loudermilch, the local mortician, for reply. Business inquiries were always handled this way because the local person in the trade was considered the best authority on it.

Of course, the system didn't promote new businesses. The local mortician replied to his fellow mortician in Arkansas that the population here was so tiny that the market wasn't very big, and there were already two mortuaries here. Then he probably took him into his confidence and told him that Alaskans who have money always go to Seattle hoping to get the very best medical treatment for their loved one's terminal illness. Consequently, rich Alaskans die in Seattle and only the indigents die at home in Alaska.

As I became acquainted with the business people who were my advertisers, I learned that they weren't really opposed to newcomers. They were opposed only to those who wanted to compete with them.

Our entire existence seemed to depend on the Alaska Railroad, the only major payroll in town. The federal government started to build the railroad in 1915 when Congress was motivated by growing tensions in the wake of World War I in Europe. The rationale was that if the United States became involved, the nation would need a strong Navy in the Pacific as well as in the Atlantic Ocean. The stated purpose in the Congressional Act emphasized encouragement of economic development. But it was also argued that the railroad would open up the Matanuska Valley coal fields to production, and the coal could be shipped from Seward to Dutch Harbor which was then the only coaling station in the North Pacific. The Alaska coal would relieve the Navy of the burden of supplying the Dutch Harbor facility with coal mined as far away as Pittsburgh, Penn.

Anchorage was born when the federal agency in charge of railroad construction, the Alaska Engineering Commission, built a temporary construction camp, actually a tent city, on the mud flats at the mouth of Ship Creek. When the railroad decided to make the site its permanent headquarters and maintenance depot, the former tent city became the city of Anchorage.

It took eight years to lay the 470 miles of track linking the ice-free port of Seward in the south to Fairbanks, the largest interior city, in the north. Much of the railroad building equipment was sent here from Panama where it was used to build the Panama Canal. But by the time President Harding drove the golden spike in 1923, marking the railroad's completion, World War I was over, the Navy had converted to oil for fuel and no longer needed the Matanuska coal. Congress lost its enthusiasm for the railroad, but reluctantly appropriated funds each year to cover its operating deficit. The railroad had become embedded enough in the economies of the local communities that shutting it down would cause major dislocations.

During its first 30 years, the railroad had to make do with the remnants of the Panama Canal project—worn-out locomotives and obsolete wooden passenger and freight cars. The track was mostly laid on the ground, light rails and no ballast. It all made for rough riding. Each spring frost heaves sometimes bulged the track upward so much that freight trains became uncoupled while en route.

In Anchorage there was one train northbound each week. It brought the passengers and mail from the weekly steamship that came from Seattle. It took two and sometimes three days for the train to reach Fairbanks, where it would turn around and come south through Anchorage to Seward in time to meet the next week's steamer.

Everybody went to the depot to meet the northbound train. It was often the most exciting event of the week to see who arrived and hear the news about what some of us called the "outer world." After stopping long enough for lunch, the train continued on to Fairbanks but the excitement continued in Anchorage. Sometime during the afternoon, postal employees would process the newly arrived mail. There was no home delivery service. Many of those who met the train gathered again and visited at the post office while waiting for the mail to be sorted and deposited in their mailboxes. As an editor I kept pretty good track of what people were thinking about by listening in on the depot and post office gatherings.

Since 1915, the railroad had provided the only major payroll supporting the town. And I soon sensed that the retailers were hesitant to take on the railroad except on the most serious issues. Otto F. Ohlson, a retired Army colonel, ran the railroad like a dictator and the communities were so dependent on the line and its services that it was hard to find a spokesman in opposition to it.

An example was the battle between the formidable Colonel Ohlson and Capt. Heinie Berger. Berger, a stocky little hustler, ran a small gasboat commuter service serving the tiny mining and fishing towns along the shores of Cook Inlet. He had won $100,000 in the Nenana Ice Pool lottery by guessing the precise day, hour and minute of the spring break up on the Tanana River at Nenana. With the winnings he bought a boat big enough to haul a couple of hundred tons of freight to Alaska from Seattle.

Berger found that the city of Anchorage owned a tiny piece of waterfront rights that weren't developed and got the city's permission to build a rinky-dink dock for his new boat. He then offered freight service for Anchorage merchants and became a competitor to the railroad. This galled Ohlson no end. So he parked a string of freight cars in the railroad yard, creating a formidable blockade to Berger's little gravel road, his access route from the tide flat to the city.

Many local residents got wind of the confrontation that would happen when Heinie's boat, "The Discoverer," docked. Eyes peeked out of windows of the railroad offices. More eyes watched from above the bluff, in apartments and offices. The event even attracted spectators on the ground.

They waited for high drama. They got it when Capt. Berger walked up from the dock and found his access closed. He had no way to go around the end of the train. Berger left briefly to make a telephone call or two and returned to his boat. He reappeared with a sack of U.S. mail in each arm. He walked up to the train and stood there in full view of the railroad headquarters establishment while his attorney called Ohlson on the phone and suggested that he look out his window and see how he is blocking the U.S. mail, a federal offense. Reports were that Ohlson called out a locomotive crew to pull those freight cars away, and Berger delivered all his freight as well as the mail,

But victory was short-lived. Ohlson took him to court on a charge that he trespassed on government property. The court fined Berger. The all-powerful railroad prevailed once more.

The town's almost total dependency on the railroad troubled me. Virtually all wage earners in town either worked for the railroad or were engaged in service industries that supplied and supported the railroad operations. It quickly became obvious to me that this city's future growth depended upon innovations and finding new areas of service. To some, this idea meant more mining ventures. Others focussed on more tourists. My editorials favored a special welcome for all newcomers who might diversify our economy and introduce new ideas.

The prevailing attitude among Alaskans in most towns was anti-newcomers. The people often said, "We don't give a damn how they do it Outside," and "We don't want Cheechakos (newly arrived residents) telling us what to do with our country." New residents generally didn't rate high on the scale of desirability and visiting federal officials were just about at the bottom of the scale.

I argued editorially that newcomers should be given a warm welcome and that federal agencies and their bureaucrats should be sought after and enticed to locate here. I urged that Alaskans view congressmen on junkets favorably. Even though most came to fish or sightsee, they nevertheless returned to Washington with a greater understanding of the territory's problems. My editorials said that Alaska had failed to attract venture capital for new enterprises largely because the federal government owned 99.9 percent of all the land and the resources and ruled it by edicts handed down by the Secretary of the Interior. Alaska offered none of the protections that capitalists find in traditional state governments.

My theme for many years was that the federal government has obligations and responsibilities that went with ownership and that the U.S. treasury should support the projects needed to open it up to private developments. I had a handy list of the growing number of areas where the feds failed to meet these responsibilities.

I was encouraged by the support of the younger people. Under the informal banner of the Booster Club, we young rebels would gather Tuesday nights in the backroom of the Anchorage Grill to discuss ways to get Anchorage moving off total dependency of the railroad. While we had our share of impatient young adventurers who came to Alaska to get rich quick and get out, the core of this group was composed of the kith and kin of pioneer businessmen.

Besides me, the son-in-law of the main banker, our group included Vic Gill, son of the mayor; Vern Johnson, a handsome young butcher and civic volunteer who "invented" the festive community party known as Fur Rendezvous to stimulate activity in the dead of winter; Wells Ervin, son of the cashier of First National Bank; J. Vic Brown, son of the city's most prominent jewelry store owner; and many others.

We saw the opportunities for commercial ski resorts in the mountains around us. We deplored the package tours sold by the railroad that allowed well-heeled tourists only one-hour stays in Anchorage. We saw opportunities for entrepreneurs to make a business of operating tours to glaciers and other points of interest. Our bush pilots could offer flight-seeing trips into the wilderness, with stops at streams where the fishing is so good you can't lie about it. By the end of the evening, some of us fortified by a bottle passed down the line, we would reach a roaring consensus. We needed more people, more hotels and more things to do.

After one year's operation, my newspaper ledger reflected further reason why Anchorage ought to look beyond the railroad for prosperity. While circulation had grown, advertising was static. Not only were there no new businesses to advertise but the railroad canceled what little lineage it ran after I refused to stop reporting its too frequent rail irregularities, including late train arrivals and derailments.

The paper made a profit of $1,800 in that first year. But Franklin Delano Roosevelt had just enacted social security. The one-year's profit would have been just enough to cover our social security tax had it been in effect. I figured from then on until something changed there would be no profit at all.

Shortly after arriving in Anchorage, Evangeline and I set a five-year time limit for our Alaska adventure. The tiny profit from the first year of work, and the bleak prospect of improving it were discouraging but we were determined not to shorten our stay. We were having too much fun to worry about the perils of publishing on America's last frontier.

A stinson Trimotor on Anchorage 9th Avenue Park Strip. Early 1930's dark house in back was the home of former Iditarod mail carrier Oscar Gill. Photo by Steve McClutcheon/Alaska Pictorial Service

A pilot lands at Kotzebue Alaska with meat for the village John Cross Pilot and Territorial Legislator with rifle on shoulder. Photo by Steve McClutcheon/Alaska Pictorial Service

Mr. and Mrs. Robert Atwood on their way to Anchorage where Mr. Atwood will be the editor of the Anchorage Times. Photo by Steve McClutcheon/Alaska Pictorial Service/May, 1935

Bob Atwood with daughter Marilyn in Anchorage 1938.

12 | CHAPTER ONE

The Anchorage Times at the time Bob Atwood bought it in 1935.

Haakon Christiansons Waco at Lake Spenard about 1937. Photo by Steve McClutcheon/Alaska Pictorial Service

"WORTHLESS ALASKA" | 13

14 | CHAPTER ONE

— CHAPTER TWO —

Initiation

My initiation into the great fraternity known as Alaska in 1935 was always exciting, sometimes puzzling or even frustrating, but never dull.

I'll never forget the hazing I got in the form of a chilly stare from Charlie Settlemeier during a conversation in the office. He mentioned placer mining and I asked, "What's that?" He gave me the stare—a quiet, cold stare much longer than necessary to deliver the message—before he undertook a patient, elementary explanation that he who kneels down beside a stream to pan for gold is placer mining, and he who builds a mill to crush rocks and then separates the gold from the rocks is hard rock mining.

Mining was a major industry in Alaska and it was obvious that Charlie questioned whether any cheechako who didn't know the difference between those two kinds of mining had any future at all.

After that experience I tried to learn without asking questions. When I went to Denali National Park, Alaska's famed wildlife viewing preserve 250 miles northwest of Anchorage, I met the park officials. It was early spring and the rangers were digging a ditch. I heard one of them mention the ditch should be just 10 inches deep. I asked what's the ditch for and they said a water line.

Now, that left me with a big puzzlement but I didn't ask why 10 inches deep. I grew up in the suburbs of Chicago where it's so cold in the winter water pipes are buried 10 to 12 feet deep so they won't freeze in the winter. Those rangers may not have known it, but they left me dangling in midair when they said they were putting a water pipe 10 inches deep.

When I got back to Anchorage I asked a friend why they would put a pipe 10 inches deep and he said, "so it won't freeze in the summer." And he left me to figure that one out. The park is in permafrost country and the ground thaws only a bit below the surface in the summer. If the pipe were any deeper it would be in ground that never thaws and the water would never flow.

My relations with Colonel Ohlson, the stern Swede who ran the Alaska Railroad, kept going downhill even after my rocky first year as editor of the Anchorage Daily Times. Socially we had correct relationships and all went well. But when his management policies for the railroad rubbed against the grain of the community interests, sparks flew. There

INITIATION | 15

were heated exchanges between the newspaper and the railroad, which could and usually were interpreted as between Atwood and Ohlson.

When Ohlson found out I was shipping in some newsprint from Seattle on Heinie Berger's boat, which was cheaper, he canceled all business, including the railroad's printing orders, with the Times.

This offended some of my friends who worked for the railroad. So they started calling the paper to tell me all the odd ball things that happened during the day on the rails. A piston fell off an engine, a car was derailed, or careless switching caused hair-raising moments and delayed the trains. I spread these little stories throughout the paper. Ohlson became particularly incensed one day at a story that simply said, "Thursday's train arrived right on time, a day late."

These run-ins with Ohlson caused considerable distress to my father-in-law, E. A. Rasmuson. He had bankrolled my purchase of the paper but the health of the Rasmuson bank depended on maintaining good relations with this vindictive man who managed the railroad. Ohlson had the biggest payroll in town and controlled most of the money that flowed to our little group of Anchorage businessmen. My father-in-law pleaded for understanding. I argued Ohlson stood in the way of progress, and I knew future confrontations would be inevitable if things in town were going to change.

Though he had the reputation of a hard-swearing dictator, Ohlson was not an evil person. It was simply that he placed service to the federal government above service to the territory. About 10 years back when the railroad's steady losses led some in Congress to talk about tearing up the track, Ohlson was brought in to run the railroad with instructions to stop the deficits. He did so by the late 1930s. But at what a price.

He got Congress to raise freight rates 50 percent and passenger fares to six cents a mile, about three times the going rate in the Lower 48. Then freight rates steadily crept up further without even the fairness of a hearing. Government-owned, the railroad needed no permission from the Interstate Commerce Commission or any other body except a willing Congress to hike rates.

By the time I arrived, Alaskans were paying more than five times as much as northwest states to haul basic foods by rail. And this was the chief means to get provisions to us. The railroad and the Alaska Steamship Co. had joint tariffs on railbelt cargo, and the freight charges were a major cause for the high retail prices in Alaska stores. Most of us felt we were being gouged.

When Congress enacted the bill creating the railroad, it said its purpose was to help the economic development of interior Alaska. Alaskans used that statement as supporting their contentions that the freight rates were so high they were defeating that purpose. Ohlson responded by saying Alaska is now developed and should pay its own way, which created a howl of protests from all Alaskans.

The squeeze had inspired several small trucking firms to start hauling food to Fairbanks, the most distant stop on the railroad. They would go up the Richardson highway after meeting vessels diverted to Valdez, an ice-free port northeast of Seward. Ohlson countered this threat to his railroad profits by persuading the Interior Department to turn the Richardson into a toll road, forcing the truckers to pay nine dollars a ton at a ferry crossing on the highway.

For a time, an Alaska rebellion ensued, culminating in a takeover of the tollbooth. The truckers locked the fare collector in the tollhouse and ran boats across the water themselves. Several arrests were made but Alaska juries refused to indict anyone. However, the courts deemed the tolls legal and the railroad won its way again.

The effect of this profit-hungry rail monopoly on anyone trying to develop new business came to my attention early in the case of a little carpenter guy who tried to start a modest burial casket industry. He figured he could build one casket a day and over a period of a year he would be able to supply the needs of the towns along the railbelt. However, when he got the freight rates, he found it cheaper to ship a casket by ship from Seattle—about 1,500 miles—than by shipping it by rail from Anchorage to Seward—a distance of 107 miles.

This battle between the railroad and the Times continued for several months. At one point, the business community decided to send a delegation to discuss its problems with Ohlson. They asked the chamber of commerce to take the initiative to approach the formidable railroad boss. The chamber asked me to serve on the delegation. I told them I was the wrong man for this job because the colonel didn't want to do anything to help me. They thought it would do some good if I just sat in the back row looking as though I was reporting the meeting for the paper, which I would have done anyway.

It worked out pretty well, in fact, better than anyone could have expected. The colonel promised to look into the chamber's complaints and the meeting ended on a pleasant note. When we stood up to head for the door, Ohlson called to me, "Bob, could you stay for a moment? I want to talk to you."

When the committee had gone, the colonel turned to me and said, "Bob, you and I ought to find a way to get along all right." I agreed.

"How much do you think we should cut the freight rate?" he asked. I was ready with that answer and said 40 cents a hundred pounds. I had the rationale to support it. He listened, positively for a change. After some discussion he said he would see if he could get the steamship line to cut it 20 cents and if they would he would cut the rail rate the other 20 cents.

A few weeks went by before the colonel telephoned the bad news that the steamship line refused to go for the 20 cents and "all I could get them to cut was 10 cents." He bad-mouthed those steamship guys just as severely as the rest of us did when we had problems. He wound up asking if I would settle for a 20-cent reduction. With him yakking away, blasting the steamship line, the thought went through my mind that I ought to get 20 cents off the railroad even if I got only a dime from the ship line, but it would prolong the debate. So I settled and got half what I wanted, which was more than I usually got when I dealt with Colonel Ohlson.

Despite our opposite goals, the fact was that Ohlson and I needed one another. This was borne out in subsequent months after a great human experiment started by the New Deal administration in Washington had been thrust upon Alaska.

In 1935, President Roosevelt created an agency called the Resettlement Administration to wage his war on poverty by relocating those people most ravaged by the depression. Principal beneficiaries were the midwestern farmers who could no longer afford to farm their land. Prairies had been overgrazed, the trees which once held moisture in the earth had been cut and not replaced, and in many sections of the country the land was exhausted from over-cultivation. Meanwhile, the depression drove down prices of agricultural products, making it impossible for many to hold on to their farms.

Alaska was picked as one of 33 sites for the resettlement colonies, but none received greater attention. A national outcry broke out with the news that 202 families, most of them Minnesota farmers forced to live on welfare, would be shipped to develop a farming colony in the Matanuska Valley, just outside of Anchorage.

The public perception was that no crops could grow in Alaska. Cyrenus Cole, a former Republican congressman from Iowa, begged Agriculture Secretary Henry Wallace to halt "this New Deal folly," and suggested that he and his dreamers be compelled to go along and hibernate with the farmers they were sending to Alaska.

That kind of idiotic criticism could be expected from those who held imbedded false impressions of Alaska. But I was dismayed by the reactions of our own people. The Alaska Territorial Chamber of Commerce passed a resolution criticizing the idea on the grounds that Alaska might find itself with large numbers of indigents on its hands to clothe and feed. And fearful of having to appropriate money for schools for the incoming children, the territorial legislature adopted a similar negative view. It sent two memorials, which is how they termed their resolutions, to Secretary of the Interior Harold Ickes and Alaska's Delegate to Congress Anthony J. Dimond warning them not to send the settlers unless ample funds were provided to care for them and for return passage if the plan failed.

This negative thinking was appalling to the large body of Alaskans who wanted to make something of the territory. It also took us by surprise. The most cynicism came from the Panhandle, that strip of Alaska which hugs the coast of Canada down in the Southeast, a thousand miles away. This includes Juneau, the capital and at that time the territory's biggest city

Opposition from the territorial chamber in Juneau and the territorial legislature were much more significant than I realized at the time. They were a symptom of an ailment that would confront us in Anchorage for many years to come—sectionalism. The chamber purported to speak for all the Alaska chambers in all the cities and consequently the whole Alaska business community. But the resolutions emanating out of the Juneau office expressed the view of only a handful of men who talked mostly to themselves and rarely had contact with businessmen beyond the Panhandle.

Sectional interests have always been a basic problem in establishing a consensus among the people of Alaska. The state is so vast and so diverse that each area has its own economy and point of view.

In the Panhandle, the concern is fishing, timber and mining. The cities are on the narrow shoreline at the foot of a mile-high mountain range and the Pacific ocean. Roads are costly to build. Harbors and waterways are most important. Elsewhere, Alaska needs thousands of miles of roads for access to its interior land and resources. Consequently, sectional interests often dominate politics.

By opposing the colony project, those Juneau people were reflecting the wishes of their own sectional interests which usually conformed with the big money in the salmon industry. The salmon packers wanted no development in Alaska because it would require taxes, and the fisheries were the only taxable asset in the territory.

Ten years later, I found myself in a great public battle against those mighty powers in Seattle. As chairman of the Alaska Statehood Committee, the territory's official agency to win statehood for Alaska, I got to know their power all too well. The salmon packers were the only strong, organized, well-connected opponent willing and able to spend millions to fight our bid for statehood.

Adding to the discord, many Outside writers mocked the program, depicting Alaska as a controversial choice, some sort of a glory hole useless to mankind. Their stories made it appear that physical conditions were insurmountable, federal rules and regulations were indomitable. Alaska was at least 5,000 miles beyond the periphery of the interest of mankind or, perhaps, even God.

I jumped into the fracas on the issue of welcoming new people to Alaska. "Is the territory going to establish a precedent against expanding its school services to additional population?" I asked editorially. "Where would other states be if they called a halt on schools after they had received their first pioneer settlers."

I argued that the Matanuska project might well prove to be the most economically constructive idea that Washington ever had for Alaska, which up to now had been continuously exploited by the salmon and

INITIATION | 19

mining interests who didn't live here, namely the J. P. Morgan banking house and the Guggenheim brothers, who controlled the companies that owned the copper mines and 12 of the largest salmon canneries in Alaska.

And it was true. For the first time the federal government was recognizing that Alaska was livable the year around. This vast land of 365,000,000 acres had a population of only 60,000 people and half of those were Natives whose culture bound them to a life of hunting, fishing and gathering. After years of neglect, the government was now subsidizing people with agricultural skills and mechanical know-how to move up and develop Alaska's greater potentials. We were finally attracting the kind of persons who might stay here and make the state self-sustaining.

My support of the newcomers would have been an extremely lonely fight had it not been for an important ally. This appeared in the person of Colonel Ohlson. He had urged his superiors in Washington all along to include Alaska in the resettlement program and then was appointed to run it as chairman of the Alaska Rehabilitation Agency. The thought of saving fellow Swedes starving on farms in Minnesota must have melted this tough tyrant's heart. And, of course, the prospect of added business for the railroad didn't hurt either.

Each new family was allotted 40 acres and a promise of a house and barn before snowfall. However, they arrived May 10, 1935, before the surveyors had marked out their land, so the families lived in a community of white canvas tents near what became downtown Palmer. But even as Alaska's new settlers cleared fields out of the birch and spruce forests and government work crews engaged in a crash program to build their permanent shelters, the collective gave the Anchorage area an unexpected new distinction. It became a tourist attraction.

The Alaska Railroad, for once, showed some social responsibility and sponsored a special train for Anchorage people to make a round-trip excursion to Palmer in one day. The train consisted of a steam locomotive pulling flat cars loaded with automobiles while passenger coaches made up the rear. Many friendships were made as we shared experiences during these visits. The interaction kindled a spirit of community and gave us a louder voice in pleading with our federal landlords to build roads that would link our communities, expand airports to lessen dependence on the railroad, and provide recreation facilities that would give our regional development a feeling of permanence.

Meanwhile, for the VIPs coming in from the states to see the colony, the colonel became a most engaging host. He met them at the ship in Seward and spared them the jarring coach ride to Anchorage by putting them aboard his personal speeder, a DeSoto car body on railroad wheels, which better absorbed the shocks on the eternally heaving track beds.

Will Rogers and Wiley Post, the famed humorist and pilot, flew in that first summer in 1935. None of us will ever forget the visit. "Matanuska is a mighty pretty country. She looks good to me. It looks like the colonists will make good," our paper quoted Rogers as telling the crowd. Then the humorist added: "Alaska will be alright if she don't let the United States take over."

Rogers promised to return in the winter to "den up with the sourdoughs and hear their yarns." However, that would be the last speech he made in public. Two days later, on Aug. 16, 1935, we carried the tragic story that Will Rogers and Wiley Post crashed to their deaths in a fog bank just short of their destination of Point Barrow on the northern tip of Alaska.

A steady stream of visitors—congressmen, journalists, and curiosity seekers—kept a constant spotlight on those farmers trying to carve a life in Alaska. Most visitors came with open minds, but some came to reinforce their preconceived notions. Typical of these was Sen. Elmer Thomas of Oklahoma. He became an authority on the project after spending 15 minutes on the railroad depot platform in Palmer. On his return, he declared the Matanuska experiment as completely devoid of any benefit except to show "once and for all that Alaska is unsuitable for large scale colonization."

I did my best to counter these critics editorially, but it was not easy. Early dissension among the colonists themselves gave opponents ammunition. As a newspaper, we had a duty to report the frictions, but we also tried to show the underlying causes of the trouble. I concluded the program was not flawed, but the administrators back in the states seemed to have tried their best to sabotage the experiment. Along with deserving families, the caseworkers mixed in people with lots of problems and unloaded their screwballs on Alaska.

It was not surprising that a good number of deadbeats among the colonists ran up debts with the cooperative that they never intended to repay. Others welched on their contract to clear the land for farming and lit out to Anchorage to look for jobs. Some came up never intending to stay, knowing that they had free passage back within a year. It turned out that only about 10 percent of the original contingent had been actually earning their livelihood on farms.

The rocky start for the colonization project provided much fuel for its critics. Although the settlers were next door to Anchorage, they were actually isolated. No road would connect them to the city for a year. They had no telephone service. The railroad was the colony's only link to civilization. It provided the only means of transportation, and anyone needing to send an emergency message depended on the good graces of the railroad to relay it via the private telephone line that linked the section houses between Seward and Fairbanks.

The hit-and-run coverage by the national newspapers did not help the image of Alaska's farming pioneers. Outside reporters came up for a brief stay, made much of the start-up problems, and left. No one really stationed a reporter in Alaska for longer than a few days, with two excep-

INITIATION | 21

tions. The Milwaukee Journal kept its correspondent, Arville Schlaben, here throughout the first year. He wrote about it as it should have been told, both the bad and the good. The other exception was Chase S. Osborn, former governor of Michigan,who came here on his own and covered it thoroughly in his own way, for a Sault Ste. Marie newspaper that he owned. He stayed with the story for most of a year.

Alaska newspapers depended upon the Associated Press reports, as did most Outside newspapers. The AP usually carried brief summaries of whatever the Anchorage paper published.

Our little staff did its best to present the truth about the colony's successes and failures. I spent a major part of my time with the colonists in their tents and in their barns, when they got barns, and in their homes, when they got homes. The Times published at the end of the first six months a review that summarized the many achievements.

Meanwhile, outside newspapers and radios always seemed to interview the farmers who opted to quit the project and take advantage of the government's offer of a free trip home. The quitters sailed out aboard the Alaska Lines' weekly boat. They knew reporters would meet them at Seattle and ask them why they quit, so they cooked up credible stories during the six-day boat trip making themselves look like heroes and the project in Alaska a bust.

The news services then would receive inquiries from the hometowns, asking, "Our man is coming home, why did he quit?" So the stories went far and wide into the fabric of the nation and, generally, made Alaska look almost hopeless. The other side was rarely mentioned. Or so it seemed us in Alaska.

A purge in the summer of 1936 rectified much of the trouble. The 40 replacement families sent here were chosen with considerably more care, thanks to the help of Congressman Marion Zioncheck of Washington. As a frequent visitor, he shared our concern and persuaded the Works Progress Administration to oversee the selection process.

The fact is that the project did succeed. Agriculture was a limited success, for lack of adequate markets, for one thing. The project didn't result in a socialistic valley with each farm family subsisting on 40-acres, as the New Deal planners had wanted. Its greatest success was in opening a wilderness valley and giving welfare families an opportunity to live in dignity and rear their children to be leaders in Alaska's professions, politics and industry.

By 1939, the colonists were on there own and thriving. Besides sending the first home-grown produce to Anchorage markets, they added a new cultural element to our lives. They became stable citizens as opposed to the many who came to Alaska to tap its resources and run. In time, their descendants would add professional and political dimensions, the impact of which is felt in Alaska to this day.

CHAPTER TWO

Col. Otto Ohlson (right) manager of Alaska Railroad. Photo courtesy of the Anchorage Museum of History and Art

Alaska Railroad crossing trestle. Government Hill in the background.
Photo courtesy of the Anchorage Museum of History and Art

F.C. Hansen, Engineer for the Alaska Railroad; Jim Farley. Postmaster General, U.S. Mail; and Bob Atwood (right) on 4th Avenue in front of the Post Office. 1934.
Photo courtesy of the Anchorage Museum of History and Art

Will Rogers, Leonard Seppala, Wiley Post, Joe Crosson. Last photo taken before crash. Taken at Fairbanks, Chenal River. 1935. Photo courtesy of the Anchorage Museum of History and Art

INITIATION | 25

26 | CHAPTER TWO

— CHAPTER THREE —

Frontier Life

My inevitable showdown with Colonel Ohlson occurred late in 1936, midway through my second year in Alaska. He had me in his office ostensibly to tell me he was about to leave for Washington, D.C., to testify before Congress for the next year's railroad budget. He usually spent a couple of months each winter for that purpose. Then, quite casually, he said it is likely that there will be a maritime interruption when longshoremen in Seattle go on strike, and it looks like a long one, perhaps six months. If that happens, he said, he would order the railroad closed down.

I asked what he meant by "closed down." He said exactly that—everything closed, employees laid off, section houses closed down, drained and left cold and empty, coaling stations left without crews, water tanks drained and closed, heat and lights all turned off.

I told him that would just about choke the life out of the city. If that happened, I said I would have a page one editorial every day calling him every bad printable name I could think of, and a few that probably shouldn't be printed. I said I would charge him with whatever heinous crimes I could make out of it, showing gross insensitivity toward women and children and letting families face starvation because he cut off the town's payroll.

I said I would say he's as bad as Grandfather Smallweed in Dickens lore, where it says "Grandfather Smallweed heard the door of his office open and someone entered in the dark. 'Who is it?' grandfather called in his high pitched voice. And the young voice answered, 'David.' 'David, so it's you. Where have you been David?" David replies, 'I have been visiting with my friends.' And Grandfather Smallweed replies, 'Friends? Visiting with friends? Friends are not to visit with. Friends are to squeeze like an orange or a lemon, and when you have squeezed all the juice out of them you cast them aside for they are no good for you any more—cast them aside!'"

The colonel seemed to be listening so I kept talking. I told him I would have the emotional support of everyone and he would be the ugly monster in their lives. After all, if the railroad closed down, the town would face oblivion.

"That's what I would do." I told him. "What would you do if you were the editor?"

Ohlson looked me squarely in the eye and said, "The same damn thing."

That was the last I saw of him for the next few months. He went to Washington. The Pacific coast maritime strike occurred late in 1936, stopping nearly all area shipping, including the vessels that carried food and passengers to Alaska. Ohlson closed the railroad. Outraged, I wrote angry editorials in larger than normal type and ran them down the middle of the first page. I used all those words I said I would.

"Are the powers that be going to permit what must be outright greed for the almighty dollar to make paupers out of Alaskans?" I asked in an editorial and urged everyone to mount protests. The Palmer Chamber of Commerce wired Ohlson's boss, Secretary Ickes: "Present management continues to disregard rights and wishes of road's supporters for no other reason than to build a personal reputation for making the road pay. It has done more to retard growth and development of the territory than any other factor..."

Ohlson, who had been called to Washington, fired back a radiogram: "Had the merchants of Anchorage and elsewhere in the railbelt patronized the railroad instead of its competitors in the past, it could have operated through this emergency but under present conditions it cannot without a deficiency appropriation."

The statement created a new uproar and gave me cause to write another editorial criticizing Ohlson's motives. Then Delegate Dimond joined the fight. On the floor of Congress, he called for the colonel's ouster.

However, the colonel didn't budge until an anonymous postal clerk in Seattle unwittingly gave us the ultimate weapon. Seeing the mail to Alaska piling up because the ships weren't running, he managed to persuade a Navy destroyer bound for Seward to carry the load to Alaska. When word got around that a pile of undelivered mail was sitting in Seward, a hue and cry went up: "The railroad reneges on its contract to deliver the mail ... this is a federal offense ... prosecute the colonel!" Naturally, the protests were front page news.

The order to close down the railroad was quickly rescinded. The railroad moved the mail and never again tried to close down. (It is interesting that years later when the huge Alaska earthquake of 1964 wrecked railroad tracks and bridges most of the way from Anchorage to Seward, the railroad, although inoperative, laid off nobody. Instead, when it had no other work for its employees it assigned them to do restoration work for their local communities. In Seward they were a godsend for the town.)

When Ohlson returned from Washington, I was in the crowd at the train station to report his return. "Bob, you are going to get your block knocked off when he gets off that train," one businessman quipped.

Ohlson picked me out of the crowd and headed in my direction as soon as he got off the train. But, with a wry smile, he shook hands with me first, surprising me and just about everyone else at the station.

These events took place in the first few years of Evangeline's and my "five year adventure to Alaska." My effort to produce a balanced account of the colonization project made me realize the enormous responsibility my newspaper had. It was the only daily publication in southcentral Alaska, an area bigger than most states. And it had mainly me as the news staff.

Running the paper sometimes became a sideline instead of my vocation in Anchorage. So many of the people I talked to during the day or the evening were newsmakers that it was hard to draw the line between working and socializing. Building a city was much more difficult and involved hard judgmental decisions that were offensive to some and pleasing to others.

Of course, newspapering had many of the same involvements. We always said that in Alaska it is essential to remember that those you are opposing today on the blue issue may be your greatest supporters tomorrow on the red issue. So it was inadvisable to write anyone off as a total loss. An enemy today could turn out to be your friend tomorrow, and I would learn this in interesting ways.

In those first years, Evangeline didn't show much enthusiasm in her new role as a mother and homemaker. A professional social caseworker, she took a personal interest in every social problem. She joined various groups and enjoyed organizing others, but her civic ardor sometimes raised hackles.

When she found no Parent-Teacher Association in Anchorage, she proposed to start one. The school superintendent said he didn't want one and if one was started he would leave. She started one and he left. Very simple.

I suggested Evangeline should be a reporter and she liked the idea. We got a very nice lady as babysitter for our infant daughter, Marilyn, and Evangeline became the first major improvement of my regime at the Anchorage Daily Times. She was truly marvelous. One of her famous stories was about a murder. A cannery worker had killed another worker by chopping him up with a double-bitted ax then tried to burn the body in the wilderness area that is now Government Hill. Evangeline went with the coroner's jury to the site of the crime and the bonfire and came back to the office with a report much more detailed than we had ever contemplated—all in excellent psychiatric social worker's style.

Unfortunately, I lost my reporter after a few happy months. She told her editor that in the evening when she came home the babysitter often told her with great enthusiasm of something new the baby had done that day. The baby was becoming a little personality. Evangeline wanted to be a part of that emerging personality, not a newspaper reporter. She quit and stayed home. (Some years later she wrote a definitive

FRONTIER LIFE | 29

book, titled "We Shall Be Remembered" on Alaska's unique farm colonization in the Matanuska Valley.)

One great, unexpected benefit from farm colonization project occurred with the visit of Jim Farley, the affable Democratic Party chairman, who as U.S. Postmaster was President Roosevelt's No. 1 patronage dispenser. Amid much fanfare, Farley decided, despite the possible rigors, to see the great humanitarian experiment in distant Alaska for himself on July 22, 1938.

Anchorage rejoiced at the news and plotted how to turn this visit into a bonus. The town badly needed a federal building. It also needed to send a message to Washington about the suffocating restraints of indifferent federal rule. During most of the 72 years the United States owned Alaska as a territory, there was no governmental authority other than the local municipalities and the territorial government, which was not much. More than 99 percent of the land and all of the resources in Alaska were owned by the federal government.

The only government that responded directly to Alaskans was the city administration. However, not only did its feeble authority stop at the city limits, it had to go to Congress for permission even to build water and sewer lines, schools and other essential facilities. And its requests were sometimes turned down because some congressman, usually from a distant state where understanding of the territory was minimal, felt it was too much of a burden on Anchorage to borrow money.

To get Farley's attention, we planned a gala welcome plus a little subterfuge. A few days before our guest arrived, Clyde R. Ellis, president of the rejuvenated chamber of commerce, arranged to place a few tin pails in the middle of the floor of the leaking, dilapidated cottage that housed our federal offices. Then he bronzed a shovel and set it in a closet. Since I covered Farley while working on the Worcester Telegram in Massachusetts, Ellis picked me to be chairman of the reception committee. I had orders not to let Farley depart until we got him to the potato patch, where we hoped to put up a federal building, and put the shovel in his hand.

A big crowd gathered to meet Farley at the train station. The high school band was there, fresh in new flashy uniforms purchased by public subscription. Over the band, like an arch, was a banner saying in big letters, "Welcome to Anchorage," and beneath it, "Our band looks like a million dollars but our federal building looks like hell."

Unfortunately, Farley never got to see the banner. Colonel Ohlson's speeder carrying the Farley party lost a wheel and jumped the track a mile and a half short of the station. Farley arrived on the outskirts of town by foot, sweating and swatting mosquitoes. He was picked up and delivered by auto directly to the luncheon in his honor put on by the townsfolk at Helen Vail's dine-and-dance place on the shore of beautiful Lake Spenard.

Farley grew restless during the luncheon. He called me to the head table and asked how he could get out of there. I told him to use the back door that was right behind him. After making a few remarks, he excused himself, saying he had to get out to the farm colony, and slipped out the back.

Warren Cuddy, driving his new LaSalle, and I in my second-hand Buick, drove up to the back door and whisked Farley away. This upset a number of high-ranking state Democrats who had yet to get to the podium. (They had been in a coach car delayed by the speeder derailment.) In effect, two Republicans, Warren Cuddy, who drove Farley, and I, who drove the others in his party, snatched away their national leader.

We drove to the Matanuska farms via a newly bulldozed gravel road, barely fit for travel. The tedious ride gave us time to tell the visitors about our problems with the unresponsive feds. We pulled up to the Trading Post at the entrance to the colony. Farley met a few farmers and shook their hands with great flourish and spewed flattering comments about their pioneering spirit. But as an inspection trip of the New Deal experiment, the visit was a sham. The stop lasted about 10 minutes before Farley asked to head back. I don't think he saw a single farm.

When we returned to Anchorage, a special train was at the depot waiting for him. Farley seemed to be relieved in seeing that it had steel wheels and a steam engine to pull it. Before dropping him off, we asked if he would mind having his picture taken at a ground breaking for a new building. He readily acceded, without asking what the new building might be.

We took him to the potato patch beside the federal jail and handed him the bronze shovel. He dug up a shovel full of dirt and held it in mid-air as Alaskans on the Fourth Avenue sidewalk snapped pictures. While Farley posed with the shovel, local dignitaries, who appeared out of nowhere, including the postmaster, the mayor and Delegate Dimond, surrounded him for more picture taking.

On the drive to the railroad, Farley asked what the new building was going to be. We told him it was the site of the new federal building. It must have been puzzling to him because he and his department were in charge of building federal buildings all over the country. I explained it was the building I had been telling him about, the one we have been wishing for 20 years. It hadn't been authorized yet, we explained, but we were confident it was something he would support.

The new federal building was authorized several months after Farley returned. Construction started in 1940, and the handsome structure was completed in 1941. We always speculated that our new friend, Jim Farley, ordered it built, but we never had proof that he did.

The building still stands, proud and permanent on Fourth Avenue, although the federal establishment in Anchorage long ago outgrew it and built a bigger headquarters on Eighth Avenue at A Street. But that first building gave the town a spiritual uplift that was never contemplated in the planning. The fact that it is solid concrete was important in that it convinced many Alaskans that Uncle Sam was here to stay—Anchorage would be a permanent city. Until that first federal building, everything the federal government had built in Alaska had been of wood-frame construction on temporary foundations. Many early Alaskans feared Congress might, without notice, close down everything and abandon the place. Some congressmen had talked that way.

Soon after it was built, a flurry of home improvements became noticeable. Homeowners seemed to say that if Uncle Sam stays I'll stay too, and they put in new foundations, new roofs and, those without, put in inside plumbing.

Ernest Gruening became territorial governor of Alaska late in 1939. He had the potential of becoming an enemy. A liberal with a Harvard background, Gruening was sent here by his New Deal pal in the White House, President Roosevelt. Gruening had all the qualities I had been accustomed to hate. He was an outsider, opinionated and sovereign. Fortunately, I resisted my first impressions. When I got to know him, he became my leader, my main inspiration and my mentor.

I trusted Gruening and he trusted me in many areas of activity and thought. But not when it came to partisan politics. He was an outright avant-garde liberal Democrat, and I could tolerate none of the free spending, give-away economic schemes of that era. Except, perhaps, some of the surprising ways they found to spend money in Alaska.

One fun illustration of mutual trust occurred at my house when the governor was a dinner guest with only my family present. In our after dinner conversation, we joked about the vicious campaign to discredit him being waged by the Juneau Daily Empire, owned by John W. Troy, the former territorial governor. Gruening replaced Troy when the latter came under fire for steering government printing contracts to his own firm.

The capital city's newspaper was so mad at the new governor that it banned the publication of his name anywhere in its columns and went out of its way to dig up any kind of a story that might make him look bad. Can you imagine the newspaper in any state capital trying to report the news of the day without mentioning the governor? The Empire made itself the laughing stock of the town by its devious and convoluted headlines and stories to keep Gruening unmentionable.

After dinner on that evening, we played a game making up our own headlines on how to more effectively skewer a governor by keeping him nameless. Gruening, a former editor of The New York Herald Tribune, handily topped every suggestion I made. He came up with some humdingers, several of which would have been dynamite in the hands of the Juneau editor. I never leaked them to anyone, and it is a tribute to the man that Gruening simply bided his time to fight back.

32 | CHAPTER THREE

Even after Troy died in 1942, the Juneau Empire kept up its vicious campaign. It tried to brand Gruening a Communist in the prevailing national hysteria in the late 1940s that led to the McCarthy era. But the paper overplayed its hand by charging also that Gruening was a partner in diverting territorial money into a private account in a Juneau bank. Gruening sued for libel and won, one of the rare instances that a public figure ever prevailed in a battle against a spiteful press.

One of the many pleasures of being the editor in an Alaska town was the duty to meet and greet visitors in all walks of life and grades of prestige and prominence. In Anchorage, it was common to have a visitor "stuck" for as long as a week when he ventured here to or from somewhere else. All he wanted to do in Anchorage may have been to transfer from one mode of transportation to another, but when it involved a steamship it was a week between boats and hence a delay.

I met Robert Marshall, the famed Arctic explorer, a founder of the Wilderness Society and author. Marshall had found his way to Anchorage and was waiting here for the next steamship in Seward. Evangeline and I had a delightful luncheon with him at our house after I had found and interviewed him at the Anchorage Hotel.

He told fascinating stories of his Arctic explorations, and especially of the year he lived at Wiseman, a Native settlement above the Arctic Circle. He wrote about that year in his book, "Arctic Village," and upset many of the residents with his candid reports of their local customs and habits, notably the acceptance of promiscuity as a normal sexual relationship.

Rex Beach, the famous author of novels with an Alaska setting and the gold rush days, impressed me as a substantial character, physically and mentally. When he discovered an Alaskan couple barred from their gold claim in Glacier Bay National Monument, he went directly to President Roosevelt and convinced him to amend his executive order creating the monument to permit this old couple to enjoy their property unhampered by the Park Service.

As our region grew in the late 1930s, so did the Anchorage Daily Times. We expanded the paper from five columns to six, adding about 100 column inches daily for news, features and ads. Norman Brown, editor of the Cordova Times, came on board as managing editor.

But now events far beyond my control were creating a new national awareness of Alaska. War clouds were gathering. Hitler was marching across eastern Europe, the military aggressiveness of Japan was receiving nervous attention, and many feared a ground war was imminent in Russia. Suddenly people were talking in terms of strategic Alaska, the U.S. land mass nearest both to the shores of our closest enemy and our most powerful ally.

FRONTIER LIFE | 33

City of Palmer May 1968, some years after the resettlement project of 1935. Photo by Steve McClutcheon/Alaska Pictorial Service

Early farm in the Matanuska Valley. Logs were utilized by some new settlers to hold down costs.
Photo by Steve McClutcheon/Alaska Pictorial Service

Early settlement of the Matanuska Valley stressed root crops and dairying. Photo by Steve McClutcheon/Alaska Pictorial Service

People of the resettlement program to Palmer in the Matanuska Valley arriving on the train in the spring of 1935. Photo by Steve McClutcheon/Alaska Pictorial Service

March 15th, 1945 at Palmer approximately 10 years after the Matanuska Valley colonists settled there. Mail and passengers are headed toward Anchorage. Produce was often carried in the baggage car. Photo by Steve McClutcheon/Alaska Pictorial Service

Left is Ed Baldwin of Baldwin Seed Company and his son (right) with Glen Wood on Wood's spud ranch in the Matanuska Valley. Potatoes are one of the valley's best crops due to the siltaceous soils; a result of near by glaciation. Photo by Steve McClutcheon/Alaska Pictorial Service

FRONTIER LIFE | 37

38 | CHAPTER THREE

— CHAPTER FOUR —

Era of Neglect Ends

As the 1930s waned, economic, social and political challenges were plentiful in Alaska, and especially Anchorage. Little did I realize that the 60,000 Alaskans—including me and my 2,500 townspeople—were to be witnesses to the end of one historic era and the beginning of another that would plunge Alaska posthaste into the mainstream of concerns and make it an integral and inseparable part of the nation's economy.

The era of benign neglect that prevailed from the time of the purchase of Alaska by the United States in 1867 ended abruptly when the Army moved in to defend it from all enemies.

I was active among the younger Alaskans, most of whom were eager for economic development in all its ramifications. We were sometimes called young Turks, mavericks and sometimes even the Rebels.

My tiny newspaper organization (total staff: five including me) was under pressure to increase productivity to keep pace with growth in circulation, advertising and the need for more and more news coverage of the events around us. We added a Linotype to our shop but were limited in space and could undertake only minor improvements.

I was trying to give some leadership to the community, mainly through editorials, to maintain enthusiasm for growth and all the accompanying commotion, despite the impacts that brought temporary discomforts. But the tiny population of wage earners, most of them railroad employees, had few men and women who could afford time and effort for civic projects. Too often, if I sought action in a special direction, I had to serve as committee chairman or do it myself.

The news scene in Alaska was always fascinating with major stories breaking almost daily. There was frequent drama at sea as our ships and fishing vessels were challenged by the mighty storms of the North Pacific Ocean, Gulf of Alaska and Bering Sea. There were heartrending tales in the wilderness as man, alone on foot or supported by a bush pilot, sought to push back the wilderness to make way for the things of civilization.

It was a rough frontier country. Alaska was 50 to 100 years behind the western states. With inadequate tools, clothing and in the Arctic cold, it took brave men to go forth on a mission. Once they left their hometown they were on their own—like the man who sewed up a 12-inch tear in his arm by himself. There was no one near to help. Eskimos were reported to have eaten their dogs when facing starvation on the shores of the Arctic Ocean at the top of the world.

The world around us was also taking on new patterns and shapes, some of them frightening to the nation. War news was growing tenser and was often crowding out our page one Alaska stories, amazing as they were. The spread of war in Eastern Europe was involving Russia, our next door neighbor across the Bering Strait.

For many years Alaskans had cited the need for northern defenses, but their pleas went unheeded. In Congress, the stingy attitude of 1867, when the members balked on appropriating funds to pay for the purchase of Alaska, had hardly changed in all the years since. In the 1930s they still refused to appropriate funds to defend Alaska.

Obviously, the leadership was oriented toward Europe from whence had come all the military threats in U.S. history. Delegate Dimond introduced bills and made powerful and sometimes emotional speeches pleading for Congress to take an interest in defending Alaska from Pacific Rim threats. The body refused over and over again. Even as tensions continued to grow, with Admiral Yamamoto and General Tojo on the loose in the Pacific occupying nation after nation to create the Southeast Asia Co-prosperity Sphere, Congress refused to respond to the exposure in Alaska.

The United States gratuitously gave up the right to arm Alaska at the time of the 1922 treaty that limited arms in the Pacific. At the same time Congress was appropriating millions of dollars building the military power center in Hawaii. The islands are not as close to Japan as Alaska is.

Alaska was left alone in the north, exposed to all comers. In the vast territory there were 200 infantrymen stationed at Chilkoot Barracks near Haines. They had a 20-year-old tugboat for transportation.

It must be remembered that in those years Alaska was, in the minds of most people, located far out there somewhere, beyond the periphery of active public interest or understanding. News was hard to come by. Newspapers and radio stations usually depended upon reports they picked up from travelers who returned from "out there" and there weren't many travelers.

In the summer of 1935 my newspaper was reporting that employees of the U.S. Coast and Geodetic Survey parties reported seeing signs of Japanese survey parties on Aleutian islands. Schoolteachers, weather bureau employees and others reported the resident Aleuts sometimes mentioned seeing strangers. These reports, true or not, fanned fears that the Japanese were preparing to invade.

In Anchorage, there was already an awareness of the need for military defenses. Civic leaders had prevailed on the municipal government to appoint a commission to document the reasons defenses were essential and why Anchorage was the strategic location for them. The commission's report languished on a dusty closet shelf in city hall. When I came across it in 1935, it became my operating manual for editorials on that subject. The document was a key factor in attracting federal attention in Washington, D.C.

As international tensions built in Asia and Europe, Alaskans kept beating the drums for some sort of a defense program. We carried stories on the exposures and quoted any person with military experience and background who had comments to make.

We leaned heavily on Gen. Billy Mitchell, former assistant chief of U.S. Army Air Corps, who, in 1935, made his historic statement, "Alaska is the most central place in the world of aircraft, and that is true either of Europe, Asia or North America, for whoever holds Alaska will hold the world, and I think it is the most important place in the world."

As the tensions increased, we had stories from various sources, such as the time a fisherman reported seeing an unmarked vessel with a periscope close to Annette Island near Ketchikan. But the one that drew national interest came from a bush pilot who said the Russians were "building something" on Big Diomede Island. The Associated Press distributed the story widely and people generally were concerned.

Delegate Dimond was pressing constantly for defense appropriations. He delivered a speech on the floor of the House about what the Russians might be building. Only a half mile of ocean separates that island from the U.S. island called Little Diomede. The international dateline runs between them. The two Diomede islands are in the Bering Strait with the Alaska mainland to the east and East Cape, Siberia, to the west.

Dimond was persistent. When they turned him down in committee, he would bring it up in another committee and get another rejection. When the chance came, he brought it up on the floor of the House. And got yet another squelch.

Some of the congressmen were frank to tell Dimond outright that they would never vote to spend federal funds defending worthless Alaska.

Things started happening soon after our story on the Russians on Big Diomede. An Army board came to Anchorage under the leadership of Col. John C.H. Lee. They were sent to Alaska by Gen. George Marshall, Army chief of staff, to make a plan for military defense installations. They would make Anchorage their base and operate out of our city for two weeks.

The board landed on the grass strip of Merrill Field, which is still owned and operated by the city of Anchorage. They were in two big, clumsy amphibious planes that could land on lakes, rivers, sandbars, short gravel runways or whatever.

We townspeople, always quick to spot a strange plane in our air, met and greeted Colonel Lee and his board members with glee. We were ready to tell him where to locate the defenses. Naturally, we thought they

ERA OF NEGLECT ENDS | 41

were here because of our efforts to get defenses built.

Every morning, the board in its two ungainly planes took off from Merrill Field and flew off to somewhere in Alaska, and returned in the evening. Lee and his people would give no hint where they had been or what they were observing.

We wined and dined those officers. They became our friends, and friends of our families. We thought they were mighty fine people and we turned on all our charms hoping they would like Anchorage and the people here. Before they left, they had heard first hand all our best sales pitches on why whatever the military builds it should be built here.

Never once did they give us a hint but we observed their planes each morning and noticed that, after leaving Merrill Field, they circled quite a while over the wilderness outside of town, and when they returned in the evening they circled that area some more. That area is now the site of Elmendorf Air Force Base and Fort Richardson, the headquarters of the military establishment in Alaska.

On their final departure, there were farewells from all off us at the airport. I asked Lee, "Are you going to leave us without telling us anything about what might happen?" He replied, "Well, Bob, all I can say is that we think well of Anchorage."

On April 29, 1939, President Roosevelt signed a land withdrawal order that set aside 50,000 acres adjacent to Anchorage for the exclusive use of the military. That was the first official recognition of the strategic importance of Alaska. It also marked the approach of the end of the years of federal neglect of Alaska.

The decision to send U.S. military forces to Alaska was momentous in its consequences. In Alaska we saw it as an announcement to the world that Alaska was a part of the United States and would be defended as such.

For the first time Alaskans thought they had evidence that Uncle Sam was their guardian and would protect them from evil forces such as Admiral Yamamoto, General Tojo or Adolph Hitler or even Joe Stalin if ever necessary. Our spirits were bolstered. It wasn't until some time later that we realized the federal government was using our land to defend the rest of the country. Really, there was minimum concern for our security as Alaskans.

Enemy bombers, vintage 1930s, were incapable of reaching the industrial heart of America nonstop from Japan. They would require a refueling stop en route, and Alaska could serve as that stop. The defenses in Alaska were to prevent that from happening.

News of the land withdrawal electrified our sleepy town. It would take a while for the full significance to become known, but those acquainted with American history knew growth and prosperity were at hand. Major western cities grew from tiny communities that had been supply centers for early day Army posts.

CHAPTER FOUR

The Alaska economy became dynamic overnight. Real estate prices shot up. Housing costs climbed. Long before anything actually happened toward building an airbase in Alaska, the atmosphere was pervaded with a mood of excitement and optimism.

There was some dismay with federal procedures, however. Early in 1940 Gen. George C. Marshall, Army chief of staff, asked Congress for $12,734,000 to build "an operating air base in Alaska ... a project of major importance." Major Gen. H.H. Arnold and others testified to the necessity. The War Department subcommittee in the House eliminated the entire appropriation. Instead they appropriated $750,000 for an airport in Tampa.

General Marshall, with Maj. Gen. Arnold and Delegate Dimond and others, pleaded for reconsideration, but found the committee adamant in opposition. That was April 4, 1940.

On April 9 Hitler invaded Norway and Denmark and occupied those two countries. Army records note that there was a different atmosphere when General Marshall and Maj. Gen. Arnold appeared before the Senate subcommittee on April 30 and asked for restoration of the Anchorage base item.

Before the committee completed its hearings on May 17 the Luftwaffe had bombed Rotterdam without provocation or warning. Hitler's armies had seized The Netherlands, had swept through Belgium and had begun the invasion of France.

The Army historical records show, "The Senate restored the Anchorage base. The House concurred. Thus Fort Richardson and its air establishment, Elmendorf Field, came to be."

The headlines and news stories in the Anchorage Daily Times during June 1940 give an idea of how the program to fortify Alaska accelerated with the pace of the war:

June 8 — "Twenty-five men sent out to Whitney station to start slashing and clearing land for air base. European war was becoming more fierce. Norway, Netherlands and Belgium surrendered; Nazis invaded Paris; Italy entered on Nazi's side. President Roosevelt pledged help to allies."

June 12 — "Crew of 100 Building Tent City for Army."

June 18 — "570 Troops from Ft. Lewis Sail for Anchorage to Defend Air Base."

June 19 — "France Signs Armistice with Germany; Naval Air Base Being Constructed at Kodiak."

June 27 — "First troops Arrive — 400 Men, 16 Officers, Long Troop Train from Seward."

ERA OF NEGLECT ENDS

The arrival of that troop train was a community event. The railroad depot platform was jammed with greeters. It was a nice, sunshiny day and the old wooden passenger cars had the windows open. Many of the windows had heads sticking out as the soldiers had their first glimpse of the city that was to be their new home.

The townspeople stood mostly silent, but giving friendly waves and responding to the greetings from the troops. A long line of flat cars carried trucks of all sizes and shapes, tanks, and special purpose vehicles.

When the train stopped the soldiers stood on the platform, each with his duffel bag as though waiting for whatever was to happen next. They had come from Missoula, Mont., so the climate and terrain at Anchorage was not strange to them.

It was at this awkward moment when the first words were exchanged between the Alaskans and the new neighbors they were so anxious to have.

The sergeants got the unloading process under way. There was no station facility at Elmendorf, a couple of miles beyond the depot, so everything was unloaded at Anchorage. The whole contingent loaded into trucks and then headed out to the air field over the crooked, dusty, wagon-track road that was the outgrowth of the dog team trail carved out in 1914 by Bud Whitney, the first homesteader.

When they arrived at the air base site they found it was only a potato patch of Mr. and Mrs. Marsh, the homesteaders. The soldiers' first task was to erect tents, which would be their first shelter in Alaska. They lived in them through the next winter.

Some townspeople, trying to be helpful, suggested that the commanding officers—Lt. Col. Earl Landreth, Maj. Francis Maslin, quartermaster, and Capt. John G. Hill, chief of staff—should live downtown in hotel rooms that had been reserved for them, but the officers declined, saying they must stay with their men.

A few days later, another train brought from Seattle, via Seward, 150 carpenters, plumbers and other workers, and carloads of lumber and cement. The construction of the air base was moving ahead.

Anchorage residents were fascinated. The sight of 10-wheel automobile trucks was strange to them. Their canvass covers were reminders of the covered wagons of the pioneers on the Oregon Trail.

They weren't used to seeing things done in such a big way. There were more people on their downtown streets than they had ever anticipated. Virtually all retail stores were busier than ever. Bars had standing room only.

In the next few months the civilian and military communities got acquainted. The townspeople were thrilled when the soldiers marched in the July 4th parade, spic and span in their uniforms, puttees, Sam Browne belts, rifles and all. There was special excitement after the parade when a saloon at C Street and Fourth Avenue caught fire and the volunteer fire department responded. At the request of the mayor, they permitted soldiers to help police the area, maintain police lines to hold back spectators and allow the Anchorage volunteer firemen work. It was the community's first civilian/military cooperative venture.

The holiday afternoon saw an interesting mixture of soldiers and civilians working together on the Delaney Park Strip staging the usual July 4th races for all the kids in town. In Mulcahy ballpark there was the traditional holiday game only this time soldiers and civilians enjoyed their first Independence Day together.

A new element was added to local society on July 23, 1940, when Col. Simon Boliver Buckner, Jr., arrived to take command of the Army in Alaska. He was an over-aged colonel, probably partly because he argued too much with generals, and would remain a colonel until August 31 when his promotion to brigadier general became effective. Buckner was an upright, powerful man, ebullient, crusty, bellicose. He was outgoing in his friendliness and made friends rapidly although he impressed some as a braggart. His voice was loud and resonant. For a time he had a Kodiak bear hide on the wall of his quarters and scuttlebutt said he had yelled at it and "it just up and died of fright."

Officers, who were cadets at West Point when Buckner was commandant, said he was tough on them. Fortunately for Anchorage and Alaska he knew the importance of close military/civilian relations and set out from his arrival to bring the two communities together.

This was his first major command in 33 years as an officer. He declined invitations for comfortable quarters in a downtown hotel in order to live with his men in tents on the reservation. His genial manner and warmth of friendliness made him a popular dinner guest in local homes and he laid the groundwork for close liaison between the civilian and military communities.

When he became brigadier general civilians learned the old Army tradition of "star parties" to pin the stars on the epaulets of the officer. It was the first of three star parties his friends were to hold for Buckner, for he was promoted two more times to lieutenant general before he was assigned to command the Tenth Army for the invasion of Okinawa.

Buckner was great in setting up challenges for himself and those around him. They ranged from simple "dares" to rigid physical undertakings. When nobody else set up a challenge he was known to have challenged himself, like his handling of the cigarette problem. He said, "If I don't smoke my friends tell me I am afraid to because I'll become addicted and can't quit. But when I do smoke people say it is because I don't have the will to leave cigarettes alone. So to prove I can take them or leave them alone, I smoke only on pay day and during lent."

There were dinners in the homes for soldiers as well as officers. Buckner encouraged all to fraternize. Churches invited the soldiers to join their groups. Pastors reported new life and enthusiasm in their young people's groups as the GIs became members. Some of the high school boys took a dim view of the new uniformed competition that confronted them seeking dates.

One local lady entertained wives of Army officers at a luncheon in her home and much to her surprise her guests arrived wearing cute hats, the style of the day, and white gloves. That was unheard of in local social groups. The local women, sans hats or gloves, felt underdressed. There followed a run on the stores for hats and gloves. The market endured and Lorene Harrison took on a new career by opening Lorene's Hat Shop, which was a downtown landmark for years.

Dr. J.H. Romig, one of the town's patriarchs, had a dinner at his home for the top officers and some of the town's civic leaders. To the delight of the ladies, the officers showed up wearing full-dress uniforms—dark blue uniforms with bright gold stripes down the legs, jackets covered with brass buttons, medals, and over it all a gorgeous dark blue cape lined with satin in the colors of their branch of service—sky blue for the infantry, bright golden yellow for the cavalry, firecracker red for the artillery, crimson for the engineers. In that regalia, any officer could make himself look like Superman just by inhaling with his arms akimbo.

The Romig dinner had social implications that brought enduring changes in Anchorage lifestyles. Civilians at the dinner party were told by their ladies they must bring out the tuxedos that had been packed away in mothballs all these years.

So they dug out the tuxes, sent them to the cleaners to get rid of the mothball smell, if that's possible, and showed up at the next dinner at Henry Emard's house, ready to face up to those Supermen.

And you know what? Those officers showed up in civilian clothes. They looked awful. Those civies had not been worn for years. They were out of style. And some looked like they had been rolled up in a duffel bag all that time.

Buckner was wearing an old tweed suit. It needed pressing. It had an ugly sewing job on one pant leg where it had been torn. A big tear. The general said it was the only civilian suit he owned.

It was a happy evening—very helpful in getting acquainted. I asked Colonel Maslin how it happened that they all show up dressed the same—blues last week, civies this week. He said they (the officers) just find out what the general is wearing and they all wear the same. I asked him to tip me off about what they were wearing when a dinner comes up, and I would pass the word along to the civilians to avoid these embarrassing situations.

That became my responsibility. For some time, I was the messenger. People would call me to ask what to wear to parties I had never heard of. Sometimes the military would call in regard to a civilian event.

Maybe the fact that I did that and other liaison chores was a factor in my being selected in 1946 to serve on the commanding general's Civilian

Affairs Board that came into being when the Alaska Command was established. I have been a member all the years since.

From June 1940 until December of 1941 the Army and civilians learned it required patience for the two communities to live together in harmony. When the Army erected tents they needed poles, stakes, flooring, siding and other lumber items. They cleaned out the local lumberyards. Townspeople found they would have no lumber for a week or two until a new supply arrived by steamboat.

Other items disappeared from local store shelves. Plumbing supplies were exhausted. Grocery items disappeared. When the Army needed craftsmen—like carpenters, plumbers, painters—they would hire them all and the town would have none for home jobs.

The war increased its tempo in Europe; tensions increased in Anchorage. Buckner did what he could to encourage local residents to live their normal lives and plan ahead. He cautioned them against unplanned, hasty development.

On Feb.7, 1941, he told the Anchorage Rotary Club, where he was a member, to plan on doubling the size of Anchorage in the next four years. "Don't let the town go into mushroom growth," he said. "This town can be planned like the nation's most beautiful city—Washington, D.C." He encouraged wide streets, plenty of parks and parkways, better homes, better architectural design and high standards of living. "In the past," he said, "people have come here to get what they can, leave as little as possible, and go somewhere else to spend their money."

What motivated that kind of talk at that particular time is hard to know. Buckner was convinced an invasion was imminent but he also knew his words were exactly what Alaskans liked to hear.

By the fall of 1941, Anchorage had a 143-foot yacht standing at anchor in Knik Arm. It looked beautiful in the long evening sunsets. It was sent north by the Army for Buckner to use as transportation on inspection trips, and as a place for doing business.

It was a yacht that had been owned by Jack Zellerbach of San Francisco and was taken over by the federal government under emergency wartime powers. Buckner used it up and down the inlet a few times, enjoying dinner parties, but then got rid it. There was no adequate dock and he had no need for it, he said.

In those pre-war days, the Army table of organization was said to have provided a yacht for each general. When another yacht showed up in the inlet, assigned to General Whitaker, he spent heavy money trying to design a dock and gang plank that would rise and fall with the 30-foot tides, safe enough for loading his dinner guests in evening clothes. Whitaker was ultimately busted and exported from Alaska as a colonel.

The impact of war continued and grew worse. Before Pearl Harbor, the mayor, as chairman of the civil defense council, ordered a Home Guard organized to be composed of the able bodied men who were left in town after much of the male population had been taken by voluntary enlistments, the draft and activation of the Alaska National Guard. He had 500 rifles coming from national civil defense sources. The guard was to protect vital municipal facilities, such as water and power plants, key buildings and plants. Sabotage was the big fear.

When Pearl Harbor was bombed, Buckner ordered blackouts every morning from 5 a.m. until dawn, the most likely time for an air raid here. Dim lights were permitted the rest of the night. It is easy for me, many years later, to write about the blackouts. The one sentence seems to cover the subject, but it gives no indication of the enormous impact Buckner's order had on the lives of each one of us, at home, at the office, in our stores and shops, and on the streets.

To begin to appreciate life with blackouts, one must become aware of just what blackout means. It means not a pinpoint of light must show anywhere, with no exceptions. Even burning tobacco at the end of a cigarette was a violation. The light that escapes with the opening and closing of a door is taboo. The purpose of the blackout order was to make the Anchorage townsite a pure black spot on the map that a pilot would have no way of knowing he was over or near human civilization.

The Civil Defense programs taught that windows and doors had to be overlaid with heavy paper to seal off the light from door jams, thresholds and around windows. Most homes and stores were lined with ugly building paper, tacked or taped to cover walls, including doorways.

That permanent masking made most doorways useless. Householders and businesses selected a certain few doors for entrance and exit, and these had to have light traps like doorways to photographic darkrooms.

The fussing around with building paper caused people to grumble but that inconvenience was minor compared to the big, permanent change it brought to the entire family at home, to business associates at work and to people wherever they were. They all had to learn to live with very little or no ventilation.

Homes were stuffy. Only in the daytime could the homemaker open doors and let in fresh air, hoping it would last all night. You can believe it, the blackouts made the long winter nights much longer and the incidence of cabin fever more frequent. Some offices, stores and shops, but not too many, were in buildings equipped with ventilation systems that worked well.

The blackout nights in Anchorage were a permanent feature for months. While families huddled in their stuffy homes, with only radios for entertainment, the streets were made even more dangerous by the armed guards that were on duty in so many places. The guards included the usual municipal police, augmented by Chief Huttle's extra cops, occasionally some military police and especially the Home Guards, many of whom never walked on the streets of a blacked-out community, carrying a loaded weapon that they may or may not be acquainted with, and feeling great responsibility to protect the entire establishment from a mighty monster that might drop on them from the black sky above, or confront them in the dark suddenly like an ambush.

It's not hard to understand why mom and pop and the kids were under stress. They ran out of things to do at home in the evenings. In the daytime, the stress continued in different forms. Mother found shopping difficult or impossible. Civilian supply lines were overloaded and no longer reliable. Groceries frequently went long stretches with no fresh produce and shortages in staples. Dad found his co-workers in various stages of pouting or even on the verge of something drastic due to the upset in lifestyles and the lack of a feeling of security.

The school population grew out of hand as kids from military and construction families enrolled. Classes were run in shifts to enable double use of the available classrooms. Teachers as well as the kids were stressed out.

The normal ambience in schoolrooms and work places as well as homes and even churches was lost somewhere in the war commotion. Streets were one big cloud of dust with so much traffic, most of it big and small trucks. Sightseeing was no fun. The only scenic road out of Anchorage, the 21-mile Loop Road, was closed since it became part of the military reservation. The road to Palmer was cluttered with military trucks. There was no southbound exit from the city. The Seward road had not yet been built.

Alaska was different politically from other parts of the United States because it was a territory. The federal presence here was always prominent. Now the Army was moving in on the civil government with its own rules and restrictions. Nothing was normal in Anchorage. The streets were crowded with soldiers and transient construction people, mostly young people who were away from home and the normal restraints of home and families. Life was rough and often tough, particularly in late evenings after hours in the bars. Minor tiffs and sometimes major scrimmages were not uncommon.

Police walked downtown beats in pairs, one city officer and one military policeman. Only a combination of authority like that could handle the imbroglios generated in barrooms jammed with GIs and civilians. Social life was crippled. Streets were uninviting and dirty. Houses were stuffy and dirty. Everything was covered with dust. Patience of everyone was stretched to the limit.

Hundreds of permanent families decided this was no place to try to live and rear children. They packed up families and kids and exported them to the Lower 48, to their former homes, or to their parents or to brand new homes where they thought living conditions would be more nearly normal.

Families contemplating departure were encouraged by governing officials. Departures meant there would be fewer mouths to feed and fewer bodies to protect or provide for in the events of the uncertain future.

The emigration made for yet a rougher and tougher community in Anchorage. The transient elements became more dominant, the community atmosphere rougher. That encouraged more families to leave.

The panicky situation was based mostly on local rumors, but it was abetted by the antics of civilians as reported in Seattle, Portland and San Francisco where rumors also were rampant

The Marsh and Whitney homesteads east of the city were taking on strange new shapes as a small army of imported construction workers cleared the ground of its scrub brush, scraped up the topsoil, and hauled it away to leave vast fields of bare gravel. This was the building site for giant concrete runways, hangar buildings, supply shops, warehouses, commissaries and all the other things that comprise and support a major air base. Alaskans found it mind-boggling.

Originally, the plan was to build an air field to be named Elmendorf Air Force Base, honoring Capt. Hugh M. Elmendorf who was killed in 1933 testing a new aircraft for the Army Air Force at Wright Field, Ohio. Early on the order was changed. The overall installation was designated an Army post, Fort Richardson, named in honor of an Army engineer who built early day roads in Alaska. Elmendorf Field became a part of the fort.

Anchorage residents were ecstatic with the visit of Rep. J. Buell Snyder, chairman of the congressional subcommittee on War Department appropriations. He announced that the military would spend $10 million to $12 million annually for the next three years to make the Alaska defense system impregnable.

It turned out Anchorage had hit the jackpot in its bid for the military to locate near the city. Fort Richardson and Elmendorf would be the two main installations for Alaska and be headquarters for the top command.

A festive spirit prevailed. Colonel Ohlson hosted a dinner-dance at the Idle Hour Country Club on the shores of Lake Spenard to welcome high-ranking officers and their wives. My paper printed a special section recognizing the businesses that were expanding their stores and services to keep pace with the growing needs of the community.

Expansion was difficult and limited even though the war was still a year away. Alaska was already living under war conditions.

These were days of mushroom-like growth. The Times had a head-line reading, "216 Added To City Population In Single Day," which I would speculate was a report on the arrival of a boat train from Seward.

Jobs were the magnet. Anchorage was the headquarters for work and contracts. The excitement attracted gamblers and prostitutes and other camp followers. An unofficial and, incidentally, illegal red light district showed up in Mountain View, a new subdivision a short walk from the Army base.

50 | CHAPTER FOUR

Rep. Snyder returned to Anchorage after a few weeks and deplored what had happened. He said after his announcement of the big military spending program, city businesses boosted rents from 50 percent to 200 percent and prices on food and clothing had skyrocketed.

Housing was in short supply as contractors and military families grabbed every vacant space. Rents soared and landowners faced charges of greed. But the Army officers themselves sparked a part of the inflation. They had rent allowances, some of which were greater than rents paid by local residents. They were approaching landlords and asking, "How much rent are you getting on your property?" They were known to have offered to double it if they could rent it and, of course, the oldtime occupant family would be ousted to make way for the new high rent payer. The officer frequently paid none of the new higher rent because his rent allowance covered it.

There were many investigations of gouging. Quite a few instances were found, but some surprises were also uncovered. They revealed that soldiers, mostly sergeants, invested their savings in houses and rented to their fellow soldiers at unduly high rates.

Investigations led to the conclusion that when it came to gouging, Anchorage landowners were not lily white but they were not as bad as some of the military landlords were to their military tenants.

Before the first winter with our new neighbors we began to learn that the impact of growth, especially fast growth, included shortages in almost everything. Alaska's infrastructure was adequate to provide for the needs of the civilian economy, but not the crash program of military spending.

Civilian needs were submerged by the needs of the defense program. Carloads of civilian goods sat for months on sidings Outside as well as in Alaska. Military shipments came first and even they were backed up. There was a time during the war when the Alaska Railroad was 167 trainloads behind in moving cargo north from Seward.

Civilian travel became more and more difficult. Efforts to control it by voluntary means failed and the military put on its rules and required a travel permit to qualify to buy a steamship ticket. In Alaska we had wartime conditions and we were not even at war.

Alaska was fortunate in having Buckner as first commanding general. He was the son of General Bolivar Buckner of Civil War fame (on the Confederate side) after serving as governor of Kentucky. He believed in the need for close association of military and civilian communities. He preached it in Anchorage and went all out to integrate the two communities as far as possible. His genial personality did much to open Anchorage homes to his personnel. He charmed everyone around him when he turned on his gracious manners and southern ways. He was the epitome of excellence in many respects, not the least of which was as a performing extrovert.

My fascinating experiences with Buckner preceded the major problems that were to come. We in the newspaper business discovered that we had no experience in covering military news. A new problem arose almost the first week after Buckner's arrival, and my newsroom people looked to me for guidance on how to handle it. We had a report from a local source that an Army bomber had clipped a tank truck while in its takeoff run. That was our total report. We had no indication whether the bomber crashed, whether there were injuries, fire or whatever. It all had the potential of a big story. Our local news sources couldn't help. I told my newsroom I would ask Buckner directly, and headed for Army headquarters two miles from town.

The headquarters office was in the only building left on the homestead, the Marsh homestead house. From the exterior the house looked proud and happy, with a tall flagpole flying the American flag in the front yard and a snappy soldier, with rifle and Sam Browne belt, marching 20 paces to and fro. He looked me over as I approached the door and he let me proceed.

There was no doorbell so I turned the knob to enter unannounced. As I pushed the door it bumped Buckner off of his chair, which was a simple orange crate standing on end. He jumped to his feet and welcomed me with his booming voice that stopped all other activity in room. I found myself standing, suddenly rather lonesome, in the presence of the five top officers, some sergeants who were apparently their secretaries, and three or four of their dogs stretched out on the floor around the pot-bellied stove.

I noted all the furniture was makeshift stuff like the general's office chair. The work of U.S. Army headquarters in Alaska was at a standstill now that I had entered the room. Buckner greeted me warmly and I felt I had better state my business and get out of there fast so their business could resume. There was no "chair" for a guest so he couldn't invite me to sit. So we all stood for this transaction.

I told him I needed to know who to talk to about Army news stories. He asked me what kind of news did I have in mind. So I told him the report we had and I asked, "If a bomber clips a tank truck while taking off, is it news?"

His response didn't help a bit. "No, I don't think it would be, but if a tank truck clipped a bomber after it took off, that would be news." All the other officers laughed and agreed. I was serving as the straight man in a comedy team.

So I asked, "Did a bomber clip a tank truck while taking off?" The general had another quick response, "I think it is safe to say no to that because we have a regulation that forbids bombers from clipping a tank truck while taking off." That brought another laugh from all.

I rephrased my question, "I have a report that a bomber did clip a tank truck while taking off. Is it true?"

Buckner turned to one of the colonels and repeated my entire question as though the colonel had not already heard it, and asked, "Is it true?" The colonel snapped his heels and saluted the general and said, "Yes, sir. It is true."

Buckner turned to me and said, "Yes. It's true." Buckner and his four officers stood there looking at me as though, now that I have the answer, why don't I leave. I stood my ground and asked for more details. The charade ended there. Buckner and his people told me all about it. It was so minor that it was hardly worth a paragraph in the paper. But the incident did get the attention of the command. Channels were quickly established for handling news.

I left that encounter with great respect for Alaska's first military commander. In years to come my respect would grow. I doubt whether there are many who are aware of the lasting contributions that this man made for this land that had been neglected and even scorned by the federal bureaucracy in Washington for so long.

Buckner had a sense of history about him. He was probably imbued with it by his illustrious father in Kentucky, his imposing name borrowed from the soldier-statesman Simon Bolivar who freed six Latin American republics from Spanish rule, and his burning ambition in Alaska to defeat Emperor Hirohito in Japan, to return to Alaska and have a home in Anchorage and homestead in Homer, and ultimately to serve as governor of Alaska, which he predicted would become a state.

Three top priorities he set for himself as commander in Alaska were to train his men to operate under the harsh conditions of a land where so little was known about its terrain and climate discover and develop the best clothing and footgear for operating and surviving in Alaska's extreme weather and remote conditions, and build a system of roads "because you can't defend or develop a wilderness."

He performed well in all three areas. He trained his men with emphasis on the recapturing of the Aleutian Islands. He was one of the moving factors in the development of modern Arctic clothing and footgear. And the Army engineered and built the basic road system that yet today serves the vast state.

ERA OF NEGLECT ENDS | 53

Gen. Simon Boliver Buckner Jr. Comander of U.S. Army Alaska. Photo by Signal Corps U.S. Army Official Photograph/July 23, 1940

54 | CHAPTER FOUR

Bob Atwood (right) discusses visit of a military flight into Anchorage in late 1930's or very early 1940's. Planes landed on the 9th Ave. park strip. Photo by Steve McClutcheon/Alaska Pictorial Service

Military parage in Anchorage, 1943.
Photo by Steve McClutcheon/Alaska Pictorial Service

ERA OF NEGLECT ENDS | 55

56 | CHAPTER FOUR

— CHAPTER FIVE —

War

We had just come out of church and gone to the post office to pick up mail when a man asked me if it's true that the Japanese had bombed Pearl Harbor this morning. It was noon, Sunday, Dec. 7, 1941. He said he had heard ham operators talking about it.

I called the Army public relations office and the personnel on duty had not heard about it. I called Col. Lawrence V. Castner, the intelligence officer, at his home, and he had nothing.

Meanwhile Augie Hiebert, radio station owner at Fairbanks, was trying to check ham radio operator reports. He was probably the first one to tip off the military that war was at hand.

I sent an urgent dispatch to the Associated Press in Seattle requesting confirmation. The Anchorage Times could not afford to have regular press service coverage on weekends. It cost one and a half cents a word and we had no Sunday edition. The city's sole radio station had no way of knowing because it had no news service at all. That's the way we lived in the early days of isolation. On weekends we weren't part of the informed world.

The AP confirmed Pearl Harbor and gave me some details. It also reported that a Tokyo broadcast had said Anchorage had been burned and Fort Richardson captured.

By the time we had that information the Army had come alive with the realization our nation was at war. Emergency measures were activated to cancel leaves and call soldiers back to duty. Cannons boomed on the military reservation, a signal for soldiers to return to the base. Army cars equipped with sirens and public address systems drove up and down the streets, blasting the message: "War Emergency!"

The city was well shaken up. Civilians who weren't in their homes thought they ought to be. Those with assignments as air raid wardens rushed to their posts. Home Guard members reported for duty. The Civil Defense organization braced for whatever may come. All were dashing here and there. It was a first-class panic.

We knew, of course, that Anchorage had not been destroyed and that Fort Richardson had not been captured, but we didn't know about the other rumors, and there were many.

On the streets it was said a Japanese aircraft carrier had moved up

WAR | 57

to the coast of Alaska and only fog over the Gulf of Alaska was delaying an air attack on our city. We had no way of knowing whether that was true. The Army didn't know either. But the Army behaved as though it might be true.

Everyone fully expected Anchorage to be a major target if the enemy ever got within striking distance. We had our main troop strength here, the largest airbase with its support facilities and the military headquarters. If any place was going to be hit, we expected to be hit first. The war scare here was real. This was no drill. And Alaska was alone in the Far North, far from possible assistance. We were alone and on our own.

The motley collection of civilians who were in the Home Guard, the Civil Defense organization, Volunteer Fire Department and other outfits reported for duty to a city-owned building known as "The Ark." They were assigned to guard against sabotage at power plants, water facilities, and strategic buildings, armed with whatever weapons they owned, mostly their hunting rifles and shotguns.

Each one of us scanned the sky continually, fearful that we might see the planes from those Japanese aircraft carriers. It would be some months before the Japanese would strike Alaska and occupy our soil, but the attack on Pearl Harbor started a life of hell for us. The vulnerability of Alaska forced us to accept hardships much greater than in the Lower 48 states.

The day after Pearl Harbor, the Army halted transportation to, from and within Alaska. Steamships were ordered into the nearest port to wait for the Navy to provide escorts and organize convoys. All private pilot licenses were suspended until the federal government was given proof of identification and loyalty.

When travel resumed, contractors holding military contracts were allocated most of the passenger spaces on steamships. War increased the urgency to finish runways and military buildings, so that meant more workers were rushed in. The Army decided who got the tickets. Ordinary Alaskans were often left out in the cold, as they probably should have been considering the prevailing urgencies, but it was hard to convince them.

The city became desperate for housing. Our little community of tarpaper shacks and small cottages did not have much housing to start with. Local residents were encouraged to make their garages available as living quarters. At times children's playhouses were known to have housed hapless newcomers. Even with money in their pockets, they had been unable to find a room for the night.

Police Chief Bob Huttle reported that two middle-aged ladies, well dressed, educated and not unattractive, asked to be put up overnight in the city jail. When he accommodated them, they gave him $3,600 cash for safekeeping. He said they were tourists and even by offering overly big sums they were unable to buy a room in Anchorage.

Milk became scarce as Matanuska Valley farmers couldn't get their cows to increase production in pace with the growing population. Grocers handled milk as an outlawed item, using "under the counter deals" in deciding who would get it. Stores would sell out a few minutes after opening.

We quoted one harried grocery clerk: "One mother, with one or more children, is the most deadly species to encounter with a milk problem. Kipling was right; she will just about tear us apart when I tell her she can't have milk for her child, and I can't blame her. The biggest and toughest male who demands milk for himself is easier to turn down than the mother with an infant."

Barraged by angry customers, storekeepers finally had to ask the government to help ration the supply. City council appointed Mrs. Howard G. Romig chairman of a committee to find an answer to the milk problem. She selected three members to help her: the city health officer, Dr. Leroy Flora; the city's public health nurse, Catherine Smulling; and the town editor, me.

I noted a while back that as the small town editor I got involved in all sorts of community affairs and served on committees often as chairman, simply because I was always around or because my paper got the town aroused over the problem in the first place. In frontier Alaska that was one of the added burdens of doing your stuff as a reporter.

This milk committee assignment was one of those I wanted least. Yet, if I turned it down they would say I was shirking a civic duty and "you don't hesitate to go after us when you think we are ducking." That's the same argument that many years later made me a political candidate that I never wanted to be.

The committee's work was short. We found we had 588 qualified for priority milk treatment and the city's supply at that time was 610 quarts a day. So we turned the lists over to the local Office of Price Administration, of which Mrs. Romig was the director, and federal employees gave the tickets to those on the list and the remainder to first-comers.

As wartime demands grew, I had to spend less time running the paper. I became a major in the Home Guard and went out on the military reservation for instruction and practice in guerrilla tactics, which included learning how to make and throw Molotov cocktails. Our main duty was to guard essential facilities against sabotage, but should Anchorage fall to the enemy, we were told, the Home Guard most likely would have to fight back from a guerrilla camp in the wilderness, perhaps somewhere in the Chugach mountains. So we should be prepared.

Among the new talents we acquired, or were supposed to have acquired, were five ways to kill a man without his emitting a sound. Army instructors taught us how to hijack an enemy motorcycle courier by stretching wire diagonally across a roadway. The taut wire, just high enough off the ground, would steer any passing cyclist into the ditch at the side of the road where you would be concealed, ready with your five ways to dispose of him without revealing your presence.

We had instruction on how to live off the land, knowing which berries and roots are edible and where they are most likely to be found. We practiced crawling on our bellies across a field, going under barbed wire entanglements, while bullets flew over us so close we could hear their "zing."

We'd pour gasoline from a five-gallon can into the small neck of a Coke bottle—wasting much of it—to make Molotov cocktails, which we'd throw at a mock tank in the wilds of Fort Richardson. Sometimes it seemed incongruous for us to be wasting good fuel this way. Gasoline was rationed Outside but not in Alaska. Authorities decided wisely that the possible saving by rationing fuel would not be worth the cost or the effort.

Rationing in Alaska differed from other states. While gasoline and food items were mostly exempt, other things weren't. The government severely rationed new automobiles. Only one a month was allowed to come to Anchorage and a ration board here decided who could buy it. I couldn't replace my 1936 Oldsmobile until 1948.

The possibility that food shipments to Alaska would be cut off by Japanese submarines was very real. Plans had to be made for families to survive six months or more without supplies. So the authorities encouraged residents to buy food in case lots and store them in their homes to conserve warehouse space. Virtually every home became a warehouse of sorts. Basements and spare rooms were usually stuffed full. Officials said that the cooperation of the people of Anchorage enabled them to double the storage capacity of the community.

Air raid alerts, blackouts and power shortages constantly disrupted our lives. It was a wonder that nobody got killed in this period of so many armed guards and pseudo-official security people running around with live bullets. The only casualty sustained in the first days of the war was a Naknek hotelman, Joseph DeHey, 58, a patient at Providence Hospital. He died of a heart attack when the first practice air raid sirens were sounded.

I wrote editorials regularly supporting the military and hoping to keep things in perspective. I must have found a dozen ways of writing that "war is hell" because it was my theme for so long. I reminded readers our inconveniences as civilians were minimal compared to the bloodshed and danger endured by people being bombed in Britain, France and Belgium. And we were luckier than the Greeks who awoke to the Nazi threat too late to save their nation.

Anchorage people were so united in their American loyalty and military support that I had nary a ripple of complaint when one of my reporters checked the town for light leaks during a blackout and published the addresses of offenders in the paper. "One light could lead the enemy to the target, which is us," my newspaper warned.

At the time of Pearl Harbor the Alaska military installations were just taking shape. A barracks for 4,000 men was nearing completion. The first troops of the Alaska National Guard, created by Governor Gruening five months earlier, were in training. Planes had just started to use the runways at Elmendorf, newly paved several months ahead of schedule.

Bud Whitney's dog team trail that served for years as the Post Road had just been improved. The city had extended Fourth Avenue to the city limits, and the territorial government continued it to Ship Creek with a bridge across the creek. The Army picked it up from there and continued the road all the way to what is now Elmendorf Air Force Base.

We had just started to feel a little stability when on June 3, 1942, just six months after Pearl Harbor, the Japanese attacked Alaska. In our biggest blackest headline to date, we reported: "RAID DUTCH HARBOR." The Japanese fleet struck this island in the middle of the Aleutians at around 6 a.m. Our first reports were sketchy, and the military clamped a news blackout on the invasion for the next nine days. When the Associated Press on June 12 finally delivered a detailed story, we learned that while the Japanese had been repulsed at Dutch Harbor, they established beachheads further out on the Aleutians seven days later. The invaders took possession of Attu Island and landed troops on the windy, cold island of Kiska, both of which are near the western tip of the Aleutians.

It was the first time in 130 years that an enemy had occupied American soil. The reaction across America was violent. Newspapers carried screaming headlines, "They are on American soil! Drive them off!"

In Alaska, it was quite different. A substantial segment of the hard-bitten Alaskans were saying, privately, "Leave them there. It serves them right for having landed there."

We knew that the islands were more than 1,500 miles from Anchorage and from that distance the enemy could do no harm to the rest of Alaska.

Nationally, the Japanese presence was a serious problem. The American war machine was in bad shape after the losses at Pearl Harbor. No matter that the rocky, sparsely inhabited Aleutian Islands had little strategic value, their capture by the Japanese was demoralizing. The national decision was to drive the enemy off American soil. A new billion-dollar defense program was launched. Cost-plus contracts were used to speed construction. Engineering was often only one pace ahead of the builders.

The marshalling of troops and ships to wage a battle for those little Aleutian outcroppings cost the United States more than dollars. General John DeWitt, head of the Western Defense Command, had to divert forces badly needed in the South Pacific. The Japanese had succeeded in using Alaska to slow down the stream of American troops and ships to the South Pacific, where the decisive battles over Japan's domination would be fought.

Many families fled to the Lower 48 after the Japanese landed. Dependents of the military were ordered to leave, and they were the first to go. Everybody was at the railroad depot to bid farewell to military wives and their children when an Army transport ship arrived to evacuate them. I noted that the officers were unusually tense in regard to that evacuation. Subsequently I learned why.

Military intelligence had located 27 Japanese submarines prowling the North Pacific along the steamship routes to Seattle. The military had tracked those submarines for weeks before and had concluded that the I-boats were there only to observe ship movements, not to sink any. It was thought the Japanese were checking the possibility that the United States was building up forces in Alaska to support a full-scale invasion of Japan via the Aleutian Island chain, which from their point of view was a dagger on the world map pointed right at them.

The Army officers had to stand by and hope that the ship carrying their loved ones would pass those enemy submarines undetected, their ship being just one of the normal traffic pattern. The big question was did any spy or a dissident citizen in Alaska tip off the Japanese? Most of the townspeople knew of the evacuation. Any one could have spilled it, deliberately or by accident.

The ship docked safely in Seattle. The townspeople were proud that their loyalty had not been betrayed.

Uncertain how the war would spread, civilian evacuees next filled every southbound ship and headed to their former homes or wherever they could find greater security. Reluctantly, I put Evangeline and our two daughters, Marilyn and Elaine, on a ship to Seattle, from where they went on to live in New Orleans.

I was able to survive bachelor cooking quite easily, but running the daily newspaper became a nightmare. Not only did I miss Evangeline's help, but also the Army drafted all my good young printers. I tried to locate some of the hard-drinking renegades, the ones I had fired previously, but I finally had to go for help to General Buckner.

"If you want a newspaper to keep people informed in this town, you have to get me some printers," I told Buckner. He located several of my drafted workers and assigned them to duty in the newspaper plant, in uniform. As a consequence, it looked like the Army in my shop. I wrote out their payroll checks, payable to Secretary of Treasury Henry Morgenthau. The printers had to work for Army pay, but I managed to slip them something extra to narrow the difference.

Later, Buckner saved the paper once more when I could not get shipping space for newsprint backed up on the Seattle dock. I estimated the day I would run out and told the general, "Unless the newsprint arrives, there will be no more newspapers after that date." Buckner later showed me a telegram he had sent to the Seattle Port Director requesting a space allocation for my newsprint. I was especially proud of the last sentence, which said, "Continued publication of this newspaper is highly essential to the war effort in Alaska."

However, I still had enormous problems keeping the paper from going under financially. While more people than ever before subscribed to the paper, many of my advertisers quit advertising because their merchandise disappeared from their shelves as fast as they could replace it. They saw no point in running ads when they did not have enough goods to sell.

When my very good advertiser, the Food Center grocery store, started cutting back, I called on the owners, Jack Barrett and Keith Lesh. They were among the town's most enlightened merchants in that they were always on the leading edge of marketing. I knew other stores watched them closely and copied their successful merchandising strategies. Their decision to stop advertising could have a domino effect on the others.

Jack told me it just didn't make sense for him to continue advertising. It wasn't possible to move goods he didn't have. I pointed out his store is an Anchorage institution and newcomers must be kept aware if he wants future customers. He said his store is full of newcomers already.

Then I pointed out that this volume of business must put him into the 95 percent tax bracket and since advertising is a deductible business expense, he will pay only 5 percent of the advertising bill. "Yes," he said, "and a minister just reminded me it works that way with donations to his church."

I suppose it was the same feeling of charity that kept Jack and his partner advertising. But I like to use this incident to point out that boom times, when money is flush and growth is fast, are not necessarilty the best times for newspapers.

In August another ugly phase of war came into our lives—censorship. The federal government called it "voluntary censorship," but it would have been more appropriate to call it "voluntary censorship on a compulsory basis" because it was applied whether approved or not.

Outgoing and incoming mail was all read by censors. Personal letters were delivered with holes cut in them to delete words and phrases that someone found offensive. Magazines and newspapers arrived with holes where censors had disapproved of items or pictures that, mysteriously to us, were approved for publication in the Lower 48 but not in Alaska.

In Anchorage, the Times found it difficult to live with censors. They even decided to restrict weather reports because they might help an enemy. The military requested the newspaper submit stories for approval when they touched on sensitive subjects. We got along well with that, but we battled when a sergeant in the Army Signal Corps forbid the use of the words "hell" and "damn" in press stories transmitted out of Anchorage. That eliminated important parts of the Alaska vocabulary. The sergeant stood pat on his rule even after we showed where the chaste Saturday Evening Post, then in its heyday, allowed those words. Fortunately, his commanding officer overruled him after my angry protest.

When I picked up prints made from an old roll of film, I found a shot of Mt. McKinley was missing. It was censored because it might serve as a landmark to help a pilot find a target. I had to appeal again to higher command just to get my favorite photograph of the well-known mountain released.

Besides tearing us apart by invading the privacy of our mail, the federal government treated Alaskans like alien immigrants when we traveled to Seattle. We were shunted via ugly plywood chutes from the runway into the immigration section of the terminal.

We had to produce satisfactory identification before we would be "admitted" to the United States. If there is one sure way to arouse the anger of an Alaskan it must be to question his American citizenship.

The rebels among us sought ways to make it tough on those immigration people, although we realized they were only doing what they were told. I showed up once and claimed I had nothing to prove identity. They quizzed me at length and finally asked, "Don't you have anything with your name on it?" I showed them a city of Anchorage permit to dump garbage at the city dump. They passed me and I wired a story of the incident to the Times. From then on Alaskans were showing garbage permits as their qualification for admittance to the US.

Alaskans got rather shabby treatment by the military when it came to public information. As in the case of the Aleutian invasion, they were rarely told the whole story of what was happening in their own territory. Most of their information came from reports from distant sources, usually Washington, D.C., but also from correspondents of big city newspapers, like the New York Times, Washington Post and Los Angeles Times.

Surprisingly, the first reports on a hot breaking war event in the Pacific area came from Tokyo Rose. Alaskans kept an ear turned to her by habit. Her reports not only were often the most current but they often proved to be more accurate. Official denials of her news were followed so often by subsequent corrections that her news service took on an amazing credibility, even though she was an enemy propagandist.

It must be remembered that in the 1940s there was no television news service, only radio and newspapers for current information, and when the war started the newspaper was the sole subscriber to the Associated Press in Anchorage. The local radio station read from the newspaper. When local military authorities released no news, we had to

64 | CHAPTER FIVE

rely on whatever was in the AP report from Washington.

It was my impression that local military commanders had only limited authority in public information matters and probably did not want the responsibility anyway. Alaska, being a territory, had no political power and particularly no senators, for instance, to speak up for them. The federal government simply didn't care.

The Army's local public relations office was part of the intelligence office where public information was the least of its concerns. The top information officer came to Alaska as an over-age second lieutenant with a National Guard outfit from San Francisco where he had been a book reviewer for the San Francisco Chronicle. He very quickly proved to the press service correspondents here that he knew nothing about news or how to handle it. We all complained to higher command but got no relief.

It may never be known, but that one second lieutenant might have caused the terrible wartime failures of the Army's public relations in Alaska. Although he bumbled his job, he was repeatedly promoted. He held the rank of lieutenant colonel before his commander came to realize that there was something wrong. The man was shipped Outside as a "section 8" case, affirming our suspicions of his mental instability.

The federal government did some brutal nonsensical things to Alaskans in the name of national security. It closed down the mining industry because manpower was deemed more vital elsewhere. With one edict, it wiped out not only the big gold operations in Nome, Fairbanks and Hatcher Pass, but closed down the family operated small businesses that would have been able to keep on mining even after their draft-eligible men went off to the military.

The government uprooted the entire population of the Pribilof Islands and shipped those peaceful Aleut natives to a Panhandle internment camp. This was done two weeks after the Dutch Harbor attack. These people had lived for centuries on the treeless windswept bluffs jutting out of the Bering Sea some 150 miles north of the Aleutian Islands. They ran a sealing operation for the federal government under terms of a 1911 treaty by Japan, Russia, Britain (for Canada) and the United States.

The terror-stricken Natives had only a few hours notice to pack their belongings (one suitcase each) and board a U.S. military transport ship. The government said they were being evacuated for their own security. A cadre of Army specialists moved in behind them and mined every building with orders to blow up the town if the Japanese invaded. The Japs never bothered. The famed seal population had no wartime strategic value and the islands did not even have an airstrip or harbor.

The Aleuts were quarantined in an abandoned salmon canning camp on Admiralty Island for the duration. The sudden change to life on this isle in the Tongass rain forest took a toll on the their mental and physical health. Then when the Aleuts were returned, they found that the American occupation forces had wrecked their homes on the Pribilofs. Some years later, the federal government decided they were entitled to reparations.

Again, in the name of national security, the government inflicted human indignity upon other Alaska individuals. It was painful to see the misery it caused for Harry Kimura and his enterprising family during the hysteria to remove Japanese aliens and citizens from the West Coast.

Harry had left Japan way back at the turn of the century to work as a cook in California mining camps. He and his wife came to Anchorage in 1916 when the town was in process of being built in the wilderness. Their first work was washing clothes in a large galvanized tub, rubbing out the dirt by hand on a corrugated wash board. They saved enough money to open a mom-and-pop restaurant at Fifth and C called Kimura's Chop Suey House.

Harry reared a fine family of five children on the earnings from his laundry and restaurant. The restaurant was popular and enabled Harry to practice his first love as super chef. It was an asset to downtown Anchorage and the laundry helped the war effort in that it washed blankets and sheets for the troops at the military base. All the children helped in the businesses. The oldest brother, George, left his job to join the Army.

Four months after Pearl Harbor, the FBI and local police barged into the Kimura home in the middle of the night and hauled Harry off to the stockade at Fort Richardson, ironically only a short distance from the barracks where George was sleeping as a soldier. They shipped Harry off to a concentration camp in New Mexico, like a prisoner of war, and notified his family to start packing for their internment. They would join some 110,000 Japanese-Americans herded in evacuation camps during the war.

A large segment of the community rallied behind the Kimuras and held a public farewell party to show their support. A few days later, officers shipped Mrs. Kimura and her children to Minidoka Relocation Center in Idaho and they never saw their husband and father again until the end of the war.

Fortunately, the Kimuras had the fortitude to survive. They returned to Anchorage, rescued their tax-liened properties, and later opened an even larger restaurant, the Golden Pheasant. The children went on to distinguished careers in art, academia, and public service.

While Japanese forces consolidated their foothold in the Aleutians, I had an unexpected ringside seat in the military's debate on how best to oust them. Buckner, who headed the Army's Alaska Defense Command from his base in Anchorage, had his act in shape. He trained his troops for cold-weather fighting and personally had traveled the length of the Aleutian chain, noting its crater-like terrain and radical weather changes. He wanted to coordinate the strategy to retake Attu and Kiska.

However, Rear Admiral Robert A. Theobald commanded the naval forces and the air corps from a base in Kodiak, where he arrived with a small fleet of ships from Pearl Harbor in May 1942. Though a stranger to the often fog-shrouded, largely uncharted western Aleutians, he had his own ideas on how to fight the Japanese and they were generally contrary to Buckner's.

In fact, the two couldn't agree on a damned thing. At a cocktail party at my house they went at it in front of guests, roughly as follows:

Buckner: "All you guys in the Navy have to do is deliver us there. My troops are trained to fight on that terrain."

Theobald: "We don't need your Army. I'll go down there with a handful of Marines, the big guns on the ships will destroy the Jap positions, and those Marines can take the island. "

In January 1943, five months before the battle of Attu began, the Navy relieved Theobald of his Alaska assignment. However, though his rival was removed from the plotting, this was no victory for Buckner's strategy. Rear Admiral Thomas C. Kincaid, a seasoned veteran of several South Pacific battles, took command, and he had his own ideas of how to launch amphibious assaults.

The military debacle of how we recaptured the Aleutians is well documented in history books. Despite our overwhelming forces—12, 500 Americans fighting fewer than 2,000 Japanese—we suffered 3,829 casualties on Attu. At least 1,200 were disabled by severe cold injuries, requiring amputations of limbs in many cases. I can only wonder how many of these could have been avoided had Buckner's trained arctic troops and his expert knowledge of the Aleutians had been fully utilized. (Despite Buckner's protests, the War Department assigned the Army's 7th Motorized Division, which had been training in the hot California desert, to lead the assault in driving the Japanese from the Aleutians.)

It was disillusioning, too, to discover after the war that the Japanese had evacuated Kiska in the fog without being detected by our large fleet of warships and planes. For the first two weeks of August 1943, American ships and planes bombarded the abandoned island before sending in 35,000 combat troops to battle the non-existent Japs. Nor did we learn until much later that 313 of those men were lost mainly because Americans were shooting at one another in the fog.

We could not publish a story on the retaking of Kiska until Aug. 21, a week after our troops took over the deserted island. Then the military used the press to cover up its blundering. "A goodly number of the estimated 8,500 Japs on Kiska were killed—how many it is difficult to estimate," Vice Admiral Kincaid said in assessing the operation in a press briefing. "After the Japanese began the evacuation of Kiska, I believe we sank some of their ships during the heavy fog at night."

The truth, as it emerged years later, was that not a single enemy solider was killed on Kiska, and the ships supposedly sunk turned out to be phantom blips that flickered on and off the radar screen.

Some military strategists contend that the mistakes in the Aleutians were not in vain, that they made us smarter in waging guerilla warfare in the South Pacific, and that the retaking of the islands did give us the first theater-wide victory in World War II. However, that is small comfort to an editor whose newspaper was used by the military to deceive the public.

August 15, 1943, is a date of big significance to Alaska. That was the day American forces took back Kiska Island from enemy forces who had held it for a year. The Aleutian chain of islands was once more free of invaders.

The action marked the sudden termination of national involvement in the everyday affairs of the territory. The war in Alaska was over and the military was to re-deploy its might rapidly to the South Pacific to take part in the island-hopping movement northward towards Japan.

For Americans everywhere, including Alaska, August 15 , 1943, was a day of relief and encouragement. The relief was "We got them off American soil." The encouragement, "Now we can move faster to hit their homeland."

But there were additional concerns for Alaskans. What would happen to their economy? How would they make a living without the military and civilian payrolls for construction projects, transportation and maintenance of the large establishment.

The fear was that Anchorage would once more become a railroad town, with one payroll for support. The city's population had swelled and it would take more than the railroad to support that many people.

Alaskans in other cities often chided Anchorage for its rapid growth and prosperity, saying its growth was only a bubble that would some day break. Some Juneau leaders were graphic in pointing to new buildings and shops saying, "When that happens, those buildings will be abandoned, the windows broken and pigeons will be flying through them."

Anchorage was saved by a decision in the Pentagon to make Alaska the staging area for a new phase of the war. Facilities in Anchorage and along the chain of Aleutian islands were ready and existing to support bombers taking the war to the Japanese homeland.

Until V-J Day, almost two years later, that was the mission of the military in Alaska. The Air Corps sent bombers every day the weather permitted. U.S. planes pounded the Kuril Islands mercilessly and forced Japan to divert substantial military strength to the north while American forces were closing in on them from the south.

All this was done under the heavy shroud of military secrecy. Nothing was announced. Newspapers rarely gave much information. But within Anchorage city limits, where many of the airmen and their co-workers lived in houses rented off base and were included in local civilian social groups, there was a pretty good understanding.

The Army couldn't keep it a secret that something was happening when beat-up bombers were seen flying low over town returning to Elmendorf, some with parts of the tail torn off, wing sections missing, sizable bullet holes in the fuselage and sometimes one or two engines dead. Obviously, they had been shot at.

Keeping Japan in the dark was part of the American strategy. They hoped the enemy didn't know where the bombers came from so it would be hard for him to plan a defense.

It was at this stage of the war that the military intelligence people became concerned about the war rumors that were prevalent in Anchorage, many of them accurate, of course. Efforts were made to find the source. They tried to trace the source by devious means.

They planted counter-intelligence personnel in downtown public places as waiters or bartenders to listen in on the bar talk as soldiers and civilians relaxed at the end of the day. Soldiers were living under orders to keep mum on war events. Civilians were constantly urged to repeat no rumors.

The investigators concluded that rumors downtown were identical to the rumors on base. So anything heard on base should be expected to be heard downtown.

Further study led to the conclusion that so many military people lived downtown among the civilians, and so many civilians worked all day on the base with the military, that the two communities should be considered one. That ended the problem.

The war in Alaska was over but its impacts lived on. There were shortages in capacity or output of almost every community facility or service. In Anchorage there was a shortage of classrooms in the schools, water and sewer systems needed to be extended to the newly developed residential areas, telephone service needed expansion, electric power generation and distribution were both inadequate. The city was short of money and no longer had a rich partner in Army uniform to help.

The war in Alaska had ended but the war in the rest of the world was still raging. Industries were still producing war goods. The backlog of orders for civilian needs was still held in abeyance. The queue waiting for deliveries would be long—sometimes two or more years after the war ended.

It would be two long years before the bomb was dropped at Hiroshima and Japan surrendered. General Buckner was re-assigned out of Alaska on a secret mission. He went to Hawaii where he organized the Tenth Army and trained it for the last big battle in the Pacific—the invasion of Okinawa. It was there, during the bloodiest battle of the Pacific war, Buckner was killed on June 18, 1945, by enemy shellfire. He was the highest-ranking American killed in action in World War II.

Life in Alaska continued with little relief from the war impacts. Ways had to be found to make do with virtually every community facility too small and inadequate to do its job. Virtually every expansion program proved to be too small due to the continuing influx of people to support the air warfare staged from here. Temporary steel-plate runways in the Aleutians had to be replaced with longer and wider paved runways to accommodate the newest and biggest bombers. Most ground support facilities had to be updated for the new technology.

Schools remained on their double-shift schedules. Grocers found their shelves empty almost every day and had to reload them overnight for the next day's business. There were frequent brownouts, when electric power was cut off because the demand was greater than the generating capabilities.

Many families returned to their homes in this period after Alaska was no longer an active war front. Some preferred family life here despite the inconveniences. Of course, some could not afford the extra cost of keeping Mom and the kids Outside while Daddy stayed home to work. Those who returned were factors in the further demand for more utility services, schools, supplies and recreation.

Needless to say V-J Day was hailed in Anchorage with great enthusiasm, each in his own way but no public gathering to mark it. Instead, staying home was a popular idea and most did, leaving the downtown for noisy, rougher activities. The Army limited the number of passes issued to soldiers. They were well aware of the police problems that could arise as the night wore on. Downtown bars were loaded with happy celebrants, moving from bar to bar as their celebrations continued. The later it got the noisier it got.

City and military police made themselves visible by patrolling the streets and sidewalks in pairs. The paddy wagons of old were on prominent display, ready for use. Merchants were concerned for their front windows. They removed precious merchandise. Some had plywood cut and ready for placement. My Anchorage Times office was mainly glass on Fourth Avenue. I sat at my desk in the dark wondering what was going to happen.

Rev. R. Rolland Armstrong, whose Presbyterian church on Fifth Avenue practically backed up to my newspaper building, joined me for the vigil. As we visited we could almost feel the tension on the street rising. People were too happy. One untoward incident could start trouble.

"Do you think it would be a good idea for me to play church music on my church carillon?" he asked. After a brief discussion we decided it might help. So he went to church and I stayed at my office. I could feel the prevailing temperament on the street slowing down. There was no indication that anyone was aware of the church music, but its effect was everywhere.

The city, which had so much stress and strain through the war, got through the night without being torn apart.

Helen Payne, member of the Girls Service Organization, enjoys a cup of tea with a corporal at one a USO's club houses.

Four members of the Girls Service Organization take time out for a cold drink between dances at a USO club house. Photo by Signal Corps U.S. Army Official Photograph/July 23, 1940

72 | CHAPTER FIVE

— CHAPTER SIX —

Post War Turmoil

With the war over, Anchorage, like many of its citizens, awoke with a hangover. It hurt to look into the future. Our infrastructure was hard-used and crumbling. The almost certain exodus of the military, our economic mainstay, meant we were also losing our lifeline into the federal system.

The Army had brought as many as 150,000 troops to man the northern ramparts during the war. Almost overnight, that was being reduced to 50,000. The government also suspended all military construction, leaving many thousands of well-paying civilian jobs in the lurch. As headquarters of the Alaska defense command, Anchorage would be hit the hardest of any area in the territory.

Was this the dreaded time when Alaska, and Anchorage, would once more be pushed back into obscurity, when there would be no more federal funds because we no longer served a national need?

It didn't happen. The fact is that the country discovered a new appeal in Alaska. Ex-GIs returned by the thousands, many of them heading here because they learned during their service that Anchorage has a very livable climate. Others spread out to the Kenai Peninsula and other unpeopled environs, attracted by the chance to own 160 acres under the generous GI homesteading program, the last free land in America, as touted in the Army weekly magazine, YANK.

They came in beat-up cars, their worldly possessions strapped on the roof. These were America's new pioneers. Of course, only the hardiest stayed, but those who did would in time discover Anchorage, Alaska's liveliest city, easily accessible on the railbelt.

No sooner had the war ended than the government announced a proposal to erect 1,220 new housing units in Anchorage to accommodate new federal employees. It made no mention of their mission, but rumors quickly spread about a giant radar network to be built across the top of Alaska, and the words "Cold War" were soon to become part of the vocabulary. The military thinking became clear—arming the Arctic and Alaska was the best way to defend America against Joseph Stalin's military buildup across the Bering Strait.

A $75 million railroad rehabilitation program, to be started in 1947, next raised our spirits. It entailed rebuilding the entire system because the strategic but rickety railroad was poorly constructed in the first place. Those decrepit wood bridges would be replaced by steel, the worn-out 70-pound rails would be ripped out in favor of 115-pounders. This again made Anchorage a magnet for new jobs and new people, and reinforced feelings that the federal government intended to make its presence permanent.

And a totally unexpected new industry, tourism, showed signs of blooming. Besides furnishing a gateway for pent-up travelers unable to visit our majestic scenic sights because of wartime restrictions, the city enjoyed a noticeable infusion of business when the state, acting two days after the war ended, lifted a two-year ban on big game hunting.

We ran stories about free-spending sportsmen flocking in from Outside, boosting ammunition and camping equipment sales as they outfitted for expeditions into caribou, bear, and mountain sheep country. (The grizzlies seemed geared for the invasion, because subsequent stories told of bears ripping hunters' tents to shreds and gorging on their food and hunting kills.)

By mid-September, barely a month after V-J Day, I was able to write an editorial titled "A Postwar Boom for Anchorage." Noting the developments, I prodded city officials to look ahead. "We are already struggling with a power problem . . . we are building an addition to a school that will be filled to overflowing by the time it is completed . . . our water system has long been inadequate." I pointed out the city lost many opportunities to improve these basic services in the war boom and asked "How will we handle them now?"

Unsurprisingly, the editorial stirred no one at City Hall. The mayor, councilmen and department heads were too busy feuding, trying to protect their turfs of power.

Mayor John Manders, a lawyer formerly of San Francisco, was a petty man, hardly one to recognize the long-range needs of what was becoming Alaska's fastest growing city. (At one point he refused to sign the city engineer's pay check because the engineer failed to follow his orders to wash Fourth Avenue. Another time, Manders was too miffed to reappoint the police chief, making it necessary for a councilman serving as acting mayor to make the appointment when the mayor stepped out of town.)

The city was particularly helpless in dealing with the power shortage. The power station had been built to serve a city of 10,000. As population doubled by the end of the war, outages became so severe that they were now a daily occurrence. The city managed to scrape up the money to buy two additional diesel electric generators and it borrowed another from the Alaska railroad, but rationing power still became necessary.

We appealed editorially for people to turn off needless lights, to alternate times in cooking their Thanksgiving turkeys, and to refrain from using ovens with doors open to heat their homes. (The latter was particularly important because temperatures in some winter days would dive to 25 below and the entire city would be blacked out as people resorted to any means at hand to keep warm.)

Only the unique idea of a bright naval engineer saved Anchorage in the crisis. A salvage officer on the destroyer Boxwood, Lt. Comdr. B.J. Logan, knew that an oil tanker, the SS Sacketts Harbor, had broken in half March 1, 1946, during a blustering winter gale out in the Aleutians on its way to the Orient. The front end of the 10,000-ton ship had sunk, but the stern half was still afloat, anchored at Adak. And inside this salvaged section was a functioning 5,400-kilowatt steam generator, with living quarters for a crew to operate it.

"Why not tow the ship into the town harbor and tap into its generator?" he suggested.

We led the paper with his proposal. The mayor, city council and the whole town got behind it. The city supported it, now under the leadership of a new mayor. (Manders quit when council voted to endorse the city manager form of government which we campaigned for.)

At that particular moment in time, Anchorage was a community of do-gooders, all working for their town. Delegations were going to Washington, D.C., to lobby congress for help in authorizing bond issues and even suggesting that Alaska was ready for statehood. Consequently, many local Alaskans were acquainted with key people in key offices of the federal bureaus that ran Alaska.

When Anchorage decided it could use the broken tanker, local residents very quickly had their representatives in the capital city see what could be done about it. With the help of Alaska's delegate, E. L. (Bob) Bartlett, they quickly had appointments with people in the key agencies. It required only a few days for title to the tanker to be transferred to an Interior Department agency which quickly sold it to the City of Anchorage.

That is how the city came into ownership of the stern half of the Sacketts Harbor, a Liberty ship destined to be an integral part of the community for more than a decade. The city owned it but the monster was still about 1,500 miles away and the city had no facilities for bringing it to town.

As the good beggars we were trained to be under the territorial form of government, Anchorage appealed to the Navy for help. The Navy assigned Logan to bring the ship from Adak and gave him two tugs to tow it.

I doubt whether any annals of naval history record the feat of Logan sailing that clumsy, unballasted, 300-foot floating hulk through the treacherous Shelikof Straits and into Anchorage. But he certainly deserves a place in Alaska history. With every gust of wind blowing the ragged-ended, bulkhead-exposed remnant of a ship every which way, Logan also fought eight-knot currents in Cook Inlet to reach his destina-

POST WAR TUMOIL | 75

tion. Under his direction, the city engineering forces dug out a big trench in the harbor mudflats at low tide. On Oct. 11, 1946, after waiting for the right combination of wind and tide, Logan nudged the vessel into the trench, his tugs deftly escaping entrapment in the mud.

The city then spent $125,000 connecting it to the city power system. The ship pumped 3,500 kilowatts of electric power into the city system, supplying 55 percent of Anchorage's power requirements from 1947 to 1955 when a huge hydro-electric plant built by the Bureau of Reclamation at Eklutna, about 30 miles east of town, went on line and met the needs of our growing city.

Besides serving Anchorage for nearly nine years, the Sacketts Harbor actually enabled the city to reap a sizable profit on the investment. Anchorage paid the War Assets Administration $25,000 for the vessel. The city sold off its lifeboats and machine shops immediately for $100,000, a junk dealer from Seattle paid the city handsomely for the beautiful bronze propeller and then it received another $100,000 when it disposed of the ship in 1955. The new owner, United Vintners, refitted the vessel at the Bethlehem Steel shipyards at San Francisco. It was launched again as the Angelo Petri, the nation's first wine ship. Last heard from, it was transporting 2,383,540-gallon loads of California wine to New York.

The city did not act as effectively—or you might say it wasn't as lucky—in dealing with the rampant crime that came with the new boom. During the wartime labor scarcity, federal agencies recruited many seamy characters to work on the railroad. The influx of ex-convicts, dishonorably discharged soldiers and mentally unstables created horrendous problems. The city had only 29 jail spaces but 226 arrests were made in one four-month stretch alone after the war ended. These lawless characters were hauled in for nearly every crime on the books—murder, larceny, molesting minor girls, vagrancy, assault and battery, peeping Tom, delirium tremens, and so on.

By 1946, the businessmen decided they had to do something to get the undesirables out of town. So they pooled funds to enable police to buy persistent offenders one-way tickets out of the territory. Many happily left their jail cells for a free ride to Seattle. In fact, the pool soon was running out of money. To cut costs, the businessmen tried to deport 23 men classified as "undesirables" by train to Seward, only 180 miles down the peninsula.

Seward's live-wire mayor, Clarence P. Keating, caught wind of the plan and met the train at the depot. He promptly bought the deported bums return tickets, rode back with them to Anchorage, and dropped them off at the station from whence they came. Keating billed the city for his expenses. I am not sure whether the embarrassed Anchorage administration ever honored the voucher.

However, the crime problem had deeper manifestations than these comic opera antics. The Anchorage police department was thoroughly corrupt. As editor, I was swamped with complaints. Police rolled prisoners in the paddy wagon on the way to the station, stripping them of their money and watches. Certain gambling games were protected, others were hassled by police. Madams ran their whorehouses with confidence that the fix was in.

For years, I thought I had an ongoing understanding with city administrations about gambling and prostitution. We were a frontier city developing into a hub of transportation. Miners and fishermen often had to spend days in Anchorage waiting for that one steamboat out each week. They needed something to do. But we also wanted a decent town, where families could raise kids out of sight of vice. The compromise was the city would permit modest-stake card games in pool halls out of sight and whorehouses were allowed to have two or three girls at discreet locations.

When the big federal projects started, things got out of hand. The tinhorn pool hall gaming operators complained that racketeers from Outside were moving in with high stake games. Word spread that the madams were bringing in girls over the limited number. I would run editorials deploring the trend. Token raids would follow, but the public could sense the sham.

Meanwhile, the police chief's office became a revolving door, suggesting an internal tug-of-war over who controlled or profited from the rackets. In the fall of 1948, the dissension at police headquarters broke into open warfare, high-ranking officers accusing one another of dereliction of duty—vague charges but symptoms of deep trouble.

It was about this time that an FBI agent dropped into my office for a confidential talk. I asked what I could do about the problem. He handed me a rundown of all the members of the force, detailing their records of criminal activity and kickbacks. As soon as he left, I went to the typewriter, and on Dec. 6, 1948, I believe I ran the most courageous editorial of my young career.

"The municipal government has no chance of controlling the police problems of the city while it has a department manned by disloyal persons whose background and associations disqualify them for the responsibilities that go with their positions, " I stated. "...Marijuana, Spanish Fly, and other illicit dope are being peddled locally; big time gamblers are attracted here to prey on the large paychecks of the working man; law officials are hamstrung ... we found that an efficient tip-off system warns the underworld of any plans of enforcement officials to act; there are leaks in the police department and in the marshal's office."

Then I listed the backgrounds of officers in the police department:

"One man was arrested in one state for violations of the Mann Act (white slavery), in another for molesting automobiles, and in a third for contributing to the delinquency of a minor.

"Another man was sentenced to a year and a half in the penitentiary for grand larceny and was arrested another time for auto theft and another time for felonious assault.

"Another man has a record of seven arrests over a period of four years in four states, which brought 10 days in jail once, two sentences of $100 and 50 days, and $25 and 30 days another time.

"We also discovered that the records of four men were unaccountably missing from the files of the chief of police.

"One man is serving on the police force under a phony name, adopted when he came to Alaska from the states.

"Another was thrown off an Alaska Railroad river boat by fellow members of the crew after he had been found in a compromising position with a native boy."

Good men cannot be expected to remain on a police department so polluted, I concluded, and urged the public to demand a massive cleanup to restore confidence and pride in the police force.

No one contradicted my allegations. Instead, mayhem broke out in City Hall. City Manager Don Wilson quickly fired three sergeants and the city jailer. The latter punched an officer in the mouth when he told him to surrender the keys to the jail. Other officers quietly resigned as Wilson pursued an investigation.

One person, who claimed he was unfairly fired, visited my office to ask help in finding another job. He confided that there had been a plot within the police department to get even for the editorials by burning down my house. That unnerved me a bit, but I believe Wilson's swift action in ousting the rats in the police department sent them packing before they had time to carry out a plan.

A sad part about our police mess was that Anchorage pay scales were the highest in the nation. In 1948, the typical entrance salary for patrolman, $4,800 plus benefits, was more than twice as high as those paid by cities up to 100,000 population. Yet, we couldn't put together a good police department until many years later. It was not until 1956, after much more turmoil, that John C. Flanigan of Montana beat out 50 applicants for the police chief's job. He served so well that I, among many others, hated to see him go when he chose voluntary retirement 17 years later.

In the midst of trying to keep on top of the city's internal problems, I did my best to save Governor Gruening in the intensifying battle to oust him when his term expired in 1948. With the death of President Roosevelt, his staunch supporter, Gruening's enemies put the heat on President Harry Truman, who had been non-committal about reappointing our governor.

I believed Gruening had proved his importance to Alaska, but he was clearly in trouble. Once opposed mainly by the Seattle-owned salmon cannery interests who feared new taxes and a ban on fish traps, Gruening had acquired a widening circle of foes after the war ended. An impatient New Dealer, he had sought more expenditures from the territory than many felt wise or necessary. The legislature turned down his every tax program (we had no taxes except a $5 a year school tax) and twice passed resolutions asking for his removal.

Further, Gruening offended many of the independent, non-political whites by condemning Alaskans' treatment of Natives. Appalled to find Natives barred from restaurants and saloons in Juneau and Anchorage, he castigated their demeaning window signs, some of which stated bluntly: "No Natives Allowed" and even "No Dogs or Indians Allowed."

Uncompromising and often unpolitic, Democrat Gruening lost even the support of the territory's Democratic organization. Party leaders in Alaska wanted Truman to name one of their own, either Norman Walker of Ketchikan or Edward Coffey of Anchorage. On top of that, powerful Democrats in Washington state urged Truman to replace Gruening with Herbert Algoe, the fair-haired boy of Gov. Mon Wallgren.

However, nobody set out to oust Gruening more intensely than the national leaders of big labor and the shipping industry. Gruening had riled them by trying to secure the release of ships which would give some relief to Alaska that was always held hostage in the continuing contentions between the steamship operators and the maritime unions on the Pacific Coast. Not only did rate increases after each fight retard the development of the territory, but one 69-day tie-up in 1946 just about choked our economy.

Gruening's criticism of high shipping rates and his appeals for federal intervention in the tie-ups had particularly angered Gil Skinner, president of the Alaska Steamship Co., which held the transportation monopoly in Alaska. The St. Louis Post-Dispatch commented that Skinner was said to have had more political might in Washington than all 90,000 residents of Alaska. But what about Truman's famed campaign promise to listen to the "little guy?"

In an editorial titled "Gruening Should Stay," I wrote: "Never before has the 'little guy' living in Alaska been made to realize his potentialities and powers as a builder and citizen. Gruening is the spearhead of the great statehood movement, the efforts to obtain cheap transportation and local controls essential to development … his political risks have been perilous as he taunted powerful absentee interests on behalf of the little people of Alaska … Failure to reappoint him could be the result of nothing other than a victory of absentee lobbyists over the will of the people."

I don't know whether anyone ever brought that editorial to Truman's attention. But a few weeks later, on March 12, 1948, he appointed Gruening to his third four-year term. Two years previously, Truman had accepted the resignation of Interior Secretary Harold Ickes, whose condescending attitude toward Alaskans made him an enemy of the territory. In that short time, Truman proved himself a really true friend of Alaska.

As we entered the 1950s, Anchorage was identified as the largest city on the North American continent north of Edmonton, Alberta. Our population had grown to 64,000 people, about a third of the entire population of Alaska. Real property values were rising at $10 million a year. Lots that sold for $100 before the war were now bringing $2,000. But people were streaming in despite the high costs of living and the Secretary of Interior's warning that only the hardy should come. A count taken in 1948 showed that 36 states were represented in Anchorage schools.

And as population grew, so did readership. We built a modern newspaper plant on Fourth Ave. (and paid for it without having to dip into the

$100,000 credit offered by National Bank of Alaska, now run by my brother-in-law, Elmer E. Rasmuson). We replaced the hand-fed flat bed antique press with an automatic feed that enabled us to print two sections and increase our size from eight pages to 14. I hired a stringer in Washington and opened a bureau in the nation's capital. We posted a new logo over our flag: "Alaska's Largest Paper."

An immensely important factor in our growth was the development of an air transportation center in Anchorage. I refrained from dealing with it in this chapter, because the fierce battles and many heartaches that ushered in the air age deserve separate treatment.

Anchorage Westward Hotel rises. Photo by Steve McClutcheon/Alaska Pictorial Service/Feb. 1971

Left: portion of tanker that supplied power to Anchorage. Photo by Steve McClutcheon/Alaska Pictorial Service

Banks had to expand to take care of expanding businesses. The National Bank of Alaska added several stories to their main building. Photo by Steve McClutcheon/Alaska Pictorial Service/June 1961

The Anchorage Times publishing Company found it necessary to build an addition in order to accommodate new presses and expanded advertising and reporting staff. Photo by Steve McClutcheon/Alaska Pictorial Service/Sept. 1968.

— CHAPTER SEVEN —

Air Age

In 1926 local businessmen imported a flying machine from Seattle, assembled it in Anchorage and organized Anchorage Air Transport, Inc. It was the first airline in the city that was destined to become the most air-minded of all the cities in America.

Although it was a wild gamble for A.A. Shonbeck and Oscar Anderson, two of the main stockholders, it was a good investment. Shonbeck was in business as Ford dealer, Hercules dynamite, tractors and other heavy equipment, as well as hay and feed for horses or what-have-you. Anderson had good income from his retail butcher shop and other businesses. Neither needed profit from the airline and, probably, there never was any. Introducing commercial aviation to compete with dog teams and riverboats for payloads in interior Alaska was not easy.

The airline was endowed with three precious assets: support from the enthusiastic local populace, free use of an airport made in 1923 by volunteers hoping to attract aviation, and the services of one trained pilot, Russell E. Merrill. From that small beginning grew the great air transportation industry that made Anchorage the air crossroads of the world.

Competitors jumped into the field as soon as they saw Air Transport making a niche for itself in the transportation picture. In a very few years, Anchorage was home base for a bevy of bush pilots. The roar of their engines as they departed each morning was a new feature of life in Anchorage. And, naturally, the roar of the same engines was a part of the afternoon and early evening.

By 1935 bush pilots had ganged up in companies the better to compete with each other. The early day companies were often hardly more than coalitions but the competition was stiff. These groups evolved into established institutions in Alaska history–Star Airlines which became Alaska Airlines, Woodley Airways which became Pacific Northern Airlines which merged into Western Airlines and finally became a part of Delta Airlines, and Ray Petersen Airlines which became Northern Consolidated Airlines and eventually Wien Airlines.

As these pioneer bush operators grew bigger and had greater volume of business, they could afford to improve their services. They could support a man and wife team to live in some remote mountain pass to send in weather reports by radio. This reduced the number of flights that started for somewhere but couldn't get there because the pass was impassable. To shut off their competitors from the benefits of the radio reports, intricate weather codes were invented. They were usually changed every week to discourage "spies."

When I became editor in Anchorage I needed a source for news reports from interior points. For lack of communications facilities, a stringer couldn't even send reports. I found the bush pilots an excellent source. Besides that, they were a bunch of interesting, courageous and adventuresome young men. Whether they were aware of it or not, I considered them all my "reporters," and interviewed them after every sortie into the Bush country. My paper had stories about the mines and the miners, who died, who married, who sold out, and who came in.

The biggest competitors for Anchorage bush pilots were Fairbanks bush pilots. They served interior villages down the Kuskokwim and Yukon Rivers, the routes of the riverboats in summer. The Anchorage pilots told me those Fairbanks guys were hard to compete with because the village residents, many oldtime miners and trappers, all had friends in Fairbanks, the oldtime city, and visited friends there whenever they went anywhere.

So I arranged for a promotional effort in behalf of Anchorage. I would provide free newspapers for them to deliver to each village they served if they would agree to put it on the counter of the trading post for customers to read. Everyone was hungry for news in the interior. Incidentally, under this arrangement the pilots became my carriers for delivering the paper.

This worked like a charm. The daily issues of the Times piled up higher and higher in trading posts remote from Anchorage. They would never throw them away, it seems, because someone in the bush country had yet to read them. News is still news no matter how old it is if you haven't heard it before. Pilots said when they forgot to take the papers to a village they were not welcome when they arrived.

The pilots were happy because their business of shopping for interior residents was prospering. More flew with them as passengers to Anchorage. They said they wanted to see the stores and the city they were reading about. Those bush people became acquainted with the names Carr, Gottstein, Loussac, Seidenverg, Crockers Department Store, the Green Front, Vaara's Varieties and other local merchants. They asked their pilot friends to bring them things from those stores.

This developed trade and commerce by air between Anchorage and Interior villages. The shopping orders became so numerous that Alaska Star Airlines hired a full-time shopper who would get the orders from the stores and put them in line for delivery by the next flight.

Meanwhile, I was busy writing the news stories I got from interviewing the pilots and urging my advertisers to make more pitches aimed at the bush trade. And the advertisers often let me know how happy they were to have business from the bush country.

Thus Anchorage, the new city built in 1915 and considered an intruder by Fairbanks, made a niche for itself as a supply center for the bush country.

By the time the military moved in, bush pilots knew more about the mountain passes and weather tricks than were shown on any record. Military pilots looked to them for their first Alaska training. But, of course, the Air Corps of that day soon passed up all phases of bush pilot operations as they brought in their newer, more-powerful weapons and technology.

These actions set the stage for the new life of Anchorage as a supply center and support base for two huge military establishments. Anchorage, population 3,500, was no longer to be an obscure railroad center. It was entering an age of mushroom growth, complex problems of every sort, and the dangers that come with being a prime war target and the hub of an active front confronting an enemy on American soil.

Nary a complaint was heard from the civilian community. We invited the military to come here and were delighted that they came.

Anyone who reads American history might see that events in Anchorage were no more than a repeat of the history of the opening of the West. Many prominent cities had their origins as supply centers for Army posts. Chicago can be described as the outgrowth of a sawmill that supplied lumber to Fort Dearborn. Minneapolis and St. Paul had beginnings in a sawmill that used hydroelectric power generated from St. Anthony Falls to supply lumber to Fort Snelling.

The optimists, which included most Alaskans, saw many benefits ahead. The influx of military brought many new friends and neighbors who were found to be clean, intelligent, well-disciplined and good citizens. The civilian community seemed to accept what was happening around them.

The Civil Aeronautics Authority (today the Federal Aviation Administration) kept an eye on the growth of civil aviation in Alaska and in 1939 saw the need for some federal regulation and guidance. Bush operations were unregulated, without certification and were flown by intrepid individuals helter-skelter without the aid of navigation aids provided for civil airways in all the states, but not in Alaska.

The CAA opened an office at Anchorage and called it headquarters for a new region, the Eighth. The needs were so obvious that they very quickly spent a million dollars installing navigation aids at strategic points on the main routes of flight. Radio beams were installed in 20 airports. Runways were paved in several. An administration building was built at Anchorage, and a radio range station was established.

Bush pilots loved the radio beacons that led them through mountain passes and the paved runways, but they found it hard to accept the regulations that started flowing from the new federal agency. In 1946 when

AIR AGE | 85

the war had ended, the Civil Aeronautics Board, the legislative agency in aeronautics, showed up in Anchorage and disclosed plans for establishing real civil air routes. Once selected, they would be the basic air transportation system for Alaska, equipped with navigation aids and under federal supervision. Public hearings would be held in connection with selecting which carriers would be granted certificates as air operators.

To bush pilots this was very hard to accept. They had always flown where and when they wanted to without government controls. The prospect of public hearings that would involve lawyers and documents, all of which cost money that some flyers could not afford. This encouraged sell-outs and mergers. Air operations were on the way toward big business.

Anchorage civic leaders quickly launched a concerted effort to see that Anchorage had a place in the route patterns the CAB was considering. Foremost need was direct air service between Anchorage and Seattle. The only existing service operated between Seattle and Fairbanks, with stops in Juneau and Whitehorse. Travelers from Anchorage had to change planes at Juneau. The connection usually entailed an overnight stay at Juneau and because of the uncertain flying weather the times of arrival and departure in Juneau were never certain.

Oldtimers still remember the frustrations of air travel in the early days of commercial aviation. Planes that flew from Anchorage to Juneau often could not find the airport and had to land somewhere else. Similarly, planes from Fairbanks en route to Seattle couldn't land and were forced to overfly to Seattle without a stop. Consequently, Juneau hotels were often full of unhappy Anchorage people who didn't want to be there.

The Anchorage presentations to the board were rich with facts and figures on weather, topography, terrain, weather and economics. The CAB hearing examiners were so impressed that they recommended direct service to Seattle. They also recommend that the North Pacific route from New York and Chicago to Tokyo also have Anchorage as a port of call in Alaska.

Anchorage people were elated. But in Seattle there was immediate resentment. That city would oppose the recommendation because it considered an "inside" direct route to Alaska (over Canada, avoiding Seattle) would destroy its distinction as the Gateway to Alaska. Seattle had opposed, without success, the inland route of the Alcan Highway on the same grounds. Now they saw they were losing their monopoly as an air gateway.

In Fairbanks, too, there was disenchantment with the recommendation for Anchorage. The aviation leaders there had expected the North Pacific route would go through their city. But they had failed to make presentations before the CAB hearings. They would have had good supportive arguments. The Great Circle Route from New York to Tokyo goes through Fairbanks. We, in Anchorage, thought it would go there and made no request for it. But the CAB examiner recommended Anchorage without a request.

The Seattle Chamber of Commerce named a special committee to see that the CAB would reject the examiner's recommendation and force the route from the East Coast to stop in Seattle en route to Tokyo. They enlisted Dave Beck, the nationally prominent president of the Teamster's Union, to be chairman. They also had Sen. Warren Magnuson and Sen. Henry M. Jackson, two of the Senate's most powerful members, on their side. And through donations they had a $250,000 fund to finance their campaign.

In Anchorage we were surprised and disappointed that our Seattle friends were trying to kill our new prospect for national prominence and economic security, but we should not have been. Seattle interests had opposed us for years when we tried to conserve the fisheries. They opposed us when we sought lower freight rates. They were continuous opponents to programs that would be good for Alaska.

The salmon packers didn't want Alaska to gain population and develop because it would mean they would have to pay taxes. They preferred to go to Alaska each spring, catch and pack the fish, and get back to Seattle without leaving anything in Alaska, especially money.

It happened that I was president of the Anchorage Chamber of Commerce this particular year. My board members speculated that our Seattle neighbors may not be aware of the importance of this inland air route to Anchorage and Alaska, so we should send someone to Seattle to discuss it with them. And they selected me to go.

At first I was proud that they chose me, with expenses paid. Any one of us would enjoy such a vacation. It would be a one-week cruise each way on the steamship enjoying the beautiful Inside Passage of Alaska. And at least a week in Seattle before the next ship north. Later I was sorry I had accepted it.

The Seattle chamber didn't want to hear my story and refused to listen. I was allowed to see only the chairman of the Alaska Department. Christy Thomas, the manager who was the chamber's power center, had no time for me.

I told my story to the Alaska manager but it went no farther. I presented economic figures that showed his organization was working against "its best customer, Anchorage." But that went nowhere.

I sat down at a typewriter in his office and wrote a detailed news story addressed to the Anchorage Times. It related with direct quotes what he told me and what I told him. I showed it to the Alaska manager. He agreed that my report was accurate, but he hated to see it sent. I called the Alaska Communications System. They sent a messenger and while the Alaska manager looked on, I dispatched the story.

Every day during the week I was there, I reported to his office every

AIR AGE | 87

morning, was refused permission to see Christy Thomas so I talked more with the Alaska manager. Then I borrowed his typewriter and desk to compose another detailed report to the Times.

The owners of stores in Anchorage responded by sending angry telegrams to their wholesale suppliers in Seattle suggesting boycotts and such. I spent the rest of my business day calling on Seattle bankers and other businessmen I had met, and told them the story I was sent to Seattle to relate to the chamber of commerce but couldn't. They listened and were sympathetic.

When Friday came and my northbound steamship was scheduled to sail the next day, the Alaska manager told me he had gotten a five-minute spot on the Monday program for the membership meeting of the chamber. He made like I was given a very special privilege because this was to be one of those few times each year when members brought their wives, "and we don't usually do business on those days." So I rescheduled my trip home and spent the weekend planning how I could condense my long story into five minutes.

The Monday meeting was in the main ballroom of the Olympic Hotel. I never had training as a speaker and I was scared. My townspeople tolerated and understood me, but in this huge hall, what did this bunch of hard-nosed, hostile businessmen expect of me? Those at the head table gathered in a side room beforehand. There I was introduced to the top officers of the aviation industry in Seattle, which included William M. Allen, head of Boeing, and representatives of every major airline and many lawyers. I wondered how they could handle so many at the head table.

We were assigned our positions to march into the ballroom and be seated in the right order. As I looked around me I could feel hostility. It was like a lamb being led to the slaughter. They were all older folks. I was still young in that day. They were all big names, famous for something. I was an unknown who, as far as they knew, came out of nowhere and would disappear into nowhere.

The room was full of Seattle movers and shakers. They had so many of their aviation leaders on hand that they had extended the head table, not across the end of the hall, but all the way from end to end. And I was sure in my own mind that every one of those seated at that table was against having Alaska on the new air route.

When I was introduced, I felt that the old men in the audience were cold. I saw them as scowling and fierce. They showed no sensitivity for Alaska. And I was still scared.

But their wives were relaxed and beautiful, like on a day out on the town. As I spoke, they appeared to be listening. Their faces were animated, unlike the stone faces on their husbands. So I ignored the men and talked to the wives.

I described the air route as our only hope for a new source of income

88 | CHAPTER SEVEN

to make lives more comfortable and secure for our young mothers and fathers and their children. I had the feeling they agreed with me when I suggested the insecurity of depending on the whims of fish as a source of livelihood and depending on luck in discovering something valuable by digging a hole in the ground. I said the economics of air traffic would liberate us.

My clincher was that story about Grandfather Smallweed, the same one I used in my battle with the Alaska Railroad many years before. The wives were avid listeners as I told of Grandfather Smallweed's advice, "Friends are something you squeeze like a lemon or an orange, and when you have squeezed all the juice out of them, you cast them aside, for they are no good to you any more." My punch line was something like, "I am sure you folks in Seattle would not treat your Alaska friends like that."

The hard-boiled men may have ignored my plea at the meeting, but when they got home that night they must have caught hell from their wives. I hope they did.

After my five-minute speech the Seattle chamber spent the rest of the hour answering it. They had Dave Beck, their biggest but not the darlingest personality present, pledge—as only a teamster boss can pledge—his devoted support to seeing that the route makes Seattle its hub. In his high, squeaky and not very pleasant voice he called on the entire national organization of teamsters to back him up. In those days, that was often enough to assure success of almost anything.

The president of the Seattle chamber was the man who owned the biggest part of downtown real estate. He must have also been the landlord of many in the room. They appeared to respect him but not particularly to like him. I didn't either. He was followed by lawyers and airline officials who cited the importance to Seattle to remain the only gateway to Alaska, "a service we have provided these many years and Alaska has always enjoyed." Oh, yeah.

I had to wait another week for a steamship home. I spent it downtown stirring up all the dissension I could among business leaders. When I got home, the store operators on Fourth Avenue were severe in their thoughts toward Seattle businesses. Several hoped they could switch to Portland wholesalers.

As president I planned for the next step by the Anchorage Chamber of Commerce. We felt all was lost if we didn't find a way to offset the influence of Magnuson and Jackson. We in Alaska had no money to spend. Neither did we have senators to fight in our behalf.

We figured that the Alcan Highway drew enthusiastic support from several inland states when it was built from the Midwest to Alaska via Canada. So we planned a campaign to enlist the support of 10 senators whose states might benefit from an "inland" air route direct to Alaska. To get the attention in those states we planned what we called a "Columbus Expedition" seeking trade routes to the East.

AIR AGE | 89

For that expedition we went to Alaska Airlines which was then a struggling airline with big hopes for the future and management always cooperative on community projects. The airline gave us favorable terms for a charter of a DC-3 to take us on our search. There would be overnight stops in many cities, the main ones including Edmonton, Great Falls, Fargo, Minneapolis and Chicago.

There were 21 seats in a DC-3 so we divided the charter cost among them and enlisted 21 key local leaders to go. Governor Gruening, always ready for a battle with Seattle, joined us and gave us such prestige we were met at several airports by a motorcycle escort.

We had a "road show" of speeches made by our most prominent speakers, always with Gruening our main spokesman. They were so effective in winning support that when we approached Chicago for the last stop someone suggested we extend the trip to Washington and buttonhold some senators. I remember walking down the aisle of the plane taking a poll. It was unanimous for the extension. Each one was ready to pay his proportion of the cost. The airline president, who was among us, gave us an attractive fee for the extra days.

When we arrived in the capital, Delegate Bartlett had us assigned to quarters at the Wardman Park Hotel, probably a fancier place than most of us expected. I was in a suite usually reserved for Claire Booth Luce and it was deluxe. Others were in equally luxurious quarters. But we found the charges reasonable. Ordinary rooms were sold out and the hotel management put us in the special suites at a block rate for the group.

For two days we buttonholed senators and reported our experiences to each other. I was in a group that went to see James M. Landis, chairman of the Civil Aeronautics Board. Gruening, Stanley McCutcheon and three other Democrats called on President Truman. We all came away with positive reactions, but no commitment. Then we bought watermelons and took them home to our wives. Watermelons were rarely available in Anchorage and expensive when they were.

When the federal order was issued creating the North Pacific Air Route through Anchorage we learned that it was signed by President Truman and dated the same day we had been in Washington. But we could never get a clue as to whether our Columbus Expedition had anything to do with it. I can't help but suspect that we had enough of our 10 midwest senators on our side to offset Seattle's two senators. And President Truman was always a friend to Alaska.

The CAB had hearings to select the carrier which would operate the new route. Northwest was believed to have the inside tract because Sen. Magnuson was reported to own $250,000 in its stock. That airline already flew from Seattle to Anchorage. All it needed was permission to fly the new route, too.

In Anchorage, we favored the principle of having different airlines on the routes so there would be competition. We lost that. Northwest got both.

The new air route brought new problems for the tiny community of Anchorage. We had a municipal airport with short grass runways. Airlines were going to need runways for the newest and biggest international transports which in that day was a DC-6. Big new transports, the Boeing Stratocruisers, soon came on line. Anchorage could not possibly accommodate them so from Washington came an order for the Air Force to allow them the use of Elmendorf runways. That brought a period of unhappiness for the Air Force.

Gen. Joseph H. (Hamp) Atkinson, head of the Alaskan Command, frequently lectured me on the traffic problems resulting from mixing the big, clumsy civilian airliners with the fast fighter planes on the same fields. He made it an impediment in his training programs. I had good relations with Hamp and he commented at social gatherings or public meetings, wherever he and I happened to meet.

Rather tired of hearing the same old thing, I finally responded something like, "Hamp, you and I know Anchorage ought to provide the airport, but our little town can't do it, partly because Congress won't approve of our borrowing any more through bond issues." That was one of the impediments to territorial status. The law required Congress to approve of proposed municipal bond issues. Hamp responded, "Ah, Bob, but I'll help."

Those words "I'll help" stopped me in my tracks. We then started talking turkey about how to go about it. Once more the Anchorage Chamber of Commerce became the lead agency in getting the new airport. The Defense department would remain anonymous, and in the background. Chamber members took up a collection to buy a ticket for Hugh Dougherty, a successful life insurance agent, to go to Washington. He won the support of the departments of State, Interior, Commerce, War and Navy. Hugh told them the departments had created the airport problem by being in favor of the route and now it is their duty to help resolve the airport problem they helped create.

Encouraged by that, Delegate Bartlett introduced a bill in congress providing for the federal government to build it. The House called a public hearing and we had to send witnesses to support the bill. This happened again in the Senate. We won approval in both houses.

When we started going to Washington to push the bill, General Atkinson told us if we ever got stuck to call Eugene Zuckert, a civilian employee of the Defense department. We called him several times in the course of progress through both House and Senate, and our problems dissolved each time.

I remember one instance when Fred Axford and I found an Indiana senator inaccessible to us. He was a tight-fisted conservative opposed to spending. He considered an airport pork barrel. We were allowed to talk only to his aide in the outer office. So we told Zuckert who told us to go back and see the senator tomorrow. When we went back, the aide greeted us saying the senator would support our bill. Happy day. We talked a bit and the aide asked, "How come if General Spaatz is so interested in having that airport at Anchorage, the Air Force doesn't build it itself?"

That's how we learned that Eugene Zuckert was our pipeline to Gen. Carl A. Spaatz, chief of staff of the Air Force. Zuckert was special assistant to Stuart Symington, the Assistant Secretary of War (air) and later Secretary of the Air Force.

There was one other time when we saw the secret support of the Air Force. It was at a hearing of the House Interstate and Foreign Commerce Committee. We had arrived for our 10 a.m. public hearing, each one of us primed with a presentation. The hearing room doors were locked so we waited outside When the door opened, I saw military people leaving the room by a side door.

We then made our presentations. They lasted until noon. During those two hours, there was rarely more than one of two committee members attending. The committee report was completed in written form by 3 p.m. I asked a friend on the committee staff how the report could be approved so soon when only one or two members had heard the testimony. He said the generals, including Spaatz and Atkinson, had told the committee in the secret session at 9 a.m. that they must have that airport, and we civilians were there merely to create the public record that would support the favorable report.

The bill still had glitches and pitfalls in going through the legislative maze. In the House congressmen impressed on us as Anchorage citizens that it would be unfair to allow our little Merrill Field to compete with the big new airport for landing fees, so we should close it down. We were very sure we could close it. However, months later when the bill was before the Senate committee we were advised that the new field could not provide for small plane traffic, so Merrill Field must be kept open. We agreed again with the alacrity of a politician making a campaign promise.

A more serious obstacle turned up in the Senate when the bill landed in a committee headed by Sen. Owen Brewster of Maine. This obstacle was one even General Spaatz couldn't overcome.

The senator for Maine was known as the "Pan American senator" because he always watched Pan Am's interests. He promptly consigned our airport bill to oblivion because the new airport would help Northwest Airlines but it would do nothing for Pan American which operated at Fairbanks.

When we tried to discuss it with the senator, we were treated as though it was ridiculous. "Do you think I am going to allow a bill that helps Northwest and doesn't help Pan Am?" he asked. He made us feel silly. We wondered why we went to see him.

Zuckert declined to become involved in this new problem. He said he would study it but he suggested that maybe we could think of some way to get by Sen. Brewster. So we went to see our good friend Delegate Bartlett. He was always helpful. He was this time, too.

We related the problem to him and he had a quick understanding of all its ramifications. And he had a quick suggestion. "Why don't I amend the bill to provide for a second airport to be built at Fairbanks?" he asked. We were dumbfounded. What a simple solution, but is it too costly? We quickly decided no and Bartlett went to work on the amendment. We told Zuckert and he was pleased.

When Bartlett told Brewster he would offer the amendment, the Maine senator put the bill back in line for consideration with the approval of his committee. We had a short time to present someone who could testify before the committee as to the Fairbanks airport needs and why the federal government should fund projects for them. This was not easy to do.

We telephoned friends in Fairbanks and told them we needed them here to help get approval for a new airport at Fairbanks. They thought we were pulling their legs. They wouldn't take us seriously. Bartlett finally got Mayor Hjalmar Nordale to come, even though he was under medication for some kind of fever that was never explained to me. Bartlett assured the mayor that he (Bartlett) would coach him so he would know what to say.

When our bill finally was enacted we got our new international airport built, operated and maintained by the federal government. Congressmen impressed on us that it would set a new precedent for the feds had never built, maintained and operated a civilian airport anywhere in the world outside of Washington, D.C.

The city of Fairbanks also got its international airport, but very few people in that city know the details of how it was authorized. The two airports have long since been turned over to be owned and operated by the State of Alaska.

After two major victories in behalf of Anchorage, we had the official air routes that would make us the hub of global air transportation, and we had the beginnings of the gigantic airport that would be needed to service planes from all over the world. We still had the long, hard path to follow to reach the final goal. That would be certification of airlines by the Civil Aeronautics Board to use our facilities. We took an active part in that battle.

Northwest International Service, Anchorage 1955. Photo by Mac's Foto Service.

9th Ave. park strip mid 1930's in Anchorage. Photo by Steve McClutcheon/Alaska Pictorial Service

Star Airlines, later became Alaska Star Airlines, then Alaska Airlines – one of the early Bellancas. Photo by Steve McClutcheon/Alaska Pictorial Service

AIR AGE | 95

Pioneer Pilots. Left to right: Jack Jefford, Ray Peterson, Jim Dodson, Art Woodly, TC Drinkwater, Merle Smith, Noel Wein (July 1968). Photo by Steve McClutcheon/Alaska Pictorial Service

Fairbanks: the first electra's on the passenger and mail run from Seattle to Fairbanks (early 1940's).
Photo by Steve McClutcheon/Alaska Pictorial Service

Wien Airlines lands mail and freight at Gambell, St. Lawrence Island only 45 miles from Soviet Siberia. Photo by Steve McClutcheon/Alaska Pictorial Service

Bob Reeve second from right, Judge Davis first on left. Northwest Airlines first flight to Anchorage (around 1940). Photo by Steve McClutcheon/Alaska Pictorial Service

98 | CHAPTER SEVEN

— CHAPTER EIGHT —

Black Gold

In the summer of 1953, I began growing uneasy over Alaska's future. There wasn't much economic optimism. The Korean War was winding down, reviving old fears of military cutbacks in Alaska. Salmon runs were dwindling to new lows, and still the greedy Seattle interests fought all attempts to have fish traps at the mouths of rivers moved a mile back. Gold mining wasn't recovering from the World War II closures, and it looked as though it never would.

Nature didn't help the mood on July 10 when Mt. Spurr blew up and showered Anchorage with a half inch of volcanic ash. The volcano is 80 miles away and the weather bureau says the prevailing winds are toward Anchorage only 20 percent of the time. It was just our luck to have the eruption timed to hit that 20 percent.

The volcanic cloud blackened the sky so the sunny mid-afternoon was like nighttime, causing some panic among those who interpreted it to mean that the end of the world was imminent. The blackout was short-lived, the cloud moved on and the sky cleared, but then the next belch in the volcano sent over another cloud.

It was an awesome story to cover. But not for me. It was my bad luck to miss the excitement because I was having some fun of my own elsewhere. I happened to be visiting a camp on the rim of the crater of another volcano, Mt. Wrangell, almost 200 miles east and a bit north of Spurr. It was a cosmic ray scientific camp and I was at an altitude of 14,004 feet with Terris Moore, president of the University of Alaska, as my pilot, one of the few fliers who would land in the crater of a live volcano.

I was there to interview Dr. Serge Korff, a leading authority on cosmic rays. He had set up a camp on top of the mountain, a Jamesway hut with bare essentials inside. Two college students lived there as his observers. He would check up on them periodically and give me a story on their findings. It didn't seem to me that it offered much hope for new industry in Alaska, but I was ready to report on anything with potential.

As interesting as his project was, it was hardly anything to chase the economic gloom setting in. "We need to make something happen to give this state a new shot in the arm." That became the recurring topic among our little group of businessmen who would regularly gather for lunch around the common dining table at the Elks Club. Anyone could sit there because the lodge opened it to the public for the extra income, and we regularly had a motley bunch of a dozen to 16 people.

A newspaper article that appeared one day that summer fired up the tempo of our luncheon discussions and lifted my spirits. The Bureau of Land Management reported that 17 Californians had filed applications for oil and gas leases on 224,780 acres of land in the lower Kenai Peninsula. Leases in Alaska cost only 25 cents an acre plus a small filing fee, and that puny price had attracted big oil firms and dreamers alike to hunt for oil that nearly everyone was certain was here. More than 100 hundred wells had been drilled since 1900 and no one found any oil of consequence. I was among those who would argue that the state's luck was about to change.

The magnitude of that latest filing got us thinking. Did those Californians know something that we didn't? They shelled out a total of $59,685 to lease the acreage. Shouldn't we look into what motivated that kind of investment by outsiders in our own back yards?

None of us knew about leases and oil and such, so we set out to educate ourselves. We started by talking to members of the oil exploration crews who stopped off in Anchorage, going to and returning from the field. They were mostly college geology students enjoying a summer job doing site studies for an oil company or the US Geological Survey. My uncle, Dr. Wallace W. Atwood, a prominent geologist and physiographer, started that way. In his younger days when he was an instructor at Harvard he spent a half dozen summers in Alaska compiling geological reports for the USGS. Before Anchorage existed as a town, he did a study of the townsite that identified oil seeps, coal and many minerals in the area. The stories he told me of those days remained strong in my memory and enforced my faith that the real riches of this state were yet to be discovered.

I started interviewing the contemporary field geologists for my newspaper regularly on what they were finding and what were the prospects for oil production in Alaska. They were always positive and usually as optimistic as a promoter might be.

Max Burkhouser, an oversized German geologist from Switzerland, was most generous with his time. He was the head man in Alaska for Royal Dutch/Shell oil company. He spent as much as a week or two in Anchorage each year, arriving each spring and leaving each fall. As an editor trying to understand why oil companies financed field parties each year, I found him a great instructor.

Curiosity about oil grew at our lunch table, and three or four of the regulars joined me in gravitating around Max to learn more when he hit town. Max did his best as an instructor when we kept the beer flowing, which we always did. It was in these "class sessions" that we learned about leases, including how to get the attention of an oil company and perhaps induce it to drill.

Besides planting seeds in our bonnet, these Burkhouser sessions probably were the progenitors of the group that came to be known as the "Spit and Argue Club." Fourteen of us who gathered for lunch at the Elks decided to put up a modest pool of money and pursue what Burkhouser told us we should do. They ranged from my well-to-do, banker-brother-in-law, Elmer Rasmuson, to a hustling Army-Navy surplus store clerk, Locke Jacobs Jr.

With a Korean truce near, it was important to all of us to invest in anything that might lessen dependence on the military. As businessmen, we were becoming increasingly alarmed by the prospect that one peacetime budget cutback by Congress could knock the props from under the mainstay of our economy.

Burkhouser had told us about the techniques that speculators used to make a quick buck—lease at 25 cents an acre preferably near big oil company leases, hype the prospects of finding oil there, and then sell out at a profit. But it wasn't the quick buck we were after. Our goal was set on drilling. We would prosper only if oil was discovered and our town grew. We agreed that instead of selling our leases we would give them to any reputable oil company that would commit to drilling a proper test hole.

We started leasing in November 1953. We found the law so complex that we needed legal advice to be sure we did it right. Max said we must have 60,000 acres leased before a company might take an interest. So we organized patches that size here and there on the Kenai Peninsula, the west shore of Cook Inlet, across the inlet from Anchorage and in the Copper River Valley. Each member of our group understood it was a wild gamble, not an investment, and that we should be prepared to lose our money without return.

Our first approach to leasing was like betting on a horse race. Some member had a hunch about a likely oil site, we'd argue about it, and then send Locke Jacobs with the money to the Bureau of Land Management leasing window. However, we learned very quickly we would soon run out of money doing it that way. We needed advice on how to be scientifically selective. So after much debate, we went to the extra expense of hiring a research geologist in Menlo Park, Calif., who had access to the public files at the regional USGS headquarters. He sent us reports recommending hot spots for leasing based on the known geological structures.

We continued to lease land for more than a year. We became convinced that each hot spot our researcher recommended contained the big reservoir that oil companies sought. However, by April 1955, shortly after we leased one more scientifically chosen site—the land around Swanson River—not only were our hopes dimming but also a legal problem was looming. We had so many leases we were approaching the legal limit on acreage.

It was time to take a different approach. Since no oil companies were knocking on our door seeking our leases, we decided to start knocking on

BLACK GOLD | 101

theirs. Wilbur Wester, operator of the Westward Hotel, agreed to take time off from his business and make presentations to oil companies in Los Angeles. He knew many oilmen because they would stay at his hotel. All of us had to share the costs of his trip.

Wilbur told me, when he returned, that his technique was to call a friend in an oil company and tell him what he had. If he were lucky, his friend would advise his firm's land man and the land man would meet Wilbur in the hotel and study his maps.

This process took several days. All the big oil companies that had sent field parties to Alaska showed no interest. However, one little company, Richfield Oil, wanted to know more. Richfield had established a foothold selling petroleum products in California but it hadn't had a decent oil discovery in nine years. Its diminishing supply of its own crude oil threatened to undermine its marketing progress. Among oil companies, Richfield was known as the "poor boy's company" because it was running out of money as well as oil.

"The Richfield land man, George Shepphird, studied my maps and zeroed in on the Kenai Peninsula lands and asked me our price on this patch, pointing to the Swanson River area," Wilbur said. "I told him it wouldn't cost anything—we would give it to them if they would agree to drill a hole within two years or else pay us a penalty."

Wilbur said the Richfield land man excused himself to talk to his home office, saying he had never heard of anyone giving his company oil leases free and he had to get advice.

"When he came back he said his boss said that he couldn't take the leases free, that he had to pay for them," Wilbur said.

"How much?" Wilbur asked. "The land man said at least as much as we paid for them, which was two-bits an acre."

Wilbur accepted that, although when you add the attorney's fees and Wilbur's traveling costs, it was about half our total outlay. But the oil company also provided a five percent override in the deal. Few of the leaseholders, including me, realized the significance of that override until much later.

We leaseholders were delighted with Wilbur's report. We had an oil company pledged to drill a hole and that, according to Burkhouser, is the only way you will ever know if there is oil in the ground. And that was our motivating purpose.

Richfield sent its field crew to the Kenai to do some geophysical work and bought leases in the same area as ours. After a time they reported that they still planned to drill but they would prefer to drill on one of their leases instead of ours, so what penalty would we assess?

We had to call a meeting of all 14 of us to answer that. Some of our group came to the meeting gleefully anticipating the joy of collecting penalty money from an oil company, noting it would be our first profit since we started. But in the discussion, Mickey McManamin, who ran the

Army-Navy store in town, noted that the original purpose was to get a hole drilled.

"These people say they will drill the hole," Mickey argued. "We didn't say it had to be on our ground so why are we talking about a penalty?"

Further discussion in the spit-and-argue mode led to a unanimous vote for no penalty.

Richfield started drilling a wildcat well on its own lease in the spring of 1957 and struck oil on July 15. First hints of a discovery started filtering through Soldotna and Kenai when workers returned from camp mysteriously jubilant. Mickey, while tending his store, was the first of our group to learn the strike was real but he couldn't tell the rest of us. Bill Bishop, Richfield's geologist, returned from the site, his face smeared and his clothes oil-soaked, and sought Mickey's help. Bishop needed a fresh set of clothes and asked Mickey to keep what he saw to himself until he could complete testing the volume of the oil flow.

I learned about the discovery the same as everyone else, eight days later, when Richfield held a press conference and announced it had a major oil find.The news hit the state like a bomb and set off a land rush that dwarfed Alaska's famed gold rush.

The excitement went nationwide. Oil and gas leases suddenly took on great value. All the major oil companies of the nation were soon in Alaska looking for land to lease. Homesteaders in the Kenai were awakened from their sleep by people seeking to buy oil rights on their land. At the Bureau of Land Management office in the federal building, lines of eager applicants began forming at 6 a.m. to await the 10 a.m. office opening. Before it ended, it would become the biggest land rush in U.S. history.

Locke Jacobs, the clerk in McManamin's store, had become an invaluable member of our group. An amateur geologist, he made a mission of duplicating BLM records of unsurveyed land in Alaska on a hunch it would make him rich. And it did. When the discovery occurred, his records of unleased land were more up to date than those in the federal land office. At the first news from Swanson River, Locke quit his job on the spot and set himself up in business as a lease broker. He helped all comers to file the papers to buy a lease all over the state. For the next few days, he told me that he was making as much as $1,000 an hour in commissions for as many hours as he could stay awake, filling out lease forms for oil companies and individuals.

When I heard Richfield's news, I rushed to a typewriter and pounded out an editorial. "This may be the Discovery Day everyone has been waiting for," I wrote. "The oil found on the Kenai Peninsula should mark the opening of a new chapter in Alaska history … Hang on … Alaska is going around a sharp curve and is starting down a new road of development such as has never been seen before."

Soon after, Richfield confirmed our highest hopes. It drilled a confirmation well that validated a major discovery, proving what we had long hoped for, that Alaska oil could be tapped in commercial quantities.

However, trouble brewing in Washington thwarted Alaska's blastoff into the Oil Era. Leaders of an expanding national environmental movement had been critical of President Eisenhower's Secretary of Interior, Douglas McKay. Dubbing him "Giveaway McKay," they persuaded friends in Congress to investigate McKay's no-bid leasing of wildlife refuges to oil and gas drilling in Louisiana.

In the heat that followed, McKay resigned to run for a U.S. Senate seat in Oregon, and Ike named his trusted White House assistant, Fred A. Seaton, to head the Interior department. The new cabinet officer's first act in office was to declare a moratorium on further oil and gas leasing in national wildlife refuges in order to investigate the "giveaway" concerns. Further, all operations in progress on those federal lands were ordered closed down pending studies to determine their impact on wildlife, including the effect on moose in the Kenai. Our hopes took a hit with that devastating edict.

I was on a rare vacation in Palm Springs late in 1957 when this glitch became serious. The Anchorage Chamber of Commerce asked me to help deal with it. Wilbur flew down to Los Angeles and I was to meet him there and shape up a strategy for getting federal approval to proceed with development of the Swanson River oil field.

Reluctantly, I left the soft and comforting ambiance of the clear air of the desert and went to the big city of smog. Wilbur explained the problem. We both agreed that when we wanted something in Alaska we had to convince the military that the Army or Air Force wanted it. If we could do that, we would get it. For example, our basic road system in Alaska was built for the military. Most of the airports and much of the civilian infrastructure throughout Alaska was built for military purposes.

It was easy for Wilbur and me to think up a list of reasons why the military would want oil production in Alaska. This was 1957. The Cold War still dominated the scene. And Gen. Nathan F. Twining, a friend of Alaska who was commander in chief of Alaska from 1947 to 1950, was now chairman of the Joint Chiefs of Staff in the Pentagon.

Almost every Alaskan knew Nate from the days when he was "one of us" as commanding general of the forces in Alaska. Quite a few of us went to his office to visit with him whenever we were in Washington. Even after his transfer to the Pentagon, he came to Alaska every August to visit with us, although he said facetiously he was there for military purposes—to check the level of the streams, in other words, to fish. In fact, one such "visit" earlier in 1957 got him into trouble. A lengthy report by the Air Force's inspector general's division cleared Twining of charges that he and other high officers engaged in a lavish Alaskan hunting junket.

But first Wilbur and I went to Richfield headquarters to get their views on how best to convince the feds to lift the drilling ban. They said they had reached the end of their rope and had done everything they

104 | CHAPTER EIGHT

could. They refused to become involved in politics, and they saw the moratorium as being political.

We asked Richfield for a desk where we could use a typewriter. They deposited us in a plush office with beautiful leather upholstery. The contrast to my drab, cluttered newspaper office made me gasp. With it came a secretary to do the typing.

I had to insist that I do my own typing. I have never dictated, don't know how to dictate, and have no use for a secretary. All I wanted was a typewriter and a desk. I wound up with an elegant typewriter and an elegant desk in an elegant room and a bunch of oil people looking at me as though I was something out of a circus sideshow.

Wilbur and I then put together a brief on why it was in the national interest to lift the embargo on oil production in Alaska. We had good support by telephone from Anchorage for statistics and quotes. We came up with a terse report:

—Oil revenue would lessen our poor territory's heavy dependence on federal subsidies.

—The readiness of major oil companies to invest more than $100,000,000 in further exploration represents a major private effort to make this nation energy self-sufficient.

—The government's own fish and wildlife experts conceded oil development would actually help the moose by providing new fields of browse.

However, our most telling argument was it would eliminate the precarious present supply system for the military. With oil pumped right in Alaska, our armed forces would no longer be dependent on tankers having to travel 2,400 miles a trip from the West Coast to supply Alaska's defense needs. With a refinery right at hand, a supply line most vulnerable to attack would be eliminated.

We addressed the document directly to General Twining. Putting it together took most of a week, during which the Richfield officials became fearful that we loose cannons might do or say something that would embarrass the oil industry. They set up a meeting of representatives of all the companies that had oil leases in Alaska and asked Wilbur and me to present our story to them. When we finished they approved our presentation but they thought the whole exercise futile.

"In Washington, you can't get in to see Twining," one oil executive commented. We had no satisfactory answer to that except to say that he was our friend and he had always welcomed us on previous visits.

When we were leaving for the flight to Washington, the Richfield people presented us with round-trip tickets, which we promptly handed back to them. We said we would pay our own way. They acted offended, but we explained it was important that we go as independent Alaskans, just do-gooders working for the good of Alaska.

We had found that when we went to Washington at our own expense

BLACK GOLD | 105

to testify before a committee or ask for help from a bureaucrat, it was important that we be able to tell the officials that we paid our own way.

We would get no direct benefits from whatever we sought. We took time off from our work and endured the ordeal of all-day travel to work for the good of our community or the territory. Once they were convinced we were on the level, they very often became our helpers and co-workers on our project.

Our strategy was to present our brief to Twining and urge him to ask Interior Secretary Seaton to lift the ban and issue a permit so the next well could be drilled. We envisioned seeing Twining in the morning and then calling on Seaton in the afternoon to give him a copy of the brief and tell him of our meeting with Twining.

We outlined our plan to Delegate Bartlett by telephone and asked him to make the appointments. He liked the plan and said he would help. However, on arrival we found his office had made the appointments backwards. They scheduled us to see Seaton in the forenoon and Twining in the afternoon. That meant we would have to present Seaton with our letter to Twining before giving it to Twining. By all the rules of protocol, that is not smart.

We decided we could handle it by telling Seaton we were "leaking" the report to him. Most public officials appreciate this. They like to be able to say, "I know about it" when the subject arises.

We had both met Seaton, a Nebraska newspaper publisher, on his visits to Alaska, and he greeted us warmly. I confided at the outset we wanted him to have prior knowledge of a report we were delivering to General Twining. Seaton brushed that off with a laugh and a promise that he wouldn't tell the general. Then we ran through the facts in our brief and told him we would appeal to Twining to call Seaton and request that he issue the drilling permit.

"And if he calls, I'll issue the permit," Seaton responded. "If he asked me for permission to drill on the White House lawn, I would give it to him—and I have the authority to do it, too."

After some more pleasant visiting, Wilbur and I took our leave. We paused for a bite to eat and then headed for the Pentagon, a place I have gotten lost every time I visited without an escort.

We found Twining well prepared for our visit. In his commodious office the general had a half dozen tripods, each holding a map of Alaska. One was the standard map showing cities, rivers and landmarks, another a physical map showing mountains and valleys. Some were blow-ups of regions. The general also had a part of his staff there, several of whom had served with him in Alaska. They were seated something like a jury would be, so they could see the maps, the general and us.

I handed Twining our brief and started my oral presentation. As I spoke, the general tried to follow the brief. He stopped me when he lost the trail in the document. When he asked me where something was in the

106 | CHAPTER EIGHT

brief, I walked around to his side of the desk and pointed it out. He took the brief from me and he started reading it out loud. Every time he came to a place name he stopped and had one of his colonels point the place out on the map. It was obviously his way of acquainting his colonels with Alaska.

The session became somewhat of a friendly game. I pointed to which paragraph he should read, and the general ad-libbed recollections of his experiences fishing and hunting in Alaska.

We went away from the meeting confident that we had Twining on our side. He discussed each point we made and even suggested some others. However, he gave no hint whether he would call Secretary Seaton.

Wilbur and I spent the evening talking about our day's experiences and the things we might have said but didn't. The next morning at breakfast we talked about how to find out whether Twining had made the call. We went to the Interior office building and roamed around in the huge, endless marble halls. The complexity of those Washington bureaucratic palaces never failed to befuddle me.

Every so often we met someone we knew, one of whom was Elmer Bennett Williams, the nationally prominent interior department solicitor. I had met Williams many times in the past and he stopped to talk. After a few pleasantries, I tried to lead the conversation to a place where he would ask us why we were there and I could tell him the whole story. He would be a good ally to have.

But that wasn't necessary. Out of the blue, he asked me, "How come Nate Twining is so anxious to have oil wells drilled in Alaska?"

I wasn't prepared for that and responded with something dumb, like, "Oh, is he?" I have forgotten the rest of the conversation, but Wilbur and I left him feeling we must have done our job.

Incidentally, our mission to Washington was known and approved by Anchorage Chamber of Commerce officers. Copies of the brief were given to every member. Our ownerships of oil leases in the Kenai were also public record; in fact, they were published in my own newspaper. There was no secrecy involved. It was all out in the open. I say that because the Anchorage Daily News in later years would claim otherwise.

In January 1958, a short time after our visit, Seaton reopened the Swanson River portion of the Kenai moose range for oil exploration. Richfield's potential fortunes soared, but this cash-poor company never could take full advantage. Many more wells were needed to bring the field into production, and wells cost about a million dollars apiece to drill.

Charlie Jones, Richfield chairman and CEO , traveled from coast to coast searching for bank credit to finance the project. He was turned down by all the bankers. The money crunch compelled him to sell a half interest to Standard Oil of California, (now Chevron) a big rich firm, and allow that company to become the operator.

When we leaseholders heard that Standard had paid $30 million for a half interest in leases that we had offered Richfield for free, we wondered if we had been chumps. But we didn't wonder for long. Our state was already in line for $50,000 daily in royalties and our city was optimistic that it would get a large share of the oil's prosperity. And it put our little group from the Elks round table in good stead, thanks to Richfield's insistence that we accept an override.

The Swanson River reservoir was shaped something like a frying pan. The discovery hole was on what might be called the handle of the pan. The big reservoir was in our leases that made up the big, round part of the pan, the part that holds the bacon. Our five-percent override meant that our group of 14 Alaskans would receive the value of five percent of the oil produced from those wells on our leases, and there must have been nearly 40 wells.

The fact that we 14 Alaskans were in line for handsome royalty payments roused certain unadmirable traits. These were envy, greed, jealousy—traits reminiscent of the battles over gold claims and just as ugly. Some highly regarded citizens in Anchorage searched for a technicality and top-filed our leases in hopes they could replace us and get the royalties for themselves.

None of them ever talked to me about it so I can only speculate on how they were organized. They were intelligent people, among them my friend, the twice governor and former Secretary of Interior Wally Hickel. I assume they were sold a bill of goods, probably by attorney James Tallman, who pressed the suit. They became plaintiffs in a court action that accused my friends and me of all sorts of trickery and wrongful acts in getting our leases and helping Richfield get federal permission to drill in a moose range.

The legal challenges over the validity of our leases lasted seven years and went all the way up to the nation's highest court. On March 1, 1965, the U. S. Supreme Court ruled 7-0 that the leases had been properly issued. The high court justices effectively shot our claim jumpers dead. We couldn't ask for greater vindication than that unanimous decision by the Supreme Court.

That was the last we heard of that, except for periodic attempts by my longtime rival, the Anchorage Daily News, to revise history. Early in 1990, it published a particularly malicious portrayal of our Spit and Argue group's role in the Swanson River discovery. Dubbing it "The Untold Story of Oil in Alaska," the eight-part series used every innuendo short of libel to accuse us of secret dealing and political favoritism. This despite our candor in publishing the leases and our exhausting efforts in Washington, D.C., on behalf of this fledgling Alaska territory.

The most remarkable result of the News' series was the public backlash. A scathing letter from Pedro Denton, who headed Alaska's oil and gas leasing program during the '60s and '70s, typified the tone of the protesters. Terming the series "the most irresponsible reporting I've ever read," Denton said he could see nothing in the articles indicating that anything illegal or wrong was done. "To the contrary," he wrote, "I see a story of a group of people who had the intelligence, vision, and guts to take advantage of an opportunity that was available to everyone. You have taken the same information and twisted it into a sleazy story of corruption … I wish someone could sue you and win a bundle, but unfortunately you were clever enough to build the story primarily on innuendo."

I believe there is a larger lesson in that ill-conceived series, one that speaks to why there is so much public distrust of the press. About 80 percent of the circulation of today's newspapers is controlled by chains with corporate headquarters centered far from the papers they own. For example, the McClatchy chain in Sacramento owns the Anchorage Daily News.

These are big corporations and nearly all of them are listed on the big board on Wall Street. Public image as much as anything dictates how well their stock performs. Winning journalism prizes is one way to enhance the image. In my view, this has led to a form of "gotcha" journalism in which the primary interest is to win prizes, too often at the expense of our traditional function, to inform the public in a rational and objective manner.

Most of the time these prizes are judged by jurors thousands of miles removed from the action. They have no way of knowing about the credibility of the reporting. When the Daily News oil series won a prize from an obscure press club in Atlantic City, John Strohmeyer, a former Atwood professor of journalism at the University of Alaska Anchorage who served several times as a Pulitzer Prize juror, wrote a press club official. For the purpose of seminar discussions, he asked whether judges had been informed of the public criticism of the series in advance of their decision.

Stohmeyer tells me he received no reply. However, it was comforting to see that the Pulitzer advisory board, which awards the most prestigious prizes in journalism, included for the first time in 1994 a provision in the entry form which reads: "Any significant challenges to accuracy or fairness of the entry, such as published letters, corrections, retractions, as well as responses by the newspaper should be included in the submission." I believe this should be a standard stipulation in all newspaper writing contests.

By 1994, the Swanson River fields had returned $31,000,000 in royalties to the state of Alaska. While production is diminishing, 30 wells are still producing and expect to be pumping at least 10 years more. Meanwhile, an estimated 330 billion cubic feet of gas is stored in the ground. When this is tapped, it is expected to provide Alaska with natural gas for 10 to 20 years.

I was pleased to have had a part in finding Swanson River. Creating a new industry was only part of the satisfaction. It also gave me the ammunition to pursue statehood with new confidence.

This well is nearest to the gathering center and oil pumping unit of the pipeline from the Kenai Field to Nikiska Beach tanker terminal. Photo by Steve McClutcheon/Alaska Pictorial Service

Costal Drilling Co. of Bakersfield California drill for Richfield Oil Company on the Swanson River lease Kenai Peninsula. Photo by Steve McClutcheon/Alaska Pictorial Service

Before the Nikiska dock was built Swanson River oil was trucked to Seward. Photo by Steve McClutcheon/Alaska Pictorial Service

Richfield Tanker takes the First load of Swansen River crude from the Nikiska Oil Pier on the Kenai Peninsula.

BLACK GOLD | 111

112 | CHAPTER EIGHT

— CHAPTER NINE —

Statehood Battle

It was only natural that the movement to make Alaska a full-fledged state was conceived and nourished in Anchorage, the territory's newest and largest community. The people in Anchorage had shown themselves to be united in support of any good project. That positive spirit distinguished the little town that was supposed to have been only a railroad construction camp.

Now it became the birthplace of the statehood idea that over a period of 10 years became a nationwide cause and in 1959 compelled the 48 states to move over, so to speak, to make way in the field of blue for the 49th star in the flag of the United States of America.

Statehood had been recognized ever since the purchase in 1867 as the ultimate destiny of Alaska. The first statehood bill was introduced in Congress by Alaska's Delegate James Wickersham on March 30, 1916, the 49th anniversary of the of the signing of the Treaty of Purchase of Alaska. It was quickly dismissed.

When I arrived in Alaska 20 years later, a serious push for statehood was still unthinkable. We didn't have the economy or population that Congress felt a state should have. Even Alaskans found it hard to believe that the nation would allocate two seats in the Senate to represent an area with a population under 100,000.

Statehood wasn't even a topic of conversation. The powerful business interests liked territorial status. They were getting rich by keeping things the way they were.

My early encounters with Austin E. (Cap) Lathrop gave me good insight into this entrenched mentality. He was the most powerful person in Alaska. A real muscle guy with a horn of a voice, he was called "Cap," reverently of course, because he got his big start by running a sea schooner that delivered prospectors and supplies to the gold fields in Alaska before and during the Klondike Gold Rush at the turn of the century.

By the time I got here, Lathrop owned most things worth owning—a bank, apartment buildings, movie theaters, the Healy coal mine, the Fairbanks News-Miner newspaper and a beer distributorship that netted him a nickel on every bottle of Olympia shipped from Seattle. As the territory's first homegrown, resident millionaire (the bounties of Alaska

STATEHOOD BATTLE | 113

made many millionaires but either they never lived here or else they left as soon as they made their fortune), Lathrop was a fierce Republican. He controlled a feuding wing of the party, which we called the "black" Republicans. They fought with a passion to seat their delegates at the national party nominating conventions.

I had been in town only a few months when the king summoned me for an audience. My banker father-in-law, E.A. Rasmuson, was the Republican national committeeman and he led the rival wing of the party, which we called the "white" Republicans. It was no secret that Lathrop believed that Rasmuson brought me into town for political purposes, to run a newspaper that would promote the "jackasses" challenging Lathrop's Republican leadership.

Lathrop was frontier-wise and steely eyed at age 70. He proceeded to lecture me, an uncertain 28-year-old newcomer, about the perils of running a newspaper in Alaska. He said he was about to build his own newspaper here and was ready to pour the footage, right next door to mine. He thought I might want to consider selling out, and if so, he was willing to talk.

I mustered a brave front and tried not to show that my stomach was churning.

"Well, Cap," I said, "selling to you is a possibility, but I would have to get enough out of the sale to be able to move back Outside and buy another paper."

"You figure out what you want and let me know," Lathrop snapped, ending the meeting.

A few days later, I wrote him a letter asking a ridiculously high figure, about four times what the paper was worth. In fact, I would have been a chump not to sell if he wanted to pay that much for our struggling little sheet.

Instead of writing back, Lathrop simply sent me a yellow carbon copy of a letter, unsigned, offering $10 less per share.

That was still a ridiculously high price to pay. "Damn," I thought, "if this guy is serious, I bet he will go the extra $10."

But I never heard from Lathrop again on the issue, and he never poured the footings for a plant next to mine. However, for many years thereafter he made life uncomfortable in other ways for me and anyone else who tried to change the way things were.

Lathrop let it be know that he opposed building the Alcan highway, which the military eventually did during World War II. I thought everyone would appreciate having Alaska linked to the Lower 48 via a road system across Canada. Lathrop wouldn't hear of it. "It would only bring in the 'Okies' and put more people on welfare," he said, referring to the southerners who emigrated here looking for work and bringing essentially only the shirts on their backs.

Lathrop talked against our efforts to start airmail service to and from

Alaska. That, he said, would be a hardship on businessmen. He claimed faster mail would deprive stores of the time lag that enabled many of them to sell shipments of goods before the checks they kited to pay for them cleared the banks in the slow steamer ship-railroad trips to Seattle and back.

And later, Lathrop used the power of his newspaper, his radio stations and his other business clout to oppose any move toward statehood. It would only mean higher taxes, he said, and besides he hated New Dealer Gruening who espoused it.

Each time new laws or an amendment to old laws came up for debate there was a flurry of speeches noting that the ultimate destiny of Alaska as statehood. Regardless of the beautiful oratory about the territory's great future, Alaskans found Congress unfavorably inclined when it came to appropriating money for the last frontier. World War II changed all that.

The Army impressed on Congress the fact that when Alaska was without defenses, the nation was in jeopardy. The generals said an enemy must be denied access to Alaska. So the Army was ordered to Alaska in June 1940. Alaskans were astonished by the speed and efficiency of the Army in getting funds from Congress and converting them to concrete and steel to make Alaska's defense system. The huge expenditures of money and effort were in defense of the nation, not Alaska. Congress proved to be prompt and generous in response to requests from the military.

The lesson for Alaskans was that Congress cared not more than a whit about them, but they were greatly concerned with the nation. Therefore, when Alaskans asked for federal funds, their projects must benefit the nation, while benefits to Alaska may be coincidental.

Under that principal the Alaska highway system was built. It is composed of military highways such as the Glenn Highway from Anchorage to Glenallen and Tok and the upgrading of the Richardson Highway from Valdez to Fairbanks. The benefits to civilians were coincidental. Community improvements, including schools, water and sewer systems, electric power generating, and even fire and police programs, were expanded to support the military. Civilian benefits, again, were coincidental.

Now, after the war, the burning desire that was growing in the hearts and minds of Alaskans was for their land to become a full-fledged and sovereign member of the family of states. If they were to succeed, it was necessary to prove that statehood would benefit the nation, and once more the benefits to Alaska would be coincidental.

The idea of statehood became a subject for editorial discussion in 1943 when Sen. Pat McCarran of Nevada and Rep. William Langer of North Dakota introduced statehood bills in each of the two houses of Congress. There were no speeches. No fanfare. Just two short bills which, if enacted, would have transferred to Alaska title to most all the vacant and unappropriated public lands and declared it to be a state as soon as certain other formalities were completed.

That got my attention. McCarran had rarely, if ever done anything good for Alaska. He was listed by many Alaskans as one of the senators "in the pocket" of the canned salmon industry. The fact that he was proposing statehood was a signal to me that there must be something involved that those of us living in Alaska would consider undesirable. That is a polite way of labeling him a "bad guy."

I promptly got a letter off to him asking what he had in mind. I also sent the same inquiry to Rep. Langer. After a couple of weeks I got replies from both.

McCarran's reply was one paragraph. It said, "I am very serious about this and am going to see that the bill is enacted." End of letter.

Langer's reply was three pages long, obviously typewritten by him personally, probably using two fingers. It had words xxxx'd out and strikeovers to correct typos—much like newspaper reporters' copy. He gave details about his thinking. He mentioned quite a few features that would benefit Alaska. His logic was good in most instances and he rose in my estimation. It was good to discover a man in Congress who had some accurate views on Alaska.

Until then I had not thought of Alaska as a likely candidate for statehood. There was general acceptance of the view that we had to do much to build our economy and population to support state government. Trade and commerce were considered too limited to support maritime investments in modern ships with more amenities. Salmon fishing, our main industry, was the main support of our transportation system, and it was only a summer season operation. Steamship operators in the Alaska trade used ships that could no longer compete in the main line trade between Europe or South America and America.

The same kind of reasoning was applied to businesses that had minimum investments and offered minimum services yet retailed their goods or services at extremely high prices "because of the high freight rates."

It was sometimes pointed out to us that freight rates to larger cities like Anchorage and Fairbanks had to be high enough to subsidize a part of the cost of running our "big steamships" to small towns like Valdez and Skagway where they might deliver as little as four tons. That didn't make those of us in the bigger cities any happier.

The Alaska economy was small even in boom times. I recall when the Alaska Railroad was proud of its record for moving 57,000 tons of freight in one year. That would average only a bit more than 1,000 tons a week for the territory's two largest cities and the railbelt, plus the supplies that went down the Yukon River from Nenana for Interior villages. In those days the railroad had around 1,100 employees to do it.

The contentment of that day ended as World War II approached and the Army became our next door neighbors. We heard the generals and their engineers talking about doing things we had believed to be either physically impossible or financially beyond reason.

They were planning airports in far-flung places, with concrete runways. We had always been led to believe that concrete would crumble in Alaska's long winters. The engineers were undaunted by the problems of frost heaves, permafrost and other Arctic conditions. They set up construction schedules that hardly allowed for a shutdown during the winter months. And they executed those schedules effectively.

After the railroad fell 167 trainloads behind in moving military freight north from Seward, the federal government got into action. An Army railroad battalion was assigned to augment the operations. For long range relief, the Whittier railroad terminus was built, including the tunnels through the mountains, and the highway system was built around Turnagain Arm to provide overland connections to Seward. The Army wanted the security of two ocean termini.

The Air Corps, then a part of the Army, controlled air traffic. Alaska bush pilots coordinated their operations and much of the time worked for the military. The Army provided navigation aids along the main routes and otherwise improved flying conditions.

These projects, and the excitement of planning and executing them, fired up the interest of Alaskans in improving their civilian infrastructure. Alaskans became understudies of the military leaders who were constantly going to Washington for help.

Governor Gruening was quick to take up the cudgels. He had long ago seen statehood as the only solution for Alaska's problems and had spoken favorably of it everywhere he went. People brushed off his dreamy ideas as just another New Deal spending binge.

Gruening was a great and constant salesman. When I asked him about statehood as proposed by McCarran and Langer he chided me for letting those men stir my interest when he had been talking about it so long. My reply was quite inadequate, referring to the old saw about prophets not being recognized at home. But we both sensed a meeting of the minds and that exchange led to the sessions where Alaaska's real push for statehood was born.

We started meeting in our home at 534 L Street, originally a log house that had been stuccoed over and Evangeline had painted white with blue and yellow trim, giving it a cheerful look on a street of drab brown houses.

Gruening would drop by every time he came to town. He liked a Scotch whiskey before dinner and a glass of wine with it. After dinner, he would sit back, puff on a cigar and talk about the reasons for statehood. Evangeline and I were his students during many nights around the fireplace. Similar sessions would occur in Juneau where my family and I had a standing invitation to stay at the governor's mansion.

When the legislature was in session, I would often drop in, appalled by how Outside interests manipulated their puppet legislators. Inevitably, the subject of statehood always came up.

Over a short period he had cleared away all my doubts about the viability of statehood and I wrote vigorous editorials going all out in support of statehood right now, not sometime in the dim and distant future. My paper was the first in all the territory to take that stand and it was almost alone in the field for perhaps a year. The Ketchikan Chronicle was second to support statehood after its editor, William L. Baker, became a convert.

My editorials about Alaska's grievances as a territorial colony got bolder after each meeting with Gruening.

The reaction of the business community was interesting. In Anchorage it was virtually nil. The retailers, mostly mom and pop store operators, weren't concerned. They were the "bread and butter" of my support. I knew them all personally and talked to most of them daily.

However, the king-makers and the moneyed people in big business, who in that day were the salmon packers and the gold miners, were adamantly opposed and were quick to make their opposition known. They headed the industries that paid what few taxes the territory levied. People paid only five dollars a year. It was called "school tax," but I never learned why.

Statehood opponents were mostly absentee owners and they influenced Alaskans by threatening economic reprisals. Alaska's small town bankers, insurance offices, grocery, drug and other retailers had reason to fear that if they stood for statehood they would lose an important segment of their local business—supplies for the fish boats and the canneries.

The statehood cause was pure American in its history and philosophy. Thirty-five territories had been admitted to the union after the original 13 colonies had fought a war to create it. The Northwest Ordinance of 1787 was often cited as having set the criteria for admission of new states, with the population requirement at 60,000. In 1940 the U.S. Census showed Alaska's population at 72,524.

There was no adequate justification for collecting federal taxes from Alaskans and withholding designated benefits that accrued to American citizens living in the 48 states. It was taxation without representation, a reoccurrence of one of the factors that motivated the American Revolutionary War.

Editorials in the Anchorage Times hammered home these and many other impressive arguments in support of statehood. Alaskans read them and took them on as their own views. The statehood cause gained strength spontaneously before the big money in Seattle—the Alaska Salmon Industry, Inc., an organization whose members owned and operated the biggest industry in Alaska—hired Winton C. Arnold as their man to see that Alaska would not win statehood.

In Anchorage statehood enthusiasts saw the need of an objective compilation of the facts about statehood: what it would do for Alaska and what it would do to Alaska. Inasmuch as this study involved history, political science and the basic civics of government, we thought the state university would be the likely place to find the special talent to compile it.

I asked the president of the University of Alaska if he knew of a professor, or a graduate student, who could make such a study and compile a report that could be published for the enlightenment of all Alaskans. I recall even suggesting some kind of a stipend to be paid for those services, although I had no money for it and considered it a public service the university should do on its own.

Much to my surprise, the president's response took the university out of the arena entirely. He said that the subject was too "hot" politically and if it became involved the legislature might cut off its appropriations. That experience bolstered my belief that there should always be a place for private as well as public education in the scheme of things. A private institution would not be beholden to politicians.

We statehood enthusiasts decided we could raise money and do our own study. Our method was to create a statewide organization that Alaskans could join and their dues would go into a fund to finance the study. That led to the launching of the Alaska Statehood Association.

My wife was elected president and she organized chapters in most of the major cities of the territory. She would get plenty of support from such people as the politically active McCutcheon brothers, Steve and Stanley, both Democrats; Irene Ryan, a pioneer civil engineer noted for her input in building the international airport; Mildred Hermann, prominent Juneau attorney and Andrew Nerland, a Rock-of-Gibraltar Fairbanks businessman with enormous integrity.

Alaskans everywhere were interested and wanted better information. The dues were five dollars and, there being no expenses, the money enabled the association to hire George Sundborg, a newspaperman in Juneau, to make the study. The funds were sufficient also to print his report and provide it free as a tabloid supplement to all the papers in Alaska. So the study got widespread distribution.

The statehood study became the subject of conversation everywhere. While it did a reasonable job of listing the arguments against statehood, those supporting statehood obviously overshadowed those opposed.

In the 1945 session of the Legislature, Rep. Stanley McCutcheon introduced and pushed through to enactment a law providing for a referendum on statehood in the general election of 1946. While the outcome of the referendum would have no binding effect, a victory for statehood would be strategically important. It would give Gruening and Delegate Bartlett a direct mandate from Alaskans to press the issue in Congress.

Our hopes took a giant leap early in 1946 when President Truman gave his first state of the union message and endorsed statehood for Alaska, the first president to do so.

The vote was 9,630 for and 6,822 against. For the first time, Alaskans expressed their views and they wanted statehood now. The victory was great considering that the issue was so new and the opposition was so mighty.

Only the Anchorage Times and the Ketchikan Chronicle favored it. Opposed were the Juneau Empire, which was owned and operated by Helen Monsen, daughter of former governor John Troy, and the Cap Lathrop's Fairbanks Daily News-Miner. Weeklies in Nome, Petersburg, Wrangell, Seward, Cordova and Kodiak were solidly opposed.

Regardless of the success of statehood in the referendum vote, the 1947 legislature was still predominantly anti-statehood. That session marched to the drums of the fish packers and didn't get the message from the people. Gruening labeled the 1947 session the worst one in his career. It spent $4,000,000 more than it had and on adjournment left such a mess the territory had to pass the hat to get money to keep the University of Alaska operating.

The people of Alaska were aroused by this embarrassing demonstration and in the next election threw enough "rascals" out to give those for statehood the upper hand. The resulting 1949 session was acclaimed by Gruening as the best one in the history of Alaska.

By this time, statehood had become a household word among Alaskans. It was discussed in schools, business places and many public gatherings. Democrats were taking the lead in promoting it and their party was soon to be claiming to be "the statehood party."

Republicans at that time were still dormant as a political power while the remnants of the New Deal under Roosevelt held forth. There weren't many Alaskans who called themselves Republican since the territory went all out for Franklin D. Roosevelt. Democrats held most of the elective offices and controlled the big federal bureaucracy that administered most of the important government programs. Republicans were hardly more than a handful of men whose names appeared on the Alaska party's letterhead.

The heavily Democratic 1949 legislature brought dramatic changes. It created the Alaska Statehood Committee as the official territory agency to win enactment of the statehood bill, and to make plans for a constitutional convention. All of Gruening's appointments to the statehood committee cleared the confirmation process, a rarity in any Alaska legislature. Selecting a chairman created another rarity. Democrats dominated the committee and their party already was promoting itself as the "statehood party." However, the factions within party could not agree up a Democrat as chairman. To my surprise, they elected me, a Republican.

I was not comfortable being out front as chairman of a group funded by public money to promote the cause of statehood. I felt my most important contribution would continue to be reporting the issues and interpreting the consequences for the public. Therefore, I was happy to leave public appearances, philosophical debates and political lobbying to Gruening.

Gruening gave example after example of how Alaska suffered from the injustices of a colonial system. Alaska paid federal taxes for roads but got no federal road money in return, he said. Alaska did not have speedy justice because the judicial system was run by a government 3,000 miles away and court hearings were held at the convenience of underfunded federal commissioners who must worry about scrambling for a living on fees incidental to the administering of justice. He said Alaska suffered from a virtual transportation monopoly operating out of Seattle which had inadequate service and unduly high rates.

The 1949 legislature also enacted a basic revenue system for the territory—an income tax, business license tax, a fish trap tax, permissive sales taxes for municipalities and school districts, and other progressive measures.

The statehood movement had become a cause supported by most of the population. For the first time in the territory's history, elected legislators were not afraid to levy taxes on their constituents. They were essential in shaping up the political corpus to carry the responsibilities of self-government.

It was in the 1949 legislature that Alaskans for the first time had to provide their own political leaders. Until that year, it was frequently said that there were few Alaskans recognized among their own peers as proven public leaders. The territory's leadership jobs were all filled by federal appointees and, generally speaking, there were only lesser public jobs available for local appointees.

The performance of Rep. Stanley McCutcheon and his brother, Sen. Steve McCutcheon, made them stand out as leaders in enacting the revenue measures and always standing strong for statehood. Rep. Vic Rivers, a civil engineer in Anchorage, was another. They were all subsequently elected as delegates to the state constitutional convention.

The revenue system enacted by this legislature was a great boost for our statehood efforts. No longer could opponents say we had no means to support ourselves. The basic laws were in place and the revenue could be increased or decreased readily by action in future legislative sessions. That is exactly what the salmon packers did not want to happen. We had finally broken the political shackles they had put upon the territory for their own benefit. Salmon, for the first time, would now pay a share of the costs of government in Alaska.

This turn of events in legislative history did not come about easily. It was preceded by six years of public discussion of the statehood issue, during which my newspaper carried a barrage of editorials on that subject. As an editor I found it to be a complex subject that always had a lively facet exposed for public understanding.

The salmon packers, through their associates in Alaska, made it a practice to bring up anything that might be puzzling or hard to understand. It is often said that when Alaskans feel they don't know enough about an issue, or facts are being withheld, they usually vote against it. The technique used masterfully by the fish packers was the old chestnut "divide and conquer."

Alaskans are easy to divide on almost any issue because they have a history of living in isolation—isolated in their cities, separated by great distances and, until very recently, with inadequate communications services.

Each community has carved out a niche for itself by shaping up its supporting economy to fit the local environment. The prevailing sense of values, priorities or even philosophical views of each community may vary from its neighbors, especially those in distant regions where the environment is different.

In southeastern Alaska, where townsites are at the foot of mountainous fjords and flatland is in short supply, urban centers were developed historically on islands without the benefit of intercommunity roads. They depended upon the sea for travel as well as for the products that supported their lifestyles.

On the other hand, southcentral and central Alaska have the huge landmass where urban settlements are scattered over a vast sea of tundra among mountain ranges. Tundra is unsuitable in summer for walking or wheeled vehicles. In winter it is good for dog team travel or to fly over. In this expanse of Alaska, urban centers have room to grow horizontally as well as vertically. During World War II engineers found ways to build stable roads and urban facilities on tundra and permafrost.

Modern technology did much to break down the isolation that marked life in Alaska and dominated the economic and social fabric that prevailed during the formative days of the territory. Nevertheless, much of the basic economy, politics and social philosophies of the earlier days have carried over to the present generation.

All of this means that much of the sectionalism that marked regional interests still prevails today. The original Four Judicial Divisions, created by federal edict almost a hundred years ago and today of only limited or no significance in political life, still delineate the broad, general division of Alaskans in their views of the world and economic opportunities. And this often spills over into political, social and cultural attitudes.

People know each other in all areas but they don't know much about each other's way of life. Their closest ties are to their neighborhoods and towns. Their statewide ties come mostly from their common love and pride of their land and the sovereign entity that they created which won national acceptance when Alaska became a state.

Until statehood in 1959, the salmon packers succeeded in keeping Alaskans divided on contemporary issues. It was their main tool in per-

122 | CHAPTER NINE

petuating their control of the territory's politics and economics.

The packers prospered most when they could move into Alaska, catch the bountiful salmon run and pack it off to world markets, without spending money in Alaska. In the beginning they did it by bringing with them each spring their own fishermen and cannery workers to their own cannery buildings, dormitories and dining rooms with their own power generators, water and sewage systems. They transported them all to and from Alaska, and paid them only after they disembarked, usually at Seattle.

They opposed almost every effort to provide or improve civil government. They sought to discourage the growth of cities, transportation and other public facilities. To the fish packers, those things meant taxes. Until 1949 they were virtually free of taxes. Their wealth flowed into places like Seattle, San Francisco, Boston and New York, where they built lavish mansions and lived the good life.

It was a repetition, 50 to 100 years later, of the opening of the western states to settlement, when the pioneer miners, cattlemen and others found wealth in the ground and took their bonanza back to New York to build fine mansions on Fifth Avenue. The west was left with abandoned holes in the ground.

Fish runs in Alaska were showing signs of depletion. Yet the federal government let it continue year after year. Alaskans feared that their land, like the West, would be left with its greatest resource depleted.

One of the strongest arguments for statehood was that states always control their own resources and statehood was the only means for Alaskans to take control of theirs and stop the depletion.

After the referendum in 1946, statehood bills were introduced into every session of Congress. One bill passed the House of Representatives in 1950 but failed in the Senate. In 1952, a statehood bill failed by only a single vote in the Senate.

However, in the fall of 1952, an election calamity struck both the drive for statehood and the political stature of Gruening. Gen. Dwight D. Eisenhower, a Republican, was swept into office, ending 20 years of Democrat administrations. Not only did Gruening lose his valuable contacts in the administration, but also he lost his job.

Early in 1953, President Eisenhower appointed Frank Heintzleman, a regional forester for Alaska who had endeared himself to timber cutters, to succeed Gruening as territorial governor. As a friend of absentee timber interests, he was openly opposed to statehood. Further, Eisenhower chose Douglas McKay, former governor of Oregon, as Secretary of Interior. McKay had supported Alaska statehood while governor but switched his view upon taking national office, probably in deference to Sen. Hugh Butler of Nebraska, an influential Republican who vigorously did all he could to block Alaska's statehood effort as chairman of the all-powerful Committee of Interior and Insular Affairs.

The Eisenhower appointments seemed to send us a clear message: no support for statehood for Alaska. It appeared that 10 years of hard work had become undone.

With Gruening's status weakened, I knew we had to change strategy. Perhaps a saner newspaper publisher would have quit as chairman of the Alaska Statehood Committee and returned full-time to his desk. The sacrifices of time away from the paper, plus the expenses of my travel and Evangeline's, which we footed, were considerable. But that setback fired my determination to become more involved than ever, even if that required me to further cut my time at the paper. I would have to assume a political role I never relished. But I chose to start studying the flight schedules to Washington.

Below: Bob Atwood speaks at a statehood booster meeting at the Elks Club in Anchorage (February 1954). Photo by Steve McClutcheon/Alaska Pictorial Service

124 | CHAPTER EIGHT

Rep Crawford's House Committee holds hearings on Alaska Statehood in the Local Theater in 1947. Near right is Delegate to Congress Bob Bartlett. Rep. Crawford is far center. Photo by Steve McClutcheon/Alaska Pictorial Service

BLACK GOLD | 125

Right: Alaska state constitutional convention at University of Alaska, Fairbanks, Author George Sundborg, a member of the convention speaking to a point during session. Photo by Steve McClutcheon/Alaska Pictorial Service

Atwood (center right) with Gunnard Engebrith, President of Terr Senate onboard Alaska Airlines DC4 to lobby for statehood (April 20, 1950). Photo by Steve McClutcheon/Alaska Pictorial Service

Stanley J. McCutcheon Speaker of the House stands with Gov. Gruening during the signing of a bill. McCutcheon youngest ever in legislature and Speakership. Photo by Steve McClutcheon/Alaska Pictorial Service

Right: Bob Atwood on stairs with hat leaves Anchorage with an Alaskan group for Washington DC to attend hearing & to lobby for statehood of Alaska. (April 20, 1950). Photo by Steve McClutcheon/Alaska Pictorial Service/

STATEHOOD BATTLE | 127

Battle for statehood, Washington DC, 1950. Back (l-r) Manager Matanuska Hotel, unknown, Capt. Larry Flahart, Judy (stewardess); unkown; McNielly, Stanley J. McCutcheon, president of Alaska Airlines. (Left) Bob Courtemanche, copiot; Mrs. Casterns sister; Senator Steve McCutcheon. Photo by Steve McClutcheon/Alaska Pictorial Service

Statehood group arrive in Washington DC. Coming off ramp; Rachel Castner, father Paul O'Connor, Essie Dale. To the right of Atwood (with his back to the camera); Ellis and Engebreth; back Al Owen (1950) Photo by Steve McClutcheon/Alaska Pictorial Service

128 | CHAPTER NINE

— CHAPTER TEN —

White House Visit

On a bright spring afternoon in 1954, I walked up to the West Wing door of the White House. I had come to keep an appointment to see President Eisenhower. It was Saturday and no one was there to open the door for me. I opened it myself and inwardly chuckled because the Republican palace guard that thought they were in control didn't know I was there, didn't want me there and, had they known, would have gone to some extremes to keep me out of there.

I had made an end run around the politicians to get to see the president. I was there, not as an advocate of statehood for Alaska, but as a visiting newspaper editor paying his respects to the president. There could be no objection to that. A visiting editor, by custom, is entitled to pay his respects to the president regardless of politics.

The guard at the gate let me through after no more than a quick glance at his daybook. There weren't many entries for this was a lazy Saturday—such a nice day nobody should be required to work. And that's pretty much the way it appeared to be. The guard and I were the only living bodies in sight on the White House grounds.

I followed the walkways in a big curve across the lawn, an empty feeling gnawing at my stomach as I looked up at the formidable mansion. I still had not decided what to say to the president.

Every step toward the White House enhanced in my mind the importance that I use my few moments to say the right thing. Statehood legislation was snagged politically in a Congress controlled by the Democrats. President Eisenhower had the clout to move it ahead or he could let it die. Its fate was in his hands.

Hostility in the White House was new to us after all the years when President Truman was there. When Republicans took over in 1952 it seemed to many of us in Alaska that anti-statehood office seekers came out of the woodwork to take the key jobs that set policies and administered Alaska affairs. Later we learned it was a carefully orchestrated exercise wherein the owners of the salmon industry, who were noted as generous donors to political campaigns, named their friends to those jobs.

Walker Stone, my friend who was editor-in-chief of Scripps Howard Newspapers, got the appointment for me. Through all the years of the statehood effort, his papers were always strong supporters.

Mr. Stone was the kind of a friend who would listen when you let your hair down and pondered your frustrations. I was frustrated after two months of trying to get action on the legislation. I told him I had to see the president and he was surrounded by anti-statehood bureaucrats who wouldn't let me see him.

Mr. Stone listened patiently and responded, in his slow paced, laid-back attitude, "Well, Bob, that isn't quite true. A visiting editor can always see the president to pay his respects, you know."

No, I didn't know. I was just a small town editor from remote Alaska who was in Washington to tramp the marble halls of congressional office buildings, making friends with congressmen and trying to persuade them to support the bill to make Alaska a state. Nobody ever schooled me on perks.

I asked Mr. Stone how to make an appointment—all my contacts were Democrats and they had no access. He said he would make the appointment and leave word at my hotel. For the next three days my only concern was how to tell the statehood story in a very brief visit.

None of my friends knew what the ground rules were for paying respects to the president and were little help in helping me shape up my pitch.

As I stood in the White House reception room the only fear I had was that I might fumble this opportunity. I was relieved when Jim Hagerty, the president's press secretary, walked in and greeted me. He was an old-time newspaperman who I'd met on many occasions.

During our chitchat as we sat in his office, I could see that he knew of my interest in statehood legislation and that I was eager to lay the facts before the president. Hagerty's sharp Irish eyes seemed to take on extra piercing powers as he began to brief me seriously.

"You know, Bob, when an editor comes to pay his respects to the president he doesn't bring up anything," Hagerty said. "The president decides what you talk about. You will talk about what he talks about. Those are the ground rules. Are you willing to follow them?"

Of course I was because I had to be. However, the thought flashed through my mind that the ground rules sounded like something invented in the Seattle office of Bogle, Bogle and Gates, the law firm that represented the salmon packers. Could this be their last gasp effort to stymie me?

Obviously, I was expected to go in and say some kind words and get out without a word about statehood. I had no intention of allowing that to happen but I felt inhibited by the heavy constraints Hagerty had put on me.

Hagerty ushered me into the Oval Office. I had been there many times for press conferences during President Truman's regime. But this time I was alone with the President, except for Hagerty, of course. It was very different. The room looked so large. And, indeed, formidable.

President Eisenhower got up from his desk and came to greet me. He was relaxed, informal and friendly. Instead of returning to his desk chair, he sat in a chair on the visitor's side of the desk and motioned me to sit so we could talk face to face with nothing between us. Hagerty sat to one side where he could keep his eagle eye on me.

This provided an informal setting for a visit and the president put his visitor at ease with his warm and friendly style. The Oval Office looks just like it does in the published pictures. The two flags are behind the desk, on either side of the French doors. His desk was littered with trinkets, I suspect mostly elephant figures and golf mementos presented by friends.

I felt the warmth of the president's personality and the informal friendliness that made so many citizens look to him as the nation's Big Daddy. He was easy to meet and gracious, a characteristic I have come to associate with people who are big in intellect and experience.

Ground rule constraints notwithstanding, I still was intent on getting the statehood message to the president. I was really there on business as well as to pay my respects. I felt I must get the president's help or the statehood bill would die with the end of the congressional session.

As soon as Hagerty introduced me as an editor from Alaska, President Eisenhower started talking about Alaska. He had many memories of Alaska and most of them involved visits as General Eisenhower to Elmendorf Air Force Base and Anchorage during World War II. He recalled the problems of that time and was interested in the growth of Anchorage since.

Our conversation was lively. I had been actively involved in every visit he made to Anchorage. He remembered public dinners he attended, and I was on the committees that arranged them, greeted him and I sometimes sat at the head table with him. I knew everyone he recalled.

I recalled that on one visit he sat high on the back of a jeep with its top down, like a dignitary in a parade, while his driver drove slowly the length of downtown Fourth Avenue and back on Fifth Avenue just so the local kids as well as adults could get a close-up look at him. He remembered how he thought it ingenious how Alaskans made a jeep do the job usually performed by a Cadillac convertible.

Anchorage was then a small town of perhaps 15,000 people. Everybody was on the street to see the president—daddy, mother, all the kids and most of the dogs. There was much flag waving by young and old. We had no band so it was quiet. And that quietness gave the event a reverential hush as Alaskans met and greeted him. There were verbal exchanges as well as friendly waves. He responded warmly and sometimes answered questions tossed from the sidelines. Now in the White House he obviously relished recalling that experience.

I did all I could to draw him out on these recollections because we were at least talking about Alaska and that must lead, eventually, to some mention of statehood.

For more than 30 minutes we must have talked about places like the Aleutian Gardens, the elite night club on East Fourth Avenue that was, in the war years, the most elegant eating place in town. Community banquets with Ike as guest of honor were held there.

Hagerty sat through this conversation stoically, stiff as a ramrod. I got the feeling he was just waiting to jump in case I brought up something.

I didn't have to bring up something. Ike brought it up himself. Hagerty looked dejected. The president asked me how Anchorage had grown since his visits. I had lots to report and I managed to run into my narrative some references to the unusual difficulties an Alaska community has in financing growth because in the territory cities cannot issue bonds without approval by Congress.

I am sure Jim Hagerty never saw an editor pay his respects to the president like this. I like to think that my sly pitches about the woes of territorialism prompted the President to bring up the next subject.

"Well, now, about statehood," the president said.

How happy I was to hear those words. No longer was I a visiting editor paying a courtesy call on the president. No longer was Hagerty some kind of a policeman seeing that I abide by his law. I was on my own now. I was an official representing the people of Alaska discussing statehood by invitation with the president of the United States of America, the nation we loved and cherished and we, as a territory, wanted very much to join as a full-fledged member.

"I keep hearing people say that I am opposed to statehood, but I'm not," Ike continued.

Those words fired up my hopes for something constructive to come out of this meeting. It confirmed my suspicions that the salmon packers had surrounded Ike with anti-statehood administrators. Democrats and some of the media played up whatever the bureaucrats said as the gospel according to Ike. Now I was hearing the truth and it was music to my ears. I waited to hear more.

The president said there was only one thing that bothered him about statehood for Alaska and it was a military consideration. The federal government must have a free hand for military operations in the Arctic areas, he said.

I knew why the president was saying that. The Defense department had a super secret project under way involving a search for the best locations to build silos for the nation's newest secret weapon, the Minuteman Missile. The weapon had a range of only 5,000 miles and its accuracy was enhanced the closer it could be to its targets. That made the vast reaches of Alaska's Arctic tundra, some of it a few miles from Siberia, a mighty attractive place for silos.

Federal engineers were at that moment combing the northern areas in search of something, but we could only guess what. My newspaper was carrying speculative stories about these activities. The project was so secret that even the president had no authority to reveal it.

As long as Alaska was a territory the federal government owned almost all the land and resources. Federal agencies had the power to use the land as they wished without public hearings, environmental consideration or the consequences of impact on the civilian population.

I encouraged Ike to keep talking about the importance of land ownership. Every statehood bill provided for the new state to take title to a portion of the public domain but how much and by what selection process varied from bill to bill. Statehood opponents made much of the land problems because they could muddy up the issue to make it controversial and difficult.

The bill then pending provided for 100 million acres to be selected by the state over a period of 25 years. Instead of requiring surveys, the state would be allowed to select its land in large blocks described in metes and bounds, a system that is remindful of the crude maps of pirates recording where they buried their treasures.

The president suggested a provision restricting state selections to areas of no concern to the military. That seemed reasonable. The vast Arctic areas had few resources ready for development. The land was home to large caribou herds and was important mainly in the subsistence economy of the Eskimo.

I left the White House in high spirits and went directly to Delegate Bartlett's office. He was pleased with my report. This would be an effective answer to the statehood foes who at that time were advocating statehood for a part of Alaska and leaving the rest as a territory. The idea of divided Alaska had virtually no following.

The president's proposal was a good solution. Drawing a line on the map would alter no boundaries and all Alaskans would live within the new state. It is interesting to note that in creating the Yukon-Porcupine River line, as it came to be known, Alaskans were excluding from their areas for land selection the great Prudhoe Bay oil reserves. It is probably fortunate that the oil was yet undiscovered. How the state eventually came into ownership of that oil field is told in another chapter.

I went home to Alaska feeling that we were on the verge of great achievement in our cause. The wheels in Washington were in motion to modify the bill so as to have it win the blessing of the president. The next high priority task would be to address the concerns expressed often in the halls of Congress.

One of them was that Alaskans, living in the territory, did not have the experience of governance. Political leadership was mostly federal. The men and women who set policies and administered public affairs were sent to Alaska. Too rarely were they drawn from the local population.

In response, we could point to the fact that most of the adult population emigrated to Alaska from the large or small towns where they lived in the 48 states. Before they went north they acquired an American background of education, culture and training on the rights and duties of citizens. But that kind of a response never stopped the continual questioning whether Alaskans knew how to run their own government.

It was easy to whet public interest in writing a constitution for our proposed state. The Alaska Statehood Committee was one of the agencies that took a leadership position in persuading the legislature to take the big and costly step.

The legislature did it. The bill passed by a 23 to 1 vote in the House and with a unanimous vote in the Senate. With such strong support there was no worry that the anti-statehood governor, Frank Heintzleman, would veto it.

The legislation appropriated $300,000 for expenses and carried many special provisions besides the basics for electing delegates and conducting business. It designated the University of Alaska campus at Fairbanks as the place for the convention. It provided for non-partisan elections. Thus the convention was removed from the Juneau locale where politics, politicians and all the hangers-on prevailed, and was placed in the more scholarly atmosphere of academia.

On Sept. 13, 1955, Alaskans elected 55 delegates and they convened a constitutional convention two months later, in November at the university. Statehood foes denigrated the activity as only a rump convention because it had not been authorized by Congress. Perhaps this attitude accounted for the absence of lobbyists and their special interest groups from the convention hall. However, some Alaskans speculated that it was the extreme winter temperatures, sometimes reaching -50 degrees, that froze the lobbyists out.

The Statehood Committee was vested with the duty of preparing documents and providing political scientists as consultants. The documents included a compilation of what each of the existing 48 states had in its constitution for every item. Along with the precise wording from the other states, the delegates had notes on court interpretations and sometimes commentaries from authorities.

We often observed that Alaska had only 48 bad precedents to follow. Our studies showed that each state had strengths and weaknesses written into its constitution. We were intent on allowing only the best in Alaska's.

The convention did it proud by producing one of the best constitutions ever written. Political scientists are still strong in their approval. Our delegates not only proved we could write a constitution, they also went an extra mile to establish our readiness for self-government. They included in the document a plan to elect senators and one representative to go to Washington and, figuratively, knock on the doors of Congress and ask to be seated.

This was known as the "Tennessee Plan" because it was first used successfully by that state when Congress was slow in granting admission. Several other territories used it in following years, each time with success.

The idea for the Tennessee Plan came from George Lehleitner, a history buff from Louisiana who made several trips to Alaska to talk to Alaskans and even appeared in the middle of winter before the convention in Fairbanks.

On April 24,1956, voters gave their stamp of approval to the constitution by a vote 33,343 to 6,618 and to the Tennessee Plan, 12,204 to 7,928. That giant step forward was cause for rejoicing. But not for me. I had foolishly allowed myself to be persuaded, on the basis of civic duty, to be the Republican candidate for one synthetic senator seat.

Wally Hickel did it. He called me five times one evening from the nominating convention in Juneau. I kept telling him "No," but he'd call back with another approach. Finally he said I wasn't being fair to the GOP, that I had been rough on the party editorially for its inner factions and frictions but now that they have healed those divisive wounds and are unanimous for me, I won't do my part. He was right about my being rough in editorials. I accepted on his pledge that the party was united and solidly behind me.

I found I was pitted against my friend Bill Egan, the Democrat candidate. The Republicans adjourned their convention and effectively disappeared, as far as I was concerned. I got no election support and found myself a mighty lonesome candidate. My campaign was virtually nil. I don't remember even having a manager.

The Democrats swept the election, voting in Bill Egan and Ernest Gruening as the Tennessee plan senators and Ralph Rivers as representative. Bob Bartlett, the official Alaska delegate to Congress under the territorial government, was re-elected for a seventh term.

If there was a redeeming feature to my one and only try for office, it enabled me to welcome C. W. Snedden, the new publisher of the Fairbanks News-Miner, into the pro-statehood fight. Snedden acquired the paper after Cap Lathrop was crushed to death by a runaway coal car in 1950 at his Healy River mine. Snedden had joined the News-Miner at Lathrop's behest to shake up the business end. He did his own homework on statehood and after Cap died he became a strong supporter.

Snedden gave me space on his editorial page for a piece on why the Tennessee Plan would help Alaska. The article gave me a chance to review my interview with President Eisenhower for his Fairbanks readers, and to point out how the Yukon-Porcupine River line would resolve the president's defense concerns.

When the voters elected all three Democrats to go to Washington, I backed them editorially and encouraged an aggressive campaign in the halls of Congress. After several months we praised their work.

WHITE HOUSE VISIT | 135

"A better understanding of the plight of Alaska as a territory and the reasons Alaska seeks statehood is resulting," my editorial said March 12, 1957. "Newspapers throughout the nation are carrying stories on the efforts of Alaskans to act like a state even though they do not have that status."

Despite these positive developments there were still some short-sighted territorial legislators who tried to renege on the compensation promised. That triggered a bit of editorial outrage until the lawmakers finally agreed to pay the Tennessee Plan trio $9,000 a year each and $16 a day expenses.

The plight of Alaska was indeed being discovered. I could feel for the first time that statehood was within our reach. Our synthetic senators and congressman were winning the sympathies of the nation. The battle now shifted to the 85th Congress that convened for its two-year session in 1957. Once more I prepared to pack my bags and head for Washington. As chairman of the Statehood Committee with Republican credentials, I could help in places not accessible to our Democratic delegation.

Bob Atwood of the Anchorage Times introduces Gov. Ernest Gruening; Aleutian Gards at 4th & B St. owned by Tony and Mary Pastro. Photo by Steve McClutcheon/Alaska Pictorial Service

136 | CHAPTER TEN

Bob Atwood campaigning for Tennessee plan senator in Oct. of 1956 (R) Evangeline Atwood and Joan Walker – meet held at the home of Gloria Britt. Photo by Steve McClutcheon/Alaska Pictorial Service/Oct. 7, 1956

WHITE HOUSE VISIT | 137

138 | CHAPTER TEN

— CHAPTER ELEVEN —

Victory at Last

Each new session of Congress was like the opening of a new ball game—the same playing field, usually the same rules but with some changes in players. When the 85th Congress was convening in 1957 it was that way once more. Alaska had been rebuffed by the previous seven sessions yet Alaskans had much to bolster their optimism that they would win statehood in the 85th. And they did.

Despite their many losses, they had many gains that gave them national recognition. Both houses of Congress had debated the merits of their plea for statehood and had laid it before the country as a lively issue that must be dealt with. The biggest guns of the opposition had fired their highest caliber ammunition and had failed to defeat us. At most they only delayed us.

The anti-statehood coalition composed of Taft Republicans and Southern Democrats found it difficult to maintain its solid front against us. Several of the deciding votes on procedural motions were won or lost by one vote.

There was one big gain for Alaska in the lineup for the 85th Congress. It resulted from the resignation of Douglas McKay as Secretary of the Interior who opposed statehood. Alaskans saw his departure as good riddance.

It became even more so when President Eisenhower appointed Sen. Fred Seaton of Nebraska to succeed McKay. Seaton had become a fast friend and supporter of Alaska during the year he served as senator to fill the vacancy left by the death of Sen. Kenneth S. Wherry. During his Senate tenure he delivered one speech and it was in favor of Alaska statehood.

The 85th Congress was still controlled by Democrats in both houses, but with Seaton in the cabinet I had a perfect coach to build up support among Republican minority members. We needed all the help we could get.

As we initiated a full-fledged effort to convince Republican congressmen to climb aboard our statehood bandwagon, Seaton opened his doors to me and the other Alaska Republicans who by now decided to get behind the statehood movement. It was the first time in more than 10 years of effort that I found I was working with so many Republicans as partners not hecklers.

VICTORY AT LAST | 139

In March 1957, President Eisenhower gave the movement a big boost, fulfilling all the expectations that lingered with me since my visit in his office. He sent Congress an Alaska statehood bill with the wording we had hoped for: no partition provision, a grant of more than 100 million acres, and land selection restricted only in the far north, at the aforementioned Yukon-Porcupine River line. We could see the guidance of Seaton, his trusted cabinet officer.

The news set off euphoria in Alaska and inspired a massive letter writing campaign directed by "Operation Statehood," an organization of Alaska volunteers who wanted to help win statehood. In a front page story on March 12, we reported that Alaskans were sending congratulatory letters to Eisenhower and Seaton, letters to congressmen urging them to get behind the president's plan and letters with informative pamphlets enclosed to friends Outside asking them to write their congressmen.

Too little recognition has been given this group for the invaluable campaign it waged. These Alaskans capitalized on the fact that most adult Alaskan residents who were interested in winning statehood had come from somewhere in the lower 48 states and had many friends in their former hometowns who were still constituents of the congressmen who held the fate of our legislation. At the behest of their Alaska friends, the hometowners poured it on to their congressmen.

I know they did a an effective job for Alaska because of the many times when I was trying to persuade a legislator to vote for "my bill" he would interrupt the conversation to comment on how many of his constituents felt the same way.

"Alaska is now on the 10-yard line," declared Bob Retherford, president of Operation Statehood.

Unfortunately, Congress decided to make a goal line stand. Opponents let it be known they were not about to capitulate.

We were determined to hammer our way out through those tortuous final yards. For the next 15 months, starting in March 1957, we generated a blitz of publicity that caught the attention of the nation. A steady stream of Alaskans, led by the ever articulate Ernest Gruening, testified at congressional hearings, many of them rebutting the testimony of W. C. Arnold, the clever and also articulate lobbyist for the vested fishing interests.

Newspapers, radio and television reported their appeals for statehood. National publications assigned their most skilled reporters to analyze the issues and usually came out on our side. I personally visited many newspaper editorial boards (including the New York Times, which became a strong supporter) and almost always left them impressed by Alaska's case.

Edna Ferber, inspired by Gruening to write a book about our plight, dramatized our cause in her novel, "Ice Palace," which some critics referred to as "the Uncle Tom's Cabin for Alaska statehood." Civic organizations, ranging from Woman's Club to Kiwanis, succeeded in getting club members in other states to pass supportive resolutions that landed on the desk of congressmen. And, of course, many private citizens from all over responded to pleas either from their Alaska friends or the national publicity by pressuring their representatives to vote for statehood.

By the time the administration's embattled statehood bill approached definitive votes in Congress in the spring of 1958, I believe we addressed every issue in dispute and impressed the nation with every injustice inflicted on territorial Alaska.

The most telling of all the injustices was Alaska's powerlessness in saving its largest industry, fisheries. Twenty years earlier, Alaska waters had produced 6.5 million cases of salmon a year. The catch had dropped steadily to 2.5 million cases in 1957. That unchallenged statistic told how Outside-owned fishing interests had been unmercifully depleting the stocks by setting fish traps at the mouths of rivers. The federal government controlled the fishing regulations and refused to ban the traps, despite the desperate appeals from Alaskans and despite the fact that fish traps were outlawed in every state of the union.

However, years of heavy campaign contributions—and promises for still more in the future—by the wealthy Outside owners profiting from this ruthless destruction had bought widespread support in Congress. That influence had to be overcome in any showdown on a statehood bill. We could not counter with money, because we didn't have any. But we had a national disdain for colonialism of Alaska building up for our side and we were determined to visit and pin down every congressman on where he stood on this issue.

We had some insurmountable problems that we had to find a way to surmount. Which we did. One of them was Sam Rayburn, Speaker of the House, who ruled with an iron fist. He was a Texan committed against admitting Alaska into the union. Since Rayburn was a Democrat, our three Tennessee Plan Democrats worked on his conversion.

While Congress from the outset had refused to give them privileges of the floor, the Alaska-elected representatives had other strengths going for them. Bartlett, serving his seventh term as delegate, and Gruening, never far from power bases, were seasoned players in Washington political wars.

I don't know what transpired behind the scenes, but one day Bartlett and Gruening told me not to worry about Rayburn. They said Rayburn would do nothing to stop the bill but neither would he do anything to help it. That was a triumph for us because he had the power to kill it if he wished.

Wayne Aspinall, D-Colo., chairman of the committee on Interior and Insular Affairs, brought up the statehood bill late in May 1958. The House debate lasted three days. When a motion to recommit by Rep. John

Pillion, R-NY, failed 202 to 173, we knew Rayburn was keeping his promise. On May 28, the bill passed the House 210 to 166 with 51, including Rayburn, not voting.

It was a big victory, but statehood bills had passed the House before only to be defeated in the Senate. And the same animosity that dogged it still prevailed. The senior senators, mostly from southern states, held the key chairmanships and they didn't want statehood. Their first concern was to defend their right to filibuster because that was their last-stand defense against civil rights laws, the big item on their agenda. The southerners feared Alaska would elect two senators who would be liberal and in favor of civil rights. Thus statehood might trim down their margin by a precious two votes.

Civil rights was the top news of the day. It dominated the news media and much of the time of Congress. Federal troops were called out to enforce a court-ordered segregation of the high school in Little Rock, Ark., in 1957. And it was the 85th Congress that passed the first civil rights law forbidding public discrimination on the basis of race, color, religion or national origin. These disconcerting events sometimes made it difficult for Alaskans to get the attention of Congress.

In mid-June of 1958, the week before the bill was up for debate and vote, Alaskans staged a concerted push to persuade senators to go for statehood. The team of Alaska Democrats systematically called on each Democratic senator in his office to talk about it.. Each evening they tallied their results and decided who, if anyone, should visit the senator the next day.

The same activity was under way on the Republican side of the aisle. Secretary Seaton had called for five Republicans to come to Washington to work with him. They were Mike Stepovich, the last territorial governor; Robert B. Groseclose, the Alaska chairman of the Republican Party; Walter J. Hickel, a Republican activist, and newspaper publishers C.W. Snedden and me. We made Seaton's office our headquarters. It was a new experience for me. In all my years of lobbying Congress, this was the first time Alaska Republicans as a party showed any interest at all.

Our group was increased by one when Bob Kederick, my Anchorage managing editor, joined us. He was on vacation on the East Coast and upon hearing of the excitement in Washington, responded like the old fire horse going to the fire.

Ted Stevens, a promising young Alaska lawyer Seaton had taken to Washington to be his staff counsel, worked with us full time. Stevens in later years became Alaska's senior U.S. senator and served with great distinction.

We were hyped up by the excitement. We were tallying more and more favorable votes and we felt our bill was going to win if we could bring it to the final vote. It made us feel good to find ourselves among so many of our national leaders and that they were responding to us so warmly.

During this critical week, I was with my Republican allies day and night, but I would run into my longtime friends, Alaska Democrats, while making the rounds in the office buildings. We shared reports on how we felt we were progressing, they with the Democrats and me with the GOP. They found it hard to believe that I was finding GOP support. In one discussion, I predicted there would be more GOP votes for statehood than Democrat. That was a rash prediction inasmuch as the Democrats claimed statehood was their idea and Republicans were the anti party. The Democrats scoffed and said I was being "brainwashed" by the Republicans. "Let's wait and see," I said.

At the end of each afternoon our Republican team met in Seaton's office for a debriefing and to talk about tomorrow. From there we usually went to the Statler Hotel for a drink in the Terrace Room. One day while the six of us were seated at our table Bob Kederick noted that a pretty young lady sitting with a friend over yonder was the secretary to a senator who would not commit to statehood.

We suggested that Bob, having met her when he called on her senator, invite her and her male friend to join us at our table for a drink, which they did. We proceeded to give her our statehood pitch. Her man friend, seated to the left of Wally Hickel at the end of the table next to the dance floor, kept butting in, saying Alaska didn't deserve statehood—too backward, too poor, already a drain on the welfare system and so on.

That guy did this repeatedly. I was on the opposite side of the table and his comments irritated me. It seems that they must have irritated Hickel as well. With scarcely a body movement, Hickel, a former amateur boxer, flicked a left uppercut to the man's lower jaw so forceful he actually catapulted into the air and landed sprawling on the dance floor.

In the commotion that followed, Hickel sat idly by as though he was wondering what the commotion was all about. The poor guy got up and, of course, made like he was ready to defend his honor and such. Groseclose moved in to keep Hickel from doing anything more. The rest of us bundled our territorial governor, Mike Stepovich, out of the bar. It wasn't easy to do because Mike didn't want to go and miss whatever was about to happen. But we told him it wouldn't help the statehood cause to have the governor of Alaska involved in a bar room brawl. We slipped him out the door with minimum public attention.

The next day when I gave my presentation to a senator and ended up with my plea for him to support our bill, he responded, "Oh, yes, I understand that if I don't vote for statehood I'll have my block knocked off." He laughed at my discomfort. I tried to brush it off. He had heard enough about the incident in the Terrace Room the night before and he kept me there until I told him the whole story. Apparently he knew the senator whose secretary was with us. He slapped his knee and guffawed loud and long. Others had similar experiences that day.

There is no book of rules or even guidelines setting up procedures for a territory to attain statehood. Each of the 37 states that followed the original colonies into the union had to invent its own. I wonder if our quick, neat barroom brawl might not have been a help. It won favorable attention from so many senators. They enjoyed it.

In the Senate, another problem appeared to be insurmountable. It was another Texan, Sen. Lyndon Johnson, Democratic majority leader who controlled which bills went to the floor for a vote. He was frank in saying that he would "never" allow a bill for Alaska statehood.

Again, our Democrats on the committee handled it in their own way. I was never privy to any sort of a deal, but I doubt it was a happenstance that when the statehood bill came up for floor consideration in the Senate late that June, Senator Johnson was absent. He was far away, somewhere on the Gulf of Mexico, inspecting an aircraft carrier at sea.

The next senator in line behind Johnson was Sen. Henry M. Jackson, D-Wash., a friend of Alaska. He took charge of the floor and pushed the bill along. The final speeches by senators who wanted to make a record of their views took most of a day. Alaska was bashed and denigrated by some, as being a haven for fugitives, lawless ruffians, oddballs and connivers.

The inflammatory comments of some of the most bitter opponents were shocking. It hurt us to hear our beloved territory slandered in such harsh terms. I recalled my interview with Dr. Jaimie Benetez years before when he explained why Puerto Rico would not dare ask for statehood.

"We could not stand the unjust criticism that comes from the opposition" Benetez, president of the University of Puerto Rico and certainly one of the greatest intellects on the islands, said. "Look at what they call you in Congress. You folks can take it because you are all brothers. Brothers fight and still love one another. But we are not family. We are Spanish and our hot blood would boil over under such criticism."

The Senate debate went on for a week until a final showdown occurred on June 30. Three powerful Democratic southern senators—James Eastland, Strom Thurmond, and John Stennis—each tried last-minute motions to derail the bill. Each was soundly defeated. Shortly after nightfall, the Senate voted in favor of statehood for Alaska, 64-20 with 12 members, including Senator Johnson, not voting.

Spectators in the gallery, many with tears in their eyes, rose to their feet applauding, in violation of Senate rules of decorum. Senators followed suit, standing at their desks as the whole room applauded. It was a warm reception for the new baby state.

I witnessed the final drama from the press gallery among my newspaper friends. It was truly a traumatic experience for me as I listened to the voting. By this time, I was acquainted personally with every member of the Senate. I knew much about many of them, especially their special interests and confidantes. In most cases I knew the real reason, as well as the reason stated publicly, that the senator was for or against statehood. The final vote had few surprises.

144 | CHAPTER ELEVEN

When it became obvious we were winning, I felt a new, strange burden. Statehood was at hand. As a newspaper editor who spent the last 15 years fighting for it, I began to realize we now were going to have to do the great things we said we would do. Could we? What kind of a state would we make?

While the roll call was still under way, reporters near me in the press gallery started peppering me with questions, "Okay, Atwood, now that you got it what are you going to do with it?" They didn't realize what a moment this was for me. I was so overwhelmed with it all that my throat tensed and I couldn't talk. To this day I have never successfully told the story of that roll-call experience without choking up with emotion.

At adjournment, newspapermen seemed to come out of the woodwork. Any Alaskan was instantly a news source and was subject of endless quizzing. There had to be a certain amount of socializing as we thanked our Senate leaders who made it a reality. Alaska Democrats, under the leadership of Gruening and his wife, obviously as emotional in their reaction as I was, went to the Capitol chapel and prayed for the new state.

I regret that I was not with them. But the Republicans allowed me no time for meditation or prayer. Along with the other Alaska GOP group, I spent the rest of the evening sitting uncomfortably in the hot lights and confusion that goes with TV cameras and reporters. The Washington media put us on live and unrehearsed to tell the nation something about the new state. Alaska was, at the moment, the nation's top news story.

The next day we were drafted to fly to New York for more media events. Overnight, the network studios had dredged out their file films showing Alaska scenes and activities, like fishing, mining, farming, some cities and scenic landmarks. They were silent films and they used us as the soundtrack to explain what was in the picture.

I would much rather have been celebrating with my friends in Anchorage, dancing around the bonfire on the Delaney Park Strip or watching the hanging of the 49th star in the huge American flag that was draped over the Fourth Avenue federal building.

However, if our "sound track" comments put a more pleasant or attractive veneer on the impressions listeners got from those old films, I suppose our efforts in the studios were worthwhile. It seemed to me they were overloaded with horse and wagon day stuff.

When I rejoined my Democrat friends and co-workers and studied the roll call vote, I was proud to point out that Republicans had truly outvoted Democrats in supporting the bill, 33 to 31. The GOP had fewer members who voted against it, 8 to 12. And the GOP had more members who abstained, 7 to 5.

So, I would say that although Republicans did little to help in all the years when they were the minority party, Republicans came on strong and made the final touchdown once their man was in the White House and they could claim some of the credit.

VICTORY AT LAST | 145

Democrats when contending that theirs was the statehood party must also remember that in all those years they were in control of both houses of Congress as well as the White House they failed to enact it. In that long period, Republicans were not asked to do anything. Some Republicans even say that if their party had gained control earlier, Alaska would not have had such a long wait for statehood. Take your pick.

Regardless of the triumph of enactment, there was to be no rest for statehood proponents yet. The Alaska Statehood Act required that Alaskans hold a referendum vote to ratify it. I objected to the senate committee and asked why another referendum was necessary since Alaskans had already voted for statehood in 1946.

Their answer to my objection was clear and convincing. It was a statement I was to hear from more than one senator. Sen. Clinton P. Anderson, D-N.Mex., told me that the vote was necessary because the previous referendum endorsed the concept of statehood but it had not endorsed the terms of statehood.

"This statehood act is more than an ordinary law," the senator said. "It is a compact, an irrevocable contract. It sets out the terms under which Alaska will become a state. By approving it, the Congress has accepted these specific terms, now Alaskans must show by a referendum vote that they are willing to accept statehood on these same specific terms. Once two parties have accepted these terms, they are irrevocable and can be changed only with the approval of both parties."

Thirty-six years later I was to recall these words when Wally Hickel, as governor of the State of Alaska, filed a court action against the U.S. government to enforce that compact. Some members of Congress were pushing legislation that would renege on the Statehood Act's provision for splitting revenues from oil production. The litigation was pending at this writing.

Statehood passed in the Senate June 30 and the referendum was to be in August 1958 along with the primary elections when political parties nominated their candidates. Alaskans would vote for governor and lieutenant governor, as well as a full legislature. It would be the first time Alaskans were ever permitted to participate in the selection of their top leaders.

Among statehood supporters, the election was seen as the last chance for the salmon packers to delay or stall statehood. Spirits were high among statehood supporters but there were fears that the euphoria of the triumph in Congress might give way to second thoughts, especially if the salmon industry pursued its usual tactics of deviously dividing Alaskans against themselves.

So we came home from Washington to face the final battle at the polls. The pro-statehood forces had no funds for a concerted campaign and fortunately not much was needed because our opponents had apparently given up and had no organized campaign. Yet, the anti-statehood

146 | CHAPTER ELEVEN

forces had one thing going for them. Alaskans had to approve three separate statehood questions on the ballot: 1. Shall Alaska be admitted to the Union as a State? 2. Shall the boundaries of the new State, as prescribed by the Statehood Act, be approved? 3. Shall all the other provisions of the Act be approved?

If one failed, the entire statehood victory in Congress would be nullified. We ran probably an excess of editorials urging Alaskans not to weaken their support. Not knowing what the fish packers might come up with, I tried to defuse any last minute surprises with an editorial that set forth the financial facts of statehood.

Our new expenses for setting up our executive, legislative, judiciary departments and other state-funded functions would cost $3,580,000 annually. Our income from oil and gas receipts, public land sales, timber harvests, sports fishing licenses, and the Pribilof Island seal harvest would total $5,000,000, more than compensating us for our added expenses.

Alaskans voted five to one in favor of accepting all three terms of the statehood act on Aug. 26, 1958, thus completing the protracted legislative process. Now all we were to do was wait until Jan. 3, 1959, when President Eisenhower would sign the proclamation to formally mark the admission of Alaska to the Union.

That waiting period was anything but dull. Although nothing had changed yet, the territorial economy became dynamic with new activity. Excitement was evidenced especially in and around Anchorage where property values soared.

The national acceptance of Alaska had lifted a low ceiling of expectations that had hung heavily over Alaskans. Spirits of the people were high as they felt and expressed pride and keen anticipation of the changes that would come in their lives with full-fledged citizenship.

The upbeat spirit was enhanced with reports of big deals in real estate and new plans for business expansion. One day I was alerted, as a newspaperman, that for the first time Anchorage had a passenger who arrived on a plane from Hong Kong and Tokyo who disembarked here. Anchorage actually was his destination, not a stopover on the way to somewhere else.

This was so unusual that the local agent of the airline called me to tell me about it. A hotel manager called my attention to it. I tracked down the man and found he was Robert de Lasalla, a real estate developer who operated throughout Asia, owned a steamship line and had other interests. He came here to buy real estate for speculation because with statehood the values were bound to go up.

De Lasalla retained Sewell Faulkner as his real estate agent, chartered a small airplane and circled over the Anchorage townsite. Looking down, Faulkner told de Lasalla of the growth trends of the past and pointed out areas for future growth.

Faulkner told me his visitor selected vacant lots at strategic intersections and told him to buy them for him. In just one day or so, de Lasalla had opened the way to become a major property owner. And he boarded the next plane for Tokyo and Hong Kong and went home. It must have been the first injection of outside venture capital into the Alaska economy attracted entirely by statehood.

Meanwhile, we had the excitement that went with electing our first two senators and one representative to Congress. New senators were Bartlett and Gruening and the long congressman was Ralph Rivers of Fairbanks.. Bill Egan became Alaska's first elected governor.

When the new year came, I was invited to join the delegation in Washington for the signing of the proclamation and unfurling the nation's new 49-star flag. It was a thrilling experience to be in the Oval Office once more and to be a part of this event.

I have often expressed my amazement that a young kid in his 20s could purchase a tiny newspaper in a tiny town in a remote corner of the world and become a catalyst in making the newspaper, the town and its corner of the world grow. It was mind-boggling to realize the greatest nation in the world would tell its 96 senators to "move over" to make way for two more senators who would share their power while representing that remote corner of the world as full-fledged members of the world's most powerful deliberative body.

On the ensuing July 4th, 1959, the 49-star flag became the official flag of the nation. Appropriate ceremonies were held in many places but none could have been more joyous than those at our house in Anchorage, on a bluff overlooking an arm of the Pacific with Mt. McKinley in the distance.

Evangeline and I had a small cannon from a sunken ocean-going vessel that had been used for shooting lines to other ships at sea. We adapted home-made missiles, consisting of fresh frozen orange juice in a can the same caliber as the cannon. We had black powder donated by friendly tug-boat captains. And we had people, scores of them.

We put them all together on our lawn and fired that cannon to make a lot of noise, smoke and celebration. Our personnel manning our weapon included Lt. Gen. Frank A. Armstrong, commander of all military forces in Alaska, as the firing officer. He wore a pink-topped officer's cap. Everyone else wore the round sailor caps. Orville Dryfoos, publisher of the New York Times, was in charge of the black powder because he didn't smoke. Crewmen, each with an assigned duty, included the publisher of the Chicago Sun-Times, Bob Logan, U.S.N. (ret) and some local folks.

To the chant: "If I wasn't a sailor I wouldn't be here," we fired off my wife's supply of frozen canned orange juice and welcomed the United States of America to Alaska.

148 | CHAPTER ELEVEN

Elaine Atwood, Page Wood and Stuart Johnson hold a statehood edition of the Anchorage newspaper while attending Mills College in California.

Statehood editions of Anchorage newspapers begin fast journey to Washington D.C. within minutes after historic senate roll call admitting Territory to Union. Through the courtesy of Alaskan Air Command no time was wasted. Here, bundles are sent on their way from Elmendorf AFB to Eielson AFB near Fairbanks and then aboard a waiting b-17 for the stateside dash. Photo by Anchorage Times/July 1, 1958

VICTORY AT LAST | 149

Govenors discuss common goal. Governor Stepovich (left) of Alaska and Hawaii's Governor William F. Quinn (right). July 7, 1958

The last territorial governor, Mike Stepovich, signs the proclamation for Alaska's first state elections. July, 17, 1958.

150 | CHAPTER ELEVEN

Alaskans were overjoyed at statehood and celebrated with a 50 ton pile of wood. One ton for each state was burned, along with the old Organic Act which had governed the Territory from 1913 – this celebration turned out the largest mob ever assembled in Alaska up to this point. Reliable estimates were near 25,000 in Anchorage. Photo by Steve McClutcheon/Alaska Pictorial Service

VICTORY AT LAST

Ring for a New State. July 2, 1958. L-r: Judy Findlay, Marilee Nowacki and Romer Derr, in Juneau.

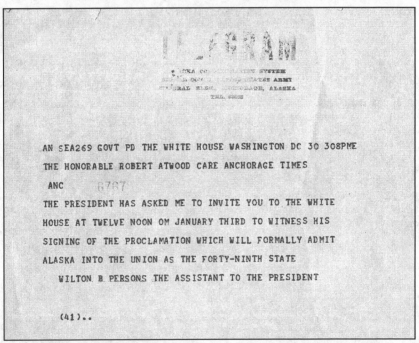

A telegram from the office of the President inviting Bob Atwood to attend the signing of the proclamation which formally admits Alaska into the union as the forty-ninth state.

152 | CHAPTER ELEVEN

LINKS ALASKA AND HAWAII—President Eisenhower poses with Barbara Leinani Kepreler, left representing the new state of Hawaii, and Marilyn Atwood of Anchorage, representing the 49th state, at a dinner in Washington during the Republican Womens Conference. They presented floral stars, background, representing the two newest states. (AP Wirephoto)

Anchorage Times Article. April 16, 1958.

154 | CHAPTER ELEVEN

— CHAPTER TWELVE —

Earthquake

About 5:30 p.m. on March 27, 1964, I drove my T-Bird toward home. It was the end of a perfect Spring day. It had been a beautiful day with the mountains sharp and clear under a bright sky. My spirits were high. My health excellent. My personal affairs were in such good shape that one could say I had the "world by the tail." I didn't know that within minutes after docking my car in the garage I would experience a cataclysm that would leave me homeless, physically hurt and mentally altered.

It was the famous earthquake that shook our town for four minutes or more and was announced as 8.4 on the Richter scale, the greatest in the history of North America we were told. It was later upgraded to 9.2, equivalent to an explosion 2,000 times more powerful than any nuclear bomb ever detonated.

The whole community was crippled, left with no light, power, water and other essential services. Substantial portions of the downtown were wrecked. Many school buildings crumbled. Some residential areas, the waterfront and the two military installations were badly damaged. Tsunami waves devastated Kodiak, Seward, Valdez and Cordova.

In those few minutes I saw my home and everything in it destoyed. My lifestyle was wiped out. My neighborhood was gone. I was buffeted about like a ping pong ball.

I was alone in the house when it started. Evangeline was just leaving the house as I pulled into the driveway. It was Good Friday and she need-ed to order flowers and pick up some yams at the grocer for her Easter Sunday dinner party. I offered to go with her but she said there was no need, she would be home again in a few minutes.

I went inside and was taking advantage of her absence to practice scales on my trumpet that I had just purchased. I had had only the free les-son that came with it and was a true beginner.

The shake started at 5:36 p.m. as I was nearing the bottom of my exer-cise page. I paid it no heed. Earthquakes are common events. But this one was different. It didn't stop shaking after a few seconds as they usually do. Scientists later determined that it continued for four minutes. That's an eternity when you are in it.

Pictures began falling off the walls of my living room. Knickknacks

EARTHQUAKE | 155

and art things were falling from bookshelves. Our big chandelier, made of the steering wheel of the historic Sacketts Harbor ship, was swinging so violently I stopped blowing the trumpet to watch in amazement. The ground motion gave me a touch of dizziness.

My house was a log structure with a high, trussed ceiling in the living room. I saw the walls give way twice, leaning over perhaps 60 degrees from upright. Each time, instead of going the rest of the way down to the ground, the walls returned upright and the house continued to stand. Odds were against that happening again so I fled out the front door.

Standing on the lawn I couldn't believe what I saw, what I heard or what I smelled. We had a big lawn and I had a sensation that I was standing in water. Waves were moving across the lawn exactly like waves in a body of water. The ground had a thin snow cover and was frozen at least three feet down from the surface. That frozen earth held fast while the waves moved across it. Even concrete curbs and the asphalt driveway held fast without cracking as the waves ran right through them.

I saw my house rise, twist, and fall apart. Something activated the automatic garage door so it opened and there was the tail end of my favorite Ford Thunderbird displayed prominently, high in the air as the garage end of the house soared while the other end of the house dipped. Then the car sank out of sight as the opposite end of the house rose.

I saw my house moving away from me. The spacing between my house and my neighbors' houses was constantly changing. Later I learned that the whole area was slipping and sliding northward into the ocean, some 90 feet below our home. All the houses were moving and so was I.

I can't describe the emotions that overwhelmed me as I stood and watched my house twist and turn, grunt and groan, as it resisted the forces that were destroying it. It was like watching a loved one die. That house went up and down with the earth movements, sometimes stretched and squeezed like an accordion. I stood helpless as my home, with most of the worldly things I cherished, was reduced to jack straws, the contents either buried or ground up into theme soil.

There was a concert grand Steinway piano and a big electric organ. We never found so much as a single note of either. Our entire library was gone. Clothes, furniture, dishes and all the things we brought back from world travel were no more. We had spent a generation or longer bringing together from all over the world the things meaningful to us. Now I was losing them in one fell swoop.

The noise was frightening and strange. There was the noise of the earthquake itself. I heard it—a guttural rumble, a roar that is unique. Tall trees were snapping and falling under the strains. Some trees appeared to be marching, in small groups, perfectly erect like platoons of soldiers. And there were many other oddities. What had been a beautiful tree was split from the base to the tip top of its trunk, with one half of its branches fallen and the remaining half still erect as though unaware that something had happened.

The intensity of the seismic shake increased by the second. The waves in the lawn grew higher. The frozen earth couldn't take it any more. It broke into jagged pieces. My front yard around me, so lovely and in my mind my very own national park, turned topsy-turvy and seemed to threaten me.

I started to move away from the big trees seeking an open space for safety. As I stepped forward I plunged into the darkness of a crevasse that had opened beneath me like a giant black hole. During that long fall into nothingness I wondered if this could be the end. My responding thought was instantaneous—even before I hit bottom—no, this could not be the end because it would be a silly way to die and my God wouldn't let that happen.

And he didn't allow it. I made a soft landing on sand. The sand was thawed. The crevasse, which might have closed and sealed me in, kept opening further. Light returned. I could see the ditch of the crevasse snaking its way westward across my lawn and the lawn of my neighbors, the Lloyd Hines family. It looked as though the Hines house was moving toward me as it tilted and appeared about to slip into the ditch that was reaching for it.

But there was no time for looking around. I was on dry ground with all sorts of dangerous things flying past me. I don't know what they were. I remember globs of frozen earth that looked like boulders, water pipes, barbed wire, mailboxes. Any one of them could have knocked me out but none hit me. As this went on, I got the impression that I was protected by an unseen screen around me. None of the flying objects came within it. Somebody was taking care of me.

But I still had problems. The earth spilling into the ditch was covering me. I had to scramble to stay on top and not be buried. But I couldn't scramble. I was held down with the right half of my body, leg, torso and arm already covered. I couldn't pull my right arm loose because my trumpet was still in my right hand. It was the last thing on earth that I owned and still had. I remember how reluctantly I relaxed my three fingers in the loops of the horn and withdrew my arm, leaving the horn to eternity somewhere in the Bootlegger Cove mud.

The next few minutes, that seemed like hours to me, were spent in the bottom of the ditch. The smell of sulfur was strong, apparently coming to the surface from somewhere down in the bowels of the earth along with blue clay that squirted out from my lawn and formed jagged ridges like miniature mountain ranges. It was as though Paul Bunyon had squeezed it out of his toothpaste tube.

The scientists who studied the earthquake said that while the shaking lasted four minutes, the ground movement in the area of my house may have lasted up to 15 minutes.

When the earth finally settled down in its new angle of repose, the noise stopped as suddenly as it started and I had another new and unusual experience. It was silence. I mean, real, total and complete silence. There was not a bird sound. No man sounds. Not a breeze. Not a thing moved anywhere I looked. It was as though the whole world was dead. Was I the only living thing left? Was I to be Mr. Adam, the only man left in the world?

I climbed up the side of my crevasse to see what I could see. It was not easy. I was caked in mud from the neck down and for the first time realized I had been injured— broken ribs. (I never learned how or when I was injured.) Every movement was painful. In spite of the pain, I climbed high enough to see my old neighborhood. It was in ruins. The beautiful lawns, landscaping and shrubs were gone. Houses were in shambles, tipped this way and that. And over it all was silence. Total silence. The silence was so intense it was frightening.

From that vantage point at the edge of my crevasse it appeared that the entire earth had been destroyed. Few trees were upright. Most were lying at angles broken and in utter disarray. I noticed that to the south I could see the tips of trees that were standing upright as though the temblor had not hit them.

While I pondered what to do next, I heard a voice calling for help. It came from my teenage neighbor, Warren Hines. His house was badly damaged. He had been home with his infant sister, Mitzi, who had a fever and had been sleeping in bed. When the earthquake came he had picked her up with what wool blankets were there, and got out of the house. He was wearing only slacks, a silk sports shirt and was in stocking feet. But he had taken good care of Mitzi.

I responded to Warren. He said he wasn't hurt. I asked him to come over and join me but he said he couldn't because he had Mitzi in his arms. Further talk revealed she was ill with fever and he had no shoes. We were only a couple of hundred feet apart but, in this broken up land that was a great distance. I told Warren to wait there and I would join him, little realizing how painful that short trek would be.

Twilight was setting in. That meant a long, cold, dark night was near. That was frightening. I didn't have the least idea what I was going to do about Warren and Mitzi. While Warren and I discussed our options, we heard calls for help coming from a broken house beyond Hines'. Across a span of jagged earth crisscrossed with splintered trees, I spotted the lady who was calling. She had five youngsters beside her, each one bundled up in mackinaws and footgear suitable for an Arctic trek.

I called to ask if anyone was hurt and she replied no. I asked what help did she need and she said she needed help to get out of there. I asked if she had warm clothes for Warren and Mitzi and she said no and she was afraid to go into her house to look. It turned out she was a baby sitter and had been left with the five children in her care. I told her none of us would go anywhere before we got something for Warren and Mitzi.

At that moment I was confronted with another new and strange experience. We were standing in the midst of the debris of my home and the broken houses that once constituted an affluent residential area. The only thing in the world that I wanted I couldn't have—something made of wool to keep Warren and Mitzi warm overnight.

While Warren, holding Mitzi, and I talked about our options, the baby sitter reconsidered. She disappeared into her broken house and reappeared with an armload of sweaters and coats that we needed. But she found no shoes so Warren faced the long hike out of the wilderness in stocking feet. He was a strong young man and optimistic that he could keep from freezing by vigorous motion.

So we set off on our journey back to civilization—the lady with the five children, Warren with Mitzi and me. Everyone was looking to me for leadership. I tried to provide it but I felt odd about it because I had very little idea where I was going to lead them. I didn't dare let them know my problem because they must have confidence in their leader.

First I told them we must all walk in single file with me in the lead. This I had learned from a dear old Swiss guide who once led Evangeline and me on a hike along the ridge tops of the Bernina Alps near St. Moritz, Switzerland. I told my people to follow me and step in precisely the same spot I step in, to grab bushes or tree limbs to hold them in case their feet slipped on steep slopes and to touch no wires because they might be hot. They followed instructions perfectly. No disciplinary problems here.

Progress was slow. Up and down the jagged, topsy-turvy jigsaw puzzle pieces of earth, climbing over and under broken tree trunks and their disheveled branches. There was no sure footing and I felt I had an extra responsibility for every step by virtue of having told my followers to step precisely in my footprint. Overhead helicopters were searching for people to rescue. They couldn't help us because the terrain around us was too rough for landing. We directed them, by pointing, to places where people needed help.

The earth was desolate along our route of travel. My navigation was based on those treetops that I had seen still standing erect after the shake. We saw many odd shapes and formations along the way.

One was a big mushroom-like clump of earth standing proud and erect amidst the devastation. On top of the mushroom was the Chevrolet station wagon driven by Margaret Hines, Warren's mother. And standing beside it, neat and clean in her color-coordinated brown outfit, was Mrs. Hines. She had been to the store and had stopped for the earthquake only to have the road and much of her world go away and leave her marooned on that tiny patch of ground, an island surrounded by desolation.

My party of nine waited while I found a way to climb to the top of the mushroom and get Mrs. Hines to come down. When I told her she would have to sit down in the mud and slide part of the way she didn't hesitate at all. She joined our safari group and we finished our journey. The end was not very impressive.

EARTHQUAKE | 159

We walked for 45 minutes picking our way through the destruction until we reached what looked like a sheer precipice. It was the point where the sloughing had stopped and the earth still stood firm. High up on the new bluff were spectators who threw down ropes and pulled us up, one at a time.

Ken Kadow was one of the two strong men who pulled me up. As he hoisted, he invited me to come to his house to relax. I thanked him but said my first job is to find my wife. Kadow walked the length of that new bluff telling everyone he met that "Bob's all right but Evangeline's lost."

That message spread through town and was even broadcast as radio news. Evangeline wasn't lost at all. When she returned from the store and found her house, husband and entire neighborhood gone, she went to the home of the Herb Hilschers which, although damaged, was still habitable. I guess she and Miriam Hilscher got so far along in grieving for me, that Herb went out for a walk. He said he went to the helicopter pads and talked to the pilots. They told him Bob and his group were all right and were walking out of the destroyed area. He cheered up things at his house by bringing that report home. I joined them there shortly, after friends told me where Evangeline was.

Meanwhile, in Washington, D.C., I had two daughters who didn't have any word from us. They, with their cousin, Ed Rasmuson, stayed up most of the night trying to find out how their parents were. They said the report that Bob was all right but Evangeline was missing was circulated back east, too. The mukluk telegraph reaches far.

Evangeline and I found ourselves welcomed by the Hilschers. We were never invited yet we stayed a week. Like every house in town, the Hilschers' had no power, heat, lights or water. But they did have a fireplace and a supply of coal. We lived around it. Herb's freezer was slowly warming up and its contents thawing. That put his collection of wild game meats in jeopardy. Those choice cuts of mountain sheep, moose, caribou and such that he was saving for special occasions when he had a VIP guest were going to spoil. So we had to eat them. We cooked in the fireplace. I brought in a case of champagne that I had stashed in the trunk of my wife's car intending it for use at the Easter Sunday dinner at my house. It went very well with our deluxe wild game menus.

During our week there we had time for contemplation and appreciation of our many blessings. Our home was gone but we had both survived the awful earthquake. The Hilschers had taken us into their home and made us feel that what was theirs was ours, too. The earthquake stripped us of our material things but that didn't hurt nearly so much as the loss of intangibles—the loss of our neighborhood, our comfortable lifestyle, the beauty of our physical surroundings that now stood in ruin or lost.

Even our family albums took on a new importance. Most of them were lost in the debris. Evangeline pointed out to me that we had two grown daughters and nothing to show that they had ever been youngsters. Each

160 | CHAPTER TWELVE

reference to intangible losses brought up nostalgic memories of others.

Later we were to find that the earthquake experience had altered our scale of values permanently. Material things never regained their previous importance. We thought of them as temporary possessions. We were only temporary custodians of them. This thought extended into land owner-ship too. Others may consider land the only permanent thing in the world. But I knew better. I had stood on it and was tossed around by it as it broke up and disappeared. From then on, the important things in our lives were love, friends, neighbors, relationships with each other, health, spiritual uplift and all good things our mothers used to drill into us when we were kids and we weren't inclined to listen.

Early Saturday morning I drove my wife's car downtown to see what happened to my newspaper plant. The direct route was still intact. I had no detours but the sites along the way were astonishing— buildings dam-aged, some completely demolished.

At Fifth Avenue and I Street, I was stopped by a tall, black Army ser-geant who stood tall and looked formidable with his rifle, bayonet fixed, slung over his shoulder and much important looking field gear hanging on his uniform. He gave me a broad smile and asked if I had identification. I had brought with me my old World War II correspondent credential card and, while I reached for it in my pocket, I asked him how come he was on this kind of duty. He gave me my first eyewitness about the disaster.

"This downtown area is busted up and we were sent here to help pre-vent looting," he said as he casually looked at my card. "Proceed sir," he said, and I found that my Pentagon credentials allowed me to pass Army check points the rest of that day."

But Sunday, it was different. I approached my plant by the same route and was stopped at the same intersection. This time it was by a soldier who stood proud and tall with the same formidable field gear, including rifle with bayonet fixed. He was an Eskimo, a member of the famous Alaska Scouts who during World War II did heroic work for the Army in western Alaska and especially the Aleutian campaign. He read even the fine print on my card and handed it back saying, "Haven't you anything to identify yourself?"

I fished in my pockets and came up with a tiny slip of pink mimeo-graph paper, about one-inch wide and three inches long, that had the words, "The bearer is a Civil Defense Worker." It was signed by the Anchorage chief of police. He allowed me to proceed.

Gen. Raymond J. Reeves, Alaska's military commander, had replaced the regular Army troops with the Alaska Eskimos after the first day, "because I thought you Alaskans would prefer to be policed by your own people rather than from some strange GI's from all over the states."

My heart sank when I saw the damage downtown. The new five-story building of J.C. Penney Co., the town's pride and joy, had been damaged beyond repair. Five hundred or more customers and employees inside were badly shaken up. The only fatality was one person who went out of the building during the four-minute shake and was hit by falling debris.

My newspaper plant, on the North side of Fourth Avenue had only minor damage. Some light fixtures had been shaken off the ceilings. Things had been strewn over the floor but there was no structural damage. The printing machinery appeared to be in good shape. It would be easy to restore the plant to operating condition.

While I was pondering these problems, Ward Sims, chief of the Associated Press in Alaska based in Juneau, walked into the plant and, on seeing me, asked that I write an eyewitness account of what happened. I begged off, saying I was busy trying to get my newspaper back into production.

He argued that the nation had not had a word from Alaska yet and my story would be the first. He said he would put it on the main trunkline and it would go everywhere. For reporters it is the acme of success if your story gets that treatment and I have always been more of a reporter than anything else. But I still begged off, saying 30,000 other people in Anchorage had the same experience and any of them could do the story. But Sims was persistent. He pressed me further, saying he would put my byline on the story—another alluring enticement for a reporter, a byline on a trunkline story that would go to every AP newspaper and would be the first report on a major disaster of the world!

That byline pitch gave me second thoughts. This story could be a way for me to tell my daughters in Washington, D.C., that mom and dad are still alive. Normal communication lines were overloaded with emergency messages. It was next to impossible to get a personal message through.

I sat down at a typewriter and, with my daughters in mind, wondered what the lead should be. I remembered how in my family every time a newspaper erred they had fun heckling me with extravagant claims, such as "newspapers are always wrong." That recollection gave me my lead.

The lead was, "I was playing my trumpet when . . ." and the narrative went on from there. I could imagine my daughters saying, "See, they are wrong again. My daddy doesn't play the trumpet." And there would come a day when I could say, "Tee-hee, they were right, I really was playing my trumpet." Of course, not suggesting how well.

Sims tore the story out of my typewriter as I completed each paragraph. As I wrote, he edited and dispatched it to the Associated Press in Seattle. I had no chance to read it over for continuity. Having mentioned the trumpet in the lead, I put in references to it as the narrative proceeded.

When that story reached the New York office of the Associated Press people there called my daughters in Washington, D.C., and gave them the word that their parents were all right. The story got the message there. It also made me an instant celebrity as a trumpet player, which I certainly wasn't.

The whole town was without electric power so there was no chance of publishing a newspaper. After finding my plant in good shape I spent the rest of Saturday looking for a portable electric generator that I could beg, borrow, rent or possibly steal to tie into my plant as a source of power. I found one in the Craig Taylor equipment yard. He was a dealer in heavy equipment and had everything on hand, it seemed. I told him my problem and he said his generator could carry that load and said I could borrow it. We were standing beside the big heavy machine and I asked him, "Who do you think I could get to move it to my plant?" He replied that he would deliver it.

Craig Taylor had his drivers bring it to the plant and parked the entire rig beside the building. That tractor with the low-boy trailer carrying the generator served well.

We published a Sunday extra that was mostly pictures, an eight-page edition with double banners: "CITY RALLIES FROM QUAKE" and 'SHOCKWAVE ONE OF MIGHTIEST." There was no incoming news from the news services because communications were either wrecked or in use for emergency services. We had a light staff because most of our people had their problems at home. Our photographers had many pictures of the major damage. So our Sunday extra was eight pages of pictures with descriptive cutlines and a few local news stories, along with the AP copy of my eyewitness story. We printed 30,000 of those on a press that would do only 3,500 an hour. We ran that press late into the night and had to run it some more on Monday morning before starting work on that day's paper.

Our newsboys delivered that little paper all over town. It wasn't much of a paper but it did much to raise the morale of a community that was very depressed from such an awful experience. Many of our customers tell us how they were sitting in their broken-down house wondering what would happen next when the carrier came across the lawn and left the paper on the porch.

"Bob, I can't tell you how grateful I was to see that boy," one man told me. "I didn't know how I was going to pay for repairs to my house. My family was broken up over the mess we were in. And I had no answers for any of them. We even questioned whether our town could pull out of this. When that carrier boy appeared, I had a warm feeling that everything isn't so bad after all—the paper is here and our town is going to recover and life will go on."

Craig Taylor left that rig in our parking lot so long I called him to remind him it was there. My little newspaper couldn't afford to pay the going rate for such equipment very long. Taylor took it back to his plant when it met with his convenience and I felt indebted to him forever. He never sent me a bill. He brushed me off saying he was glad to help get me into production again because the town needed the paper.

For lack of news service stories from Alaska, Outside newspapers were printing anything they could pick up about the disaster. Ham oper-

EARTHQUAKE | 163

ators were talking by radio to their friends who, in turn, talked to their friends and the facts got pretty well mixed up before publication.

The New York World-Telegram, one of the more respected East Coast newspapers of that day, had a headline "ANCHORAGE IN RUINS" and a subline "300 Believed Dead." It was so soon after the earthquake that it would obviously be impossible for anyone to know how many, if any, were dead.

The New York paper said the report came from the Associated Press. At my insistence, the AP tried to trace out its origin and several days later told me the report came from a ham radio operator in the mid-West who said he heard it direct from a ham in Alaska.

The actual death toll turned out to be 115 in all of Alaska. Although the greatest property damage was in Anchorage, only nine lives were lost in the city. Three of them were my neighbors who had been caught in that churning Turnagain landslide. Two of these were young sons of Dr. Perry Mead, the town's only neurosurgeon. Despite his grief, he stayed at his hospital station all night and into the day treating earthquake casualties.

Loss of life was heaviest in coastal towns where the gigantic waves washed out entire villages and extended down to Crescent City, Calif. The waves hit hardest in Valdez where a massive rush of water at high tide wiped out the town and killed 30 people. The village of Chenega on Prince William Sound was wiped out. Twenty-five of its 75 residents were killed. The city of Kodiak on Kodiak Island listed 19 dead. Eleven were washed to their deaths at the port of Whittier.

At Seward 13 died as the tsunami washed out the waterfront and much of the town. The waves were so powerful they pushed Alaska Railroad locomotives and dozens of freight cars off the tracks and inland, leaving them strewn around the railroad yards with a mixture of hundreds of small boats and dozens of sizeable commercial fishing boats mixed with them. The city's huge petroleum tanks were broken during the shaking and the leaked fuel caught fire. The huge plume of black smoke stood like a pall marking the end of a city.

Despite the loss of life and the devastation of the waterfront, Seward had much to be thankful for, especially the timing of that tsunami wave. It followed the earthquake, which was timed at 5:36 p.m. in Anchorage. It washed out and destroyed the downtown waterfront facilities including the large wharf warehouse in which a gala community dinner was scheduled that very evening. Had the wave come an hour or so later it would have washed away most of the citizens of Seward while they celebrated the great achievement of their city in winning the designation "All America City," a national honor sponsored by the National Municipal League and Look Magazine. That would have been as many as 300 people.

In Anchorage we found the earthquake only the beginning of a plague of troubles. Reporters and photographers from the Lower 48 swarmed into Anchorage like locusts as soon as they could find transportation from

164 | CHAPTER TWELVE

Seattle. It was the famous, or infamous, "mass media." And many of us in Anchorage are still trying to decide which was worse, the impact of the earthquake or of the mass media.

The Anchorage Times was automatically headquarters for many of these transients. After all, we are fraternal brothers, aren't we? And we want to help each other, don't we? Yes, of course. But it wasn't easy.

Those guys moved in on us as we were trying to put our house in order after the big shake. It took us several days to get things back to normal so we could perform in our own offices. Meanwhile our uninvited visitors were using any vacant desk they came upon, our typewriters, telephones, dark room facilities. Some of my staff people said if they laid anything down they were unlikely to see it again. They said the "big shots" from Outside stole their copy and sent it to their own papers when they got the chance. Photographers complained that some of their pictures disappeared and showed up in strange newspapers Outside. They found they had to carry all their notes and unfinished stories with them when they left the office. They kept their desks locked even when they were at work in their own newsroom.

When a better-mannered team from the National Geographic Magazine came in to interview me, I begged off again. I was tired of interviews. Many different TV and newspaper reporters had quizzed me and I was sure my story was getting to be old hat. I suggested National Geographic should get something fresh and different. I wasn't making first base with them by mentioning others they should interview until I suggested Mrs. Lowell Thomas, Jr. That scored big because her father-in-law, the world traveler and broadcast authority was honorary president of the National Geographic Society. And her husband, Lowell Jr., was known worldwide as a pilot, explorer, author and lecturer.

The Geographic team spent much time with her and did one of the most exciting stories to come out of the earthquake. The presentation in photographs and hand-drawn schematics were marvelous. Tay Thomas told how she was home alone with her daughters not far from where my house stood. They had harrowing experiences as their house was destroyed and they were buffeted about like shuttlecocks.

For the next few weeks a big effort was put into restoring the morale and the hope of people whose hometown was crippled and whose families were in jeopardy. There were plenty of stories with uplift to them. We had daily reports on what city agencies were doing to rebuild and restore the town. We told of the special groups appointed to augment the normal government machinery. Civil engineers, for instance, volunteered their services to serve on groups to set standards and procedures for repairing damaged buildings.

At that time I was one of the shareholders of the Anchorage-Westward Hotel Corp. Our downtown property was the only first-class hotel in town and when it was closed due to earthquake damage, there was an acute

EARTHQUAKE | 165

shortage of rooms. There would be an influx of building contractors and construction workers that had to have accommodations.

The corporation notified the engineers in Seattle who had designed the structure and urged them to plan for its repair. The earthquake was Friday evening. The engineering firm had their first people here on Saturday. By Monday morning they had a plan for repairs and took it to city hall, where they found nobody knew who could look at it or issue a permit to proceed.

The mayor had the engineers meet with the volunteers who were working up standards and procedures. Recognizing the need for the hotel to be reopened the engineers allowed the repairs to proceed, "provided the engineers from Seattle would sign a statement that the repaired building would be stronger than it was before the earthquake." With that kind of cooperation from the city establishment, the hotel reopened in a week.

Building morale wasn't made easier by the proclivity for local scientists and pseudo scientists to hand down gloomy statements warning people that another earthquake of equal intensity to the big one could happen at any moment, like right now. That would scare hell out of young mothers whose main concern is the safety of their young ones, and others, too, of course. Usually, by reading the fine print down at the end of the statement one would learn that another earthquake of the same intensity was unlikely to occur for 200 years.

I tried unsuccessfully to convince them to emphasize the 200-year feature and to put the possibility of an instant repeat at the end of their statements. I even got newspapers and magazines reporting the San Francisco earthquake and showed them where scientists of that day downplayed the fact that it might happen again now. But to no avail. It seems that Anchorage scientists, and those who claim to be scientists, still like to scare hell out of people.

A panicky undercurrent seemed to prevail long after the March 27 event. Seismologists at the Palmer earthquake station reported 4,900 aftershocks the first week. Most of them were so minimal that they were detected only by instruments. But there were plenty of scares day after day. It was common to find downtown offices that had hung a plumb bob on a wall and a scale showing how far the plumb bob swings, like a pendulum, as the earthquakes occurred. Many had wisecrack scales like, for a tiny earthquake, "pay it no heed." If the bob goes further it might point to "prepare to leave." And still further, "Get under the desk," or "Run for your life."

Concern for the mental health of the populace was sufficient for the town's two psychiatrists, Drs. J. Ray Langdon and Allen J. Parker to go on television to counsel the public.

To this point, I have described two traumatic experiences—first the original earthquake with its horrendous impact, and second the influx of the mass media with its mixture of good citizens and more than its share of arrogant, uncouth, unruly and selfish characters.

Now I mentioned a third awful experience—the arrival of the bureaucracy. The public servants, who are ostensibly here to help us, proved to be another frightening factor. Their impact on the community vied with the earthquake itself and the mass media for first place in the rankings.

The federal government was very generous and fast in responding to the emergency in Alaska. During the late night hours Friday, the U.S. Air Force had jets from Washington, D.C., lacing the city with special cameras to photograph earthquake damage and deliver the pictures to President Lyndon Johnson and his people Saturday morning.

Federal relief programs started taking shape immediately. Sen. Clinton, who was always one of the leading advocates for Alaska statehood, was named chairman of a committee to supervise. The Small Business Administration moved into Alaska with its disaster relief programs and under its director, Eugene Foley, cut red tape to the minimum. The SBA made 30-year loans bearing 3% interest to finance home repairs. The Federal Housing Administration excused mortgage debts on damaged homes with the payment of $1,000. Evangeline and I had no mortgage to be excused from. Hence our facetious conclusion that "thrift don't pay."

Damage in all of Alaska was estimated at $750,000,000, which in 1995 dollars amounts to about $3.7 billion. Prolonged studies of the Alaska earthquake ensued and have figured in the drafting of national building codes for earthquake-prone areas. Volumes of information on what happened and why were published.

In Anchorage it is common to find the wisdom of the scientists questioned. People are frequently heard to say that scientists sometimes aren't scientific because of events that have followed. Senator Clinton had geologists reporting to his committee. Some of their reports and recommendations haven't fared well with the passage of time.

One of the first studies concluded that certain downtown land that had sunk in a graben was permanently unstable and would never be safe for use, except perhaps as a landscaped park. City officials ignored it and rebuilt the streets that had been severed. An insurance company, Mutual Of New York, was the first to build on the blighted land by choosing it as the site for its local headquarters office.

Wally Hickel built the first tower of his Captain Cook hotel in the middle of the graben. Subsequently he added two more towers, each higher and bigger than the first. He was considered a courageous investor when he started the first tower. I asked him where he found an equally courageous banker and he told me he had engineers build a model of his building and subject it to earthquake stresses twice as great as those of the Alaska event. He said they learned how to build so that even a banker was convinced it would not collapse.

"After all," Hickel said, "why be so surprised that I can build here. Marine engineers build a thing ten floors high and make it stand up in

EARTHQUAKE | 167

water. They call it a ship. Why shouldn't I be able to build a thing 10 floors high and make it stand up in gravel?"

The government geologists also reported the land along the ocean shore of Knik Arm, west of L Street, would be permanently unstable and there was no way to restore it. That was an area that had moved 11 feet toward the west. One of the surprising phenomena that drew much attention was the fact that a six-story apartment house had moved with that land and was left undamaged and perfectly plumb. All they had to do was apply 11-foot pipes and a few wires to hook it into the city infrastructure again and, at this writing, the building was still a comfortable home for about 80 families.

The townspeople were trying to decide whether they should stay or leave, and whether it was safe to invest their money in repairing their homes. They were frightened continually by gloomy reports of the geologists and by other reports turned in by federal teams of sociologists, financial agencies, health authorities and all the others of every shade of belief, expertise and philosophy. The great preponderance of the experts were sent to Anchorage from somewhere Outside and few if any of them were acquainted with Alaska climate, logistics, economics, lifestyles or the peoples' likes and dislikes.

Some bureaucratic outfit stirred up community resistance by proposing that the entire townsite be turned over to the federal government for urban renewal. Under that program, we were told, the federal government would take title to all the real estate and do their thing to restore its stability. People—families and businesses—would have to move off the townsite but they would have a preferential status to buy their property back when the townsite stability had been restored.

For several weeks this was an issue in the city council meetings as the feds sought council approval. The people let their councilmen know of their disapproval and each week, the proposed project was trimmed down to a smaller area. In the end, the council allowed the feds to urban renewal only the land north of Fourth Avenue between B and E Streets.

For the next two or more years, the feds had contractors clear the area, excavate and haul away the gravel and soil they called unstable, build an intricate drainage system which would be covered by the stable stuff that would be hauled in, and put it on the market for sale. The new land title would ban any building more than two stories high.

The feds spent well over $20 million doing that. Private enterprise (with abundant federal financial help) cleared up the rest of the downtown area, built new buildings and restored normal life long before the urban renewal project was finished.

It is notable that most of the unstable gravel, mud and soil was dumped on the tideflats adjacent to the north side of the Alaska Railroad depot. This was a mud flat that flooded at high tide. It was deemed permanently unstable. But a few years later, the railroad built its new headquarters office building smack in the middle of the so-called unstable area. And life goes on.

The federal government spent many millions of taxpayers dollars on studies and reports about the physical affects of that earthquake. But I have never been aware of any study made of the effects of such an earthquake experience on people.

I know from my experience that the stress was enormous and the lessons were indelibly imprinted on my mind. Even today, more than 30 years later, those experiences are vivid. I have already mentioned how the experience altered my attitude today material things, and magnified the importance of intangible things.

Evangeline and I found it relatively easy to replace material things. Most of them simply involved money. The intangibles, such as relationships, were not readily replaceable. We lost our physical neighborhood, which we loved and miss, but an even greater loss was the loss of our neighbors and our relationship as neighbors. We socialized together, and took care of each other. Even their dogs liked our dogs.

After the earthquake every family had to solve its own housing problem. They settled widely scattered over the growing townsite.

Like about everyone else, we had no earthquake insurance. But the possessions I lost were more than offset by a valuable discovery about life in Alaska. It was the strength of what I have often referred to in editorials as our fraternal relationship as Alaskans. We help one another in time of distress. We are dependent upon each other and perhaps it takes a disaster to make us realize it.

Our staying for a week with the Hilschers without an invitation reminded me of Robert Frost's poem, "The Death of the Hired Man." In that poem a farmer's young son is asking why the hired man, gone many years, has returned now. The farmer explained, "He has come home" and the youngster says this isn't his home, he hasn't been here for many years, why do you call this his home? And the father says because "Home is the place where, when you have to go there, they have to take you in."

After the earthquake we had many "homes" where, if we went there, we could be sure they'd take us in. I have often thought how many friends I have who, if they ever had such a misfortune, I would want to come to my home. When I ask friends who live Outside how many friends they have in their neighborhood or city who would take them in, they stop and think. Rarely do they have a quick answer. The fact that they have such hesitation means it's different from Alaska.

No matter what the scientists and the experts in their various disciplines may say about it, I have a feeling that the earthquake experience made the people of Anchorage stronger. They had temptations to pick up and leave this city when it was shattered. Some did leave. But those who stayed restored it as a magnificent city. And they still have plans for making it better.

Top left: March 27, 1964, north side of 4th Avenue between C street and D street. Top right, above & left. This is the wreckage of JC Penny's new store building. The exterior walls just peeled off and cracked up on the ground. Bill Tobin, the Times managing editor, had just parked his car (one the Time's Buicks) at the curb and stepped out to help a woman who was falling down in the street, when the concrete slabs peeled off the Penny building and flattened the Buick like a pancake. Building around Penny's were also damaged.

EARTHQUAKE | 171

172 | CHAPTER TWELVE

THE WHITE HOUSE
WASHINGTON

March 23, 1965

Dear Mr. Atwood:

The approaching first anniversary of the great Alaska earthquake of March 27, 1964, gives me an appropriate opportunity, which I have long been seeking, to express something which is in my heart.

To the people of Anchorage, Seward, Kodiak, Valdez, Seldovia and the other cities in Alaska which were so tragically damaged, I wish to voice my admiration at the wonderful spirit which you have all shown in withstanding and overcoming that great disaster. All Alaskans performed in a way to make all Americans proud of them.

The assistance which the Federal government has extended to Alaska in the earthquake recovery effort, while unprecedented in our history, would have been unavailing if it were not matched by the remarkable spirit and fortitude of the people of Alaska.

Sincerely,

Lyndon B. Johnson

Mr. Robert B. Atwood
Publisher
Anchorage Daily Times
Anchorage, Alaska

Top left: Photographer Steve McCutcheono, owner of "Mac's Foto" waves to search and rescue unit. Top center: Closeup of hotel showing the crack in the side of concrete wall. Only five window panes were cracked in whole structure. At the time it was the world's tallest building ever to survive an earthquake of th intensity recorded here. Above: A letter to Atwood from president President Lyndon Johnson on the first anniversary of the 1964 earthquake. Left: Downtown Anchorage after the earthquake. Right is north and to the left is south. Fourth Avenue is the main street. You can see the two-block stretch where there was bad slumpage, something like 12 to 15 feet. The whole row of building on the north side crumpled.

EARTHQUAKE | 173

Top left: Atwood's first view of his house after the quake. It used to be atop a 100-bluff. Now it is at tidewater. High tides come over it and shift things around. He used a part of the house roof as a heliport and landed on that part nearest the upper right-hand corner of the picture. Near the lower left-hand corner is the debris that was once his bedroom. Top right: 78 home were demolished in the high class Turnagain residential area. 5 lives lost, hundreds hurt. Above: Elmer Rasmuson's house on bluff in Turnagain, a bit east of Atwood's house. The house went straight down, his wife, his 84 year old mother, a nurse and a maid all rode the house down. Left: Bob Atwood's home in Turnagain subdivision before the 1964 earthquake.

Send me a new trumpet
Address: Anchorage, Alaska

Robert Atwood, Alaska newspaperman and amateur musician, had just put his trumpet to his lips when the earthquake hit. Running outside, he found himself on the ground, arm and trumpet buried shoulder-deep in rubble. To extricate his arm, he had to surrender the trumpet.

One trumpet: a small loss. Perhaps.

The earthquake damage was confined, fortunately, to limited areas. Alaskans are fighting back. Engineering tests are being made to locate safe sites for rebuilding. Materials and equipment are pouring in. Despite a short building season, Alaskans plan to have rebuilding well along by Christmas. Ambitious — but very Alaskan!

Alaskans are going about their jobs. In damaged areas, merchants are supplying their customers. Schools, hotels and public services are functioning. Alaska's splendid visitor attractions and accommodations are open and inviting.

Standard, too, lost heavily, but our service did not stop. Within hours of the earthquake, our products were supplying heat and energy to distressed communities. Today, even as *we* rebuild, they supply energy for Alaska's reconstruction. We've served Alaska almost 80 years. We intend to go forward.

Bob Atwood's impatience to have a new trumpet is symbolic of all Alaskans' determination to recover life's amenities. They came north-by-west to build that life in their Big Land. They mean to get on with it.

Their courage and optimism make all Americans walk ten feet tall.

STANDARD OIL COMPANY OF CALIFORNIA

Advertisment by Standard Oil Company appeared in Time magazine (July 24, 1964).

— CHAPTER THIRTEEN —

Recovery and Redication

The Atwoods, like so many others, were left uprooted by the earthquake. We were confused and under great stress from the traumatic experience of losing our home and everything in it.

We didn't own even a change of clothes. Stores were closed. Many were destroyed. A friend who was a clerk in the men's' department of the Northern Commercial Company crawled with a flashlight into the wreckage of the store and brought out two suits of my size. They were my new wardrobe.

Quite a few families simply threw in the towel and left Alaska in search of a new life Outside, but Evangeline and I had no such inclination or even thought. We had made a definite decision, a year or more before the earthquake, based on the pros and cons of living in Alaska, and had concluded that we didn't want to live anywhere else.

That decision was not made easily. The idea of liquidating our interests and leaving Alaska occurred to me seriously sometime in 1962. Our baby state was in its third year of existence and I was disenchanted with the antics of our political leaders. They weren't measuring up to the idealistic standards of performance that we had promised Congress we would adhere to.

More than that, the legislature had forced our community to become a subordinate part of a new political entity called a borough. That had some facets that were the opposite of what we sought through statehood. The borough took the power of zoning laws, building codes and health planning away from the city and vested it in the borough.

This resulted in two political entities, automatically competing with each other in accumulating political power, prestige and revenues. The borough had mostly residential properties in its domain while the city had the major tax-producing business properties in the downtown area. So the borough sought to remedy that by enacting zoning laws and building codes that made it economically more attractive for new businesses and apartment complexes to build outside the city limits. This triggered the substantial rise of buildings now in Midtown at Northern Lights and C Street. Soon after that the malls on Dimond Boulevard were built and Anchorage took on some of the sprawl characteristics made famous in Los Angeles

As I said before, I was disenchanted with these antics. Never before had we had political bickering and duplication in our everyday life. We had two levels of government assessing property. We had two taxing agencies. We had two fire departments. Two of many agencies, which we all knew in most instances were one too many. The in fighting of the local political bodies was ferocious, each trying to build a power base and its own fiefdom.

Besides these distractions, I felt the loss of my leader who was such a great influence for 30 years or more. Ernest Gruening had been elected to the U.S. Senate and, upon arriving in Washington, seemed to take on the whole world for reformation into his own image. I say that with tongue in cheek, well knowing his political enemies will agree with it and his dedicated supporters will be shocked.

Gruening was the greatest appointed governor Alaska ever had. He was an erudite scholar of government and history. He was a recognized authority on many subjects and his energy, enthusiasm and devotion to all his causes were truly spectacular.

After a short time as a senator he became what I would call a world statesman more than a guardian of his Alaska constituency. He gained national fame by being one of the two senators who voted against President Johnson's Gulf of Tonkin resolution which was the basis for much of the military action in Vietnam. Sen. Wayne Morse, D-Ore., was the other no vote but their Vietnam fame, so important nationally, did little to enhance their standing with Alaskans.

In addition to the disenchantment in politics, the disappointment in people and the loss of my leader, there was one other shortfall in my life. I had no cause. When Alaska won statehood, my goal for 15 years was achieved. I no longer had a driving cause to promote, fight for and make life interesting. I was sitting at my desk like an ordinary publisher, studying operating reports trying to make a nickel here and there. How dull!

Those were some of the things in my mind when Evangeline and I started discussing our future long before the earthquake uprooted us. She had many of the same reactions as I and was concerned with the same trends. We gradually came to an agreement that we would start thinking about where we would go if we left Alaska.

Our method of scouting for potential places to live was to attend almost every national or regional newspaper or hotel convention for about a year. That took us into most of the areas of the nation. It was fun as well as enlightening. We were members of quite a few newspaper and hotel associations and were acquainted with many of the members and leaders, so we were with friends in the most comfortable resorts.

It is also notable how fortunate we were in that we both liked to travel and our travel expenses were deductible business expenses because we were both corporate officers in our newspaper and hotel businesses. Making the travel even more painless was the fact that I was a director of an airline and could travel on passes almost anywhere. At our destination the hotel often gave us complimentary rooms or suites.

I found it fun to complain to my envious friends about the high cost of bus fares between the airports and the hotels, the one expense I never succeeded in ducking.

By 1963 we had discovered that we were happiest every time we came home. We learned we never wanted to leave Alaska.

That meant I had to find a way to make my life more interesting in Anchorage. For that I had a fascinating idea. I asked Turner Catledge, managing editor of the New York Times, if he had someone on his staff he could release on sabbatical for a year so he could come to Alaska and be my leader. I suppose I was hoping to clone Gruening but I must have known that was impossible. I suggested certain areas in which the writer should have some national recognition and credibility, such as history, economics and sociology.

My plan was to hire this writer to travel through Alaska to study the resources, people, markets, and opportunities and do stories on the potentials he saw that could make the state an integral and inseparable part of the nation. We would print his reports in the Anchorage Times and I would be free to pursue the ideas with more stories from other sources and, in the end, either support his proposals or shoot them down in flames.

I knew that if the visiting writer had even half as many ideas as Gruening, he would enhance the lives of all of us in Alaska. Mr. Catledge wrote me that he would have three candidates for me to interview during the editors' convention in April 1964. The earthquake in the last week of March wiped out my attendance at that meeting and terminated my fancy scheme.

Our first home after the earthquake was an apartment in the Anchorage Hotel which we owned. It was in the same building we lived in 29 years before when we first arrived in Anchorage. The town was filling up with paternalistic bureaucrats from Washington who professed to be here to help Alaska's recovery.

My paper tried to keep everyone informed on what people were doing in their personal problems, and what the bureaucrats were doing in their fields. We had many stories about the hardships and shortages confronting families whose homes were wrecked.

We were impatient with the pace of federal agencies, which had a proclivity for committees and study groups. We sought action and we were quite frank in saying editorially that red tape was bogging down our recovery.

Spring brought a building boom. Developers and entrepreneurs of every stripe moved into the wilderness areas outside Anchorage. New residential areas sprang up in bunches like spring flowers. Homesteaders found ready buyers for their 160-acre tracts, yielding them more money than they had ever hoped to own at one time. But they saw their buyers multiply their investment many times by subdividing the homestead into small lots and selling them at retail.

Sewell Faulkner, one of the leading real estate wheelers and dealers in town, told me more millionaires were made in Anchorage from real estate than ever were made from gold, oil or commercial fishing.

Gene Foley, head of the SBA, often asked me when I was going to apply for an SBA loan to build our new house. I explained that I didn't need a house because my daughters were adults and my wife and I weren't so inclined. He always said I was a "chump" because a federal loan at 3% for 30 years was "next to giving it to you." He said the SBA could loan me enough to replace my original home square foot for square foot. That would qualify us for big money because we had built our home years ago and costs had multiplied many times since.

Evangeline and I talked about it often in the privacy of our home and we generally agreed that we didn't need a new house. But we also agreed that the town needed a new house. We had made our Turnagain home a mecca for special events, such as entertaining visiting congressional committees, senators, other dignitaries and especially for the commanders of the military who had limited facilities for entertainment on base.

We had so many generals as guests that I sometimes chided my wife that she was running a USO for generals while I was downtown putting my energies, as a committee member, into running a USO for GIs. Her response was simple and adequate, "Well, somebody must take care of the generals, too."

The all-time peak of excitement in our "USO for Generals" must have been the occasion during the Cold War years when most of the members of the Joint Chiefs of Staff were in Anchorage and we had them as guests for dinner. It was a big, warm and friendly black-tie event with Alaskans hobnobbing with some of the big names in American history. Among those present, besides lesser generals, were the first chairman of the Joint Chiefs of Staff Gen. Omar Bradley, Air Force Chief of Staff Gen. Hoyt Vandenberg, and the chief of naval operations.

Jack Ferguson, a local businessman, told me of his big embarrassment. "My cummerbund had come unhitched and I moved over to a far corner of the living room where I thought nobody would notice me as I reached under my jacket. Just as I was bent over and got a hold of the ends and was about to hitch up, a hand was protruded into my line of vision and a voice said, 'My name is Omar Bradley and I didn't get yours.' So I had to drop everything to shake hands with General Bradley."

Evangeline and I had only happy recollections of the events that came to our house. We soon convinced ourselves that the town needed a replacement house. But she hesitated at the thought of building another log house, even though we had been so comfortable in it and it was so Alaskan.

180 | CHAPTER THIRTEEN

"That log house was good for frontier days when the town was just growing up," she said. "The new house ought to reflect the new era and the modern Anchorage by providing amenities for the social graces."

Evangeline found a man who called himself an architect and they went to work. She liked curves and wanted the whole house curvy—a spiral staircase upstairs, curved walls and all that. That guy did what she said and they ended up with a plan so complicated that they even had blueprints for the ceilings, showing the curves, coves and tricky lighting. Then we invited our choice list of favorite contractors to bid for the job. Not one would bid. The common excuse was that "I have never built anything like that in my life."

So Evangeline and her architect had to do it over. We lost a building season but simplified the design. The new house, for instance, needed no blueprints for the ceilings. But our contractors still begged off. One by one we lost them. All except one, J.B. Warrack, the son of the man who built the original Anchorage Times building on Fourth Avenue, the Westward Hotel, the Anchorage Hotel, many schools and other structures in Anchorage.

The son had inherited his father's business and felt he ought to help an old family customer. He put his bidders to work on the plans. He told me later that he prodded his people to hurry up with the bid only to be told that there were complications and they couldn't find sources for some of the building materials and gadgets in the plan.

"One day my bidder told me where the total bid stood although it was not yet complete, and I told him to cut it off there and make that the bid," Warrack said. "I could build a hotel for that. I ought to be able to build a house."

The site for my new home was an undivided 22-acre tract that had been a golf course owned by the local Elks lodge. It was available because the revenue from golf was insufficient to pay the mortgage costs. A banker, who acted in my behalf in buying it, had promised he would take care of chores of subdividing and selling the lots as subdivision. But soon after the purchase, he left Alaska and left me alone as the owner. The subdivision never came into being.

Evangeline got her spiral staircase and furnished the house in French provincial style. She traveled to San Francisco, Chicago and New York in search of furniture and interior decorators who could provide the drapes and sheer curtains of gold brocade from looms in Italy, tassels from France, and other fancy trims.

It took the contractor's workmen a long, long time to finish our project. When vandals damaged some of the interior one night, we decided to move in and live in the place even though sawhorses, stepladders and workmen were still there. Our presence proved to be a great catalyst for speeding completion. There was no more vandalism and I suspect that having Evangeline on the property all day and sometimes asking questions made the workmen uncomfortable. They seemed to finish the job must faster.

Our first guest in the new home was Gen. Curtis E. LeMay, retired Air Force Chief of Staff whose World War II performance earned him a permanent place in American history. He was in Alaska ostensibly on a fishing trip but I am sure there were hidden political purposes. He was in the national news as a possible vice presidential running mate with Gov. George Wallace of Georgia for president on the American Independent Party ticket.

Sawhorses and ladders were stacked to clear the living room for the party. We had light and heat but bare walls, no paint, no floor covering or wallpaper. And only makeshift furniture. Our military friends who were hosting General LeMay and our civilian guests were so friendly and enthusiastic about the new house that even General LeMay enjoyed the evening.

Actually, our guest of honor, even though he was a national hero, looked almost as shabby as our unfinished house. He wore an ordinary business suit, which made him appear shorter in stature and lacked the snap or formidability of a general's uniform studded with stars and ribbons of honor.

His physical condition was also odd. He had suffered a stroke that left much of the left side of his body paralyzed. One side of his face was expressionless. When I looked at the face of the man who was so well known and respected I saw half of two faces. The paralyzed side of his face was stern and cold because it was expressionless. It reflected the well-known tough and even abrasive personality for which the general had a degree of fame. But the right half of the face was upbeat and different. Even though only one side of his lips moved when he talked or smiled, he was fascinating and we found him a warm and gracious guest.

General LeMay had many phone calls that night and he accepted every one, even as they interrupted his cocktail hour and dinner. At the end of the evening he told us he had accepted the invitation to run as the running mate with George Wallace. We all congratulated him and wished him the best. To myself, I was thinking that was a hell of a way for a national Air Force hero to wind up a distinguished career, as a defeated candidate. In the 1968 election that ticket won only five deep South states.

Of more relevance to us in Alaska in the mid 1960s was the announcement by one Wally Hickel that he would enter the race for governor. Hickel was a hotel owner and building contractor in Alaska. In politics he had been active within the party and had gained some statewide prominence as Republican National Committeeman. The published announcement built him up as a friend of President Eisenhower. As national committeeman he had been among GOPs invited to the White House.

Hickel had an inauspicious beginning in Alaska. He has frequently

182 | CHAPTER THIRTEEN

said that he had little formal education, graduating with a below C average from Claflin high school in Kansas, and actually landed in Alaska in 1940 by accident. Hickel has told his friends he looked in the "A" section of an encyclopedia and was impressed with what he read about Australia, so he decided to head down under.

"But when I got to the West Coast and learned I needed a passport for Australia I switched to Alaska which I had also read something about in that book," he said.

Hickel remembers arriving in Anchorage with 37 cents in his pocket and became an odd-jobs worker and an occasional professional boxer. He appeared at smokers staged by the USO to entertain soldiers and managed to get a job as a flight and maintenance inspector at Fort Richardson. He was hard working and ambitious and he convinced Emil Pfeil, an Alaska Railroad blacksmith, to be his partner and invest in building a string of houses on Medfra Street on the east side of Anchorage. From that venture his construction talents grew and he had a building career which cut him in on the rapid growth of wartime Anchorage.

Hickel had never been elected to public office and he wasn't known for any coherent policy. He was active in the Republican party hierarchy while the party had little clout with affairs outside its own housekeeping problems, which were many. Democrats were in control of everything.

Republicans spent much of their time fighting each other, often on a sectional basis (Fairbanks vs. Anchorage). The Anchorage contingent depended upon Hickel to make points for them as one of the few who could out-shout Mike Stepovich of Fairbanks. In those days clout within a political party depended much on such things as shouting and pushing. However, he didn't need to manufacture an issue for his campaign. He was handed a big one.

The Democrat, Bill Egan, governor since statehood, was running for a third term. The Alaska Constitution limits governors to two consecutive terms. Egan argued that his first term was 34 days short of being a full term. He was first elected in November 1958, but he was not sworn in until statehood was proclaimed by President Eisenhower Jan.3, 1959. However, even erstwhile loyal Democrats weren't all buying that argument. The fact remained that Egan had competed for and won two consecutive gubernatorial elections.

"Do you want the intent of our constitution undermined by a third term?" read the Hickel election advertisements in the Times. The ads of some disenchanted Democrats were even blunter. "The Third Term is immoral and the governor knows that it is," asserted one by a Walter Keats, who signed himself as an Independent Democrat.

The characteristics of Hickel and Egan were remarkably different. Alaskans were heard to say that those who want action and excitement should want Hickel, but those who want comfort and serenity should prefer Egan.

Many considered Egan more qualified than Hickel. Egan was reared in Valdez, a town of about 400 souls, ran a grocery business and first entered public service when he was elected mayor. Obviously his small town rearing and his experiences as the town's grocer had taught him how to live in peace and harmony with his neighbors. In Alaska's small towns the job as mayor is often difficult to fill. The fame and glory isn't much, the responsibilities could require much time and attention, and the pay was usually nil.

Egan met with such approval that the Valdez people elected him to the territorial legislature. In Juneau, the territorial capital some 300 miles away, he served Valdez successfully and with dignity. He also expanded the area of his political acquaintances to other parts of Alaska, which stood him in good stead for his subsequent political career. He made everyone feel comfortable. He won the support of Republicans as well as Democrats, as his succession of victories indicated.

Hickel's entry into the political arena as candidate for governor had spectacular effects. His flamboyant style and pugilistic attitude electrified the campaign. In Hickel's world, there was no room for equivocation or inaction. He spread the feeling that with him as the leader something would happen. And that feeling was attractive to those who were sick and tired of having nothing much happen.

He beat Egan in the 1966 election and his victory had an interesting variety of interpretations. The voters were predominately Democrats and yet he was a Republican, which was seen as a sign that Alaskans vote for the man and not the party or that parties are weak and have only minor influence in Alaska politics. But the third-term issue also was seen as a significant factor. There were those who placed first emphasis on that and asserted that the voters were defending their constitution by electing Hickel.

Nothing indicated that the voters saw a flaw or were disenchanted with Egan. Just four years later he was elected governor again, this time with no issue of legality, by defeating Keith Miller, the lieutenant governor who had become governor when President Nixon appointed Hickel to be Secretary of the Interior in Washington, D.C. Politicians said that election was the first one in the history of the nation where a governor was defeated after doubling the size of his budget in one year. (During Miller's short term, the state became filthy rich from the sale of the Prudhoe Bay oil leases and went on a spending spree.)

These were the post-earthquake years of rebuilding much of Anchorage's downtown establishment and some residential areas. Also, the towns of Seward, Valdez and Cordova were restoring their huge waterfront projects lost in the tidal waves. The Alaska Railroad had to be virtually re-built from Seward to Anchorage.

Alaska had not yet reached its 10th anniversary as a state, and was still in the process of searching among its people for those with leader-

184 | CHAPTER THIRTEEN

ship qualities. Institutions were still in the process of evolving. Higher education was seeking a niche in the new society. Hospitals, churches, schools and their programs that become institutions and are so important to a society were just taking shape. The new state had no traditions, customs or culture to guide it.

Oil played a minor role in the economy at this time but its potential loomed large on the immediate horizon. The Swanson River discovery opened the oil age, but its principal impact was to attract an influx of entrepreneurs, engineers, contractors, speculators, gamblers and camp followers of every stripe. As exploration intensified, modest new discoveries of oil were found on the Kenai and in Cook Inlet, leading to the development of 14 offshore platforms. The excitement grew with oil scouts combing the Seward Peninsula and Copper River Valley as well as the North Slope in the Arctic for prospects. The Bureau of Land Management said it was the biggest land rush in the history of the nation.

We added a regular feature, "The Oil Report," early in the 1960s because of the strong appetite in Anchorage for news about leasing and drilling activities of the oil companies, dreams and schemes of engineers and others who would reveal them. As editor, I tried to remember we had the old areas of news to cover despite the consuming excitement about oil. Editorially we made it a point to direct public attention to other economic activities and opportunities, particularly tourism which has always had tremendous potential for growth but never the capital to develop it.

In my years as editor and publisher, my paper beat the drums for greater access for people to enjoy the national parks and more accommodations to support them. When I first arrived in Anchorage, the big project on the front burner of the Interior department was a new hotel to be built at Wonder Lake in McKinley Park, and the widening and upgrading of the one highway that provides access. It was mysteriously taken off the drawing boards in Washington, D.C., and never came to pass.

The prevailing frustrations with the park service were so great that in Anchorage we young Turks (I say we because I was one of them) tried to advance tourism ourselves. And we came close to having a winner.

The Booster Club bunch and Kafe Klatch bunch who met daily at the Oyster Loaf observed that one of the disappointments for tourists is that they usually see no wildlife while they are here. We figured we could correct that ourselves if we could get the right cooperation. What we needed was a big piece of land (vacant wilderness surrounded Anchorage) where we could collect and keep two each of every variety of wild animal in Alaska. It would be the biggest natural area of wildlife in the world, as we dreamed of it.

I went to Holgar Larson, the Anchorage U.S. Fish and Wildlife agent in charge. He had coffee at the Oyster Loaf and all I had to do was walk over and sit down with him at his table to talk business. After a few days

RECOVERY AND REDICATION | 185

of discussion, he agreed that Alaska animals could fend for themselves for food, winter and summer, if their areas were large enough. He agreed it would be possible to find a way to bring the animals to a local area. And we whipped up his interest in the project to a point where he promised to help us. Eventually, he and his wildlife service were our partners. They said they would keep us supplied with animals, under certain conditions, of course (none of which involved spending money—we had no money).

At the Oyster Loaf we also had Bureau of Land Management employees who liked the morning cup of coffee. I could hobnob with Lowell Puckett, the manager, and Peanuts Maine and other staffers and encourage them to study their maps to find an area suitable for the zoo. It took many days of discussion before decisions were made.

The first suggestion from the BLM was to use the Eklutna River valley for the animals. It was empty of people. It contained lots of wildlife already. It had the first beginnings of the Eklutna hydroelectric project and the animals were compatible with that. It had a wagon track that we called a road all the way to Lake Eklutna. My fish and wildlife friends rejected that area as too steep. Too little room for the animals to roam. They required more of a "U" shaped valley. Eklutna valley was a "V"

Next the BLM suggested Eagle River Valley— big, beautiful, "U"-shaped, and virtually empty. The only inhabitants were the handful of homesteaders who fronted on the wagon-track dirt highway that eventually became the Glenn Highway. The zoo could be up the valley and would not conflict with the homesteaders. My fish and wildlife friends approved, and it looked as though we had a deal.

We young Turks enlisted the help of the local chapter of the Izaak Walton League. They applied for and got the land withdrawn from the public domain to preserve it for zoo use. We then initiated efforts to get the Alaska Road Commission (the territory's road building agency) to engineer a pioneer road to make the valley accessible to tourists. And we started planning certain fencing as specified by our wildlife authorities. All of which led to the discovery that we needed some money to buy the fence material. The one thing we didn't have.

Just about then, someone pointed out that we would have to have attendants at the gate where the zoo road takes off from the highway into the game area. The attendants would open and close the gates and see that all visitors were out at closing time. That requirement just about did our project in. We might find money for fencing but we had no prospect of a flow of money to meet a payroll. But we didn't give up. We took our problem to George Shannon, Anchorage city manager, who also met us in the Oyster Loaf. Could he supply the guards by using the drunks serving time in the city's drunk farm, which was then at Russian Jack Springs (from which, incidentally, the city's greenhouses and flower gardens were an outgrowth)?

We argued that it wouldn't cost much to move the drunk farm to the zoo gate. The farm was hardly more than a Quonset hut or two. He countered with the complaint that it would cost the city too much to provide transportation for prisoners back and forth from Eagle River for their court appearances and trials. We contended that it would cost no more than from Russian Jack, but he never saw it our way and our zoo project died on the vine for lack of a gatekeeper.

I remained a champion for a zoo featuring Alaska animals. We did get one in July 1966, but it was nothing like we young Turks had planned. It seemed that the town's major grocery outlet, S&F Foodland, won a national contest staged by Zellerbach Paper Co. of San Francisco for a promotion of a chiffon tissue. The prize was "$3,000 or a baby elephant." Zellerbach never thought a store so far up in frigid Alaska would want an elephant. But Jack Snyder (the "S" in S&F) did. So they shipped him a 15-month-old elephant that had been captured somewhere in India.

Jack had a fun summer touring Alaska with his elephant Annabelle and then turned her over for tender loving care to Sammye Taplin, owner of the Dimond H horse ranch on O'Malley Road. Sammye was known as an animal lover. When wildlife agents found themselves with an orphaned baby seal that needed bottle feeding, she offered to do it. She did such a good job that the agency brought her more orphaned or injured animals. By the time Annabelle arrived, she already was caring for bear cubs, foxes, and various birds. She loved them and she welcomed parents who brought youngsters to her horse ranch to see the wild animals.

With the cost of food mounting, Sammye's friends felt sorry for her and started a fund to help her. Before long, civic clubs and businesses organized drives for money, not only to pay for food but to fix up the surroundings. It grew into a town project even without official action on anyone's part. In 1969, after three years of informal operations, a lawyer, who was also an animal buff, gave his services free and incorporated the ranch as a non-profit entity, thus creating the Alaska Zoo that grew into one of the city's major institutions.

I served on Sammye's board for a term or two. Both state and city governments contributed to its support. Today, the zoo is often called "world class," a popular visiting spot for young and old. When I was on the board, I noted that the corporation had no insurance protection for directors. It was hard to convince them to spend money for insurance, but I argued that in this litigious society there was no way of knowing when someone might sue, no matter how silly the basis for a claim. I finally prevailed and insurance coverage was put in the budget.

I suspect that insurance provided some comfort when Binky, the polar bear, tried to eat up a tourist from Australia who had climbed over three high fences to get close enough for a good picture of the bear. Upon finding the young lady in his territory, Binky reached through the bars and pulled part of her in and chewed. Zoo staffers and other visitors managed to get her out of the bear's clutches, leaving Binky with an Australian tennis shoe showing a spot of blood on it dangling from his mouth. That picture was published all over the world. T-shirts with Binky as a logo sold like hotcakes during the rest of the season. That scene also decorated coffee mugs and other souvenir items which were equally popular.

The young lady from Australia spent a week or so in the hospital. She proved herself a person of good moral standards and straight thinking. Frequently asked in interviews if she intended to sue the zoo, she said she had been foolish, it was all her fault, and she would not sue anybody—much to the disappointment of some lawyers, I suspect.

A short time after the Australian lady's experience with Binky, two local youths decided late at night to swim in Binky's pool. Once more, Binky rushed to protect his territory and thank goodness onlookers rescued the boys before too much damage was done. The boys were charged with trespassing. Alaskans wrote letters to the paper and poured out sentiments on radio and TV talk shows, all in defense of Binky even though nobody had charged him with anything. Sadly, Binky died a short time later, in July 1995 from a mysterious illness. The community mourned the loss of a cherished friend.

Annabelle, at this writing (about 40 years after her arrival in Anchorage), was still the patriarch of all zoo animals. She did the zoo proud by learning to do oil paintings. Her art is still a hot item. Her keeper sets out paintbrushes with different colored paints nearby. Annabelle takes a brush by the handle one at a time and paints exotic strokes on canvas. Her first original painting sold at auction for $2,500 and copies go for $15. The last time I checked with Sammye, who is now Mrs. John Seawell, she said Annabelle had brought in well over $30,000 for the zoo.

My new house and the new zoo were just a few of the many new developments after the earthquake. Townspeople and Outside investors, encouraged by the upbeat spirit, seemed determined to do things bigger and better than before. J.C. Penney, which lost its three-year-old building in the heart of downtown, replaced it with a structure that covered more ground and with more floor space than the original. The manager said they were just correcting mistakes, and mentioned in particular that the new store provided twice as much floor space for sports equipment, sports clothing, and hardware.

The store had learned in its first years that our town was made up of sports buffs. That was evident way back in 1915 when the town was founded in the wilderness. When government agencies refused to provide recreation facilities, the townspeople themselves built the first baseball park with donations of money, volunteer labor and borrowed equipment. Ski trails seemed to appear naturally, since many of the railroad workers came from Scandinavian countries.

As far back as 1937, we in the Booster Club saw skiing as a potential tourist attraction. Al Corey and Ralph Soberg set out to do something about it and they found me an easy mark to enlist. They called all skiing enthusiasts to a meeting at the Richmond's Café. There, sitting around a hot stove, they pointed to our mountainsides and projected good things that could happen if we just invest in minor things like rope tows. They signed up 21 members and elected me as the first president of the ski club. Membership grew swiftly because most of the Alaska population was young and adventurous.

As pioneers, we found that it took more than rope tows to develop skiing. We cut trails through brush and built a foundation for a modest ski jump on the south side of Ship Creek, just below the site occupied later by the Alaska Native Health Center. We skied there until 1940 when the military arrived.

Soldiers make good skiers and we were pleased to see that the military wanted to train ski teams. Major Marvin Marston, a dashing bundle of enthusiasm for anything exciting, took charge. He wasn't impressed with our runs on the bluff south of Ship Creek. He looked at the mountains and headed there. Using troops during off-duty times, he carved a trail up the highest slope he could find. At this writing, almost 50 years later, both soldiers and civilians benefit from his vision. This is the Arctic Valley Ski area that overlooks Fort Richardson east of Anchorage.

(One of the biggest obstacles Arctic Valley faced was man-made. The U. S. Public Health Service tried to close it down because, they said, it was within the water reserve for the Anchorage area. The military was not ready to fight it, but that edict aroused the civilian community. The bureaucrats cited the lack of sufficient toilet facilities, but the civilians crowded the public hearings and asked what about all the moose, bears, wolves and other wildlife in the area. How can it be healthy for the people of Anchorage to drink water from a watershed where four-legged animals have roamed generation after generation, and now a seasonal sortie by a few two-legged people can pollute it? The heated discussions delved into the urinating habits of four-legged compares to two-legged, including the chemical differences in substance. The Public Health Service people gave up and never issued the closing order.)

Skiers are like ducks who when they find a source of food immediately tell their friends and invite them to come and enjoy it. The intrepid pioneers, both civilian and military, urged friends to join them. Before long, Anchorage skiers were looking for bigger and better ski runs away from the crowds. Bob Bursier, Sven Johanson, Ernie Bauman and Joe Gayman will always have a place in history because their search led them to discover Alyeska mountain in Girdwood, about 40 miles south of Anchorage, which is today a world class ski resort.

Those men, like so many others, were employed somewhere in town, and became volunteer enthusiasts in skiing development. They saw the opportunity for big investments which could return big profits at Alyeska. The mountain could maintain ski conditions for about six months of the year. It rose from sea level to 2,900 feet in a short distance with peaks and valleys up yonder for future access. However, the four men did not have the finances to develop it, but they were generous to get out of the way if someone else might do it. So they persuaded Frances Richins Clark, wife of an FBI agent, who was widely traveled, worldly knowledgeable, and financially smart, to look for investors.

Sometime in the late 1950s, Mrs. Clark brought in a skiing buff named Francois de Gunzberg of Paris. He was introduced to me as a baron, and I suspected Franny was pulling my leg. De Gunzberg looked like a grubby Alaska ski bum in Levis and tank tops. He had traveled extensively in Alaska scouting for likely oil leasing opportunities for Murchison oil interests in Texas. I do not know how good he was at spotting potential oil fields, but I do know he knew a gem of a ski area when he saw one. The baron hired a helicopter to take him to the top of Mt. Alyeska. He skied down the exhilarating slopes and promptly proclaimed the mountain a skiing resource worthy of international patronage.

By 1958, the baron persuaded his Texas oil friends to buy the rights to Mt. Alyeska. He dealt with the U.S. Forest Service leasing people for permission to use that portion of the mountain within the national forest. He dealt with the U.S. Bureau of Land Management for land in the BLM domain. Then he raised the capital to bring to Alaska a French contracting crew to build a chair lift and carve out several ski trails. The lift went to the top of the mountain, enabling skiers to experience the 2,900-foot vertical drop that would challenge the world's best athletes. Besides the Murchisons in Dallas, the investors included Laurence Rockefeller of New York, Samuel Bronfman, board chairman of Seagrams, and T.L. Wynne of Dallas, owner of a hotel chain.

The excitement at Girdwood pumped new value into real estate in the area. Enterprising developers sold lots for weekend ski chalets. Like many others, I was caught up in the enthusiasm and bought a lot or two. However, the investment in the skiing facilities found tough going. Alaskans weren't used to paying ski lift fees. They always fended for themselves or stuck to the neighborhood rope tows.

Several of us agreed that something must be done to stave off bankruptcy for the first major recreational investment in Alaska. Our ad hoc group came up with a plan that we hoped would bring international fame and glory—and consequently international skiers—to Alyeska. We organized the International Airline Ski Race, an event that for the next 15 years would be a highlight of the ski season at Alyeska.

At that time, about 15 international air carriers were flying over the North Pole between Europe and Asia. They all stopped at Anchorage. Some had passenger traffic rights and all of them needed refueling and crew changes. These operations kept some 200 to 300 personnel in Anchorage at all times. These crew members, most of them young and athletic, actively participated in our local events.

With their help, we invited all the world's airlines to send ski teams here for an annual ski race, with nothing to win but a plaque or trophy. The Denali Ski Patrol volunteered its members to police the runs. We also found volunteer timekeepers. Chalet owners provided free housing for the racers. The airlines operating though Anchorage honored the teams' transportation passes. Free bus rides moved the skiers from the airport to Girdwood. The baron made his mountain facilities free to all competitors.

Teams streamed in from Japan, France, England, Sweden, Germany, the United Kingdom, and sometimes from odd countries we rarely heard of before. Major American airlines also check in. We billed the race as a world championship meet, and my newspaper covered it accordingly. We made sure each winning team returned home with clippings and pictures. The airlines also responded magnificently with worldwide promotion in their house organs. Alaska made friends with people from distant countries. The visitors became enthusiasts for skiing Alyeska.

We got the results we wanted. Skiers from the Lower 48, Europe and Asia started showing up to test the slopes at Girdwood. What most inspired them to come? Airline personnel became terrific ambassadors. I noticed this while flying with SAS in Austria. A stewardess engaged in conversation with a skier headed for Innsbruck. When they started comparing resorts, she suddenly asked, "Have you ever skied Alyeska?" He hadn't and wanted to know something about it. She gave him information packed with superlatives and noted she had many memorable moments there. He seemed sold.

As people abroad became strong supporters, local skiers caught on, too. They began to shell out for fees to be part of the excitement. In March 1965, the sixth year for the International Airline races, more than 300 team members from 20 airlines headquartered in 11 nations participated. This is when we began to worry whether we had created a monster. "We were out of everything but the mountain in trying to conduct Class A and Class B competition," Bernie Kosinski, managing editor of the Anchorage Times, told me. "We are getting too successful and better cut back to just Class A skiing."

However, there is no way for one person to stop an avalanche. Bernie's advice was buried and the race kept growing until it became an Alaska headache, and not only because of its size. We had promised the airlines no commercialism, but we found it impossible to prevent some beer outfits from plastering the place with posters. They started hospitality rooms and beer parties that were noisy and degrading. Townspeople began to complain. My newspaper put its foot down and withdrew as a sponsor after the bikini parties went too far. (One airline passed out pieces of cloth to whomever would take one and offered a prize to the woman who would make herself a bikini and return the biggest remnant of cloth. Contestants had to parade to be judged.)

Rowdiness at night came to overshadow the great performances on the slopes in the daytime. We did attract star athletes, such as Marki Haraldsen, a former Olympic competitor, who swept the women's downhill races for Swiss Air.

Our withdrawal as sponsor ended the airline races there. Baron de Gunzberg sold Alyeska to Alaska Airlines and became a big time vintner in Bordeaux, France. The airline sold the property in 1980 to Seibu Corp., whose principal investor is said to be one of the richest men in the world. The popularity and fame of Alyeska under new management began to grow and in 1994 Seibu completed a $100 million skiing development there, replete with a fabulous luxury hotel. It is today Alaska's biggest private recreation project.

Alaskans have benefited handsomely. Alyeska slopes continue to fire up the interest of skiers. Hundreds of Alaskans train and hope to make it to the big time. Community enthusiasm for winter sports triggered a campaign to bring the winter Olympics to Anchorage. Townspeople contributed $2 million to finance the effort. Anchorage did win the designation as America's choice for the 1998 and 2002 Olympics. In 1998, we lost out to Lillehammer, Norway, in the final vote when, in the opinion of many, the intrigue of international Olympic politics controlled the final selection. We lost to Albertville, France, for the 2002 games.

Many athletes in this relatively new state are climbing high in national ratings. Kris Thorsness, daughter of an Anchorage lawyer, was the first Alaskan to bring home the fame and glory of an Olympic gold medal. While in college, she was a member of a rowing team that won collegiate honors and went on to win first place for the U. S. in the Olympics in 1984. At Lillehammer, Tommy Moe, who grew up in Girdwood and learned to ski on Mt. Alyeska, took first place in downhill racing and came home with a gold medal that made all of Alaska proud.

Skiing has become so popular for Alaskans, young or old, that it might someday be called the state sport. Cross-country trails are everywhere. At least a half dozen ski hills serve the Anchorage area, and few facilities in the world can match Mt. Alyeska as the ultimate ski resort.

192 | CHAPTER THIRTEEN

Home of Bob Atwood rebuilt after earthquake.

The construction of the Capt. Cook Hotel began shortly after the earthquake of 1964.

Alyeska Ski Resort before the earthquake of 1964. Insert: Baron Francois de Gunzberg, developer of Alyeska Ski Resort.

194 | CHAPTER THIRTEEN

— CHAPTER FOURTEEN —

Filthy Rich

Discovery day for Prudhoe Bay will always be Feb. 18, 1968, but that is not the day most Alaskans remember. That was the day Atlantic Richfield's State No. 1 returned a "substantial flow of gas," as a brief company announcement said.

The news was received enthusiastically by those informed on oil prospects, but there was no great public response as might be expected. It wasn't known that the discovery well had come upon the largest oil reservoir ever found in North America. It was weeks later that the hole was recognized as the harbinger of wealth, wealth so great it would make new millionaires on the east coast of America, on the west coast and even in Alaska. Wealth so great that it would convert the state of Alaska from, perhaps, the nation's poorest state in income, into a state not only rich but filthy rich.

The first announcement was fascinating to those who realized that the discovery, no matter how big, probably would prevent the company from quitting the Arctic. Atlantic Richfield was the last of the oil companies to still be drilling there. Other majors had abandoned the field after continual failures, and Atlantic Richfield had scheduled this hole, if dry, to be its last. News of a "substantial flow of gas" was taken to mean further exploration would be pursued.

Alaskans were abuzz with curiosity waiting for the next announcement. Most were optimistic that good things for their state were in the offing. On March 7 they were glad to hear that Atlantic Richfield would drill a second well, seven miles southeast of the first one. If this was to be a confirmation well, it was obvious the oil company was thinking big.

A week later, the company put out further information. Officials were under heavy pressure from the press to clarify the situation. Rumors were so hot and heavy they were felt in the stock market as well as in board rooms around the world. A major discovery in Arctic Alaska could rock the financial world.

In a clarifying announcement the company disclosed that the first well was tested between the depths of 9,505 and 9,825 feet and oil flowed at the rate of 1,152 barrels a day with a three-quarter-inch choke, and gas flowed at the rate of 40 million cubic feet a day.

On June 25 Atlantic Richfield put out new figures showing that Prudhoe Bay State No. 1 oil production at 2,415 barrels a day with gas at

40 million cubic feet, and added that Sag River No. 1, the second well, was producing at the same level from the same formation.

That announcement set off euphoria and joy across the nation. Atlantic Richfield stock soared on the stock market. Many of the nation's major oil companies prepared for the rush to the Arctic for oil leases. The state of Alaska launched a crash program to prepare for an auction sale of leases on state lands surrounding the Prudhoe Bay discovery.

The state scheduled the sale at public auction for Sept. 10,1969, when 179 tracts would be put on the block containing 459,458 acres of treeless Arctic tundra on the shore of the Arctic Ocean. The worldwide interest of oil companies indicated it would be a mammoth sale.

The state rented the Anchorage high school auditorium downtown and equipped the stage much like the old-style New York stock market with its walls covered with stock quotations. The state showed a huge map of the Prudhoe Bay area and the location of the 179 tracts to be leased. On stage, state employees would be at desks handling the flow of documents in connection with the bidding and clerks would write on the huge map the highest bids for each tract.

The sight of money-bearing oil tycoons coming to town with their sealed bids excited the community, as did the influx of the small army of reporters anxious to report how much the rich and powerful were willing to bet on the bleak, forlorn and remote North Slope of Alaska, a place so far beyond the periphery of public interest that relatively few knew where it was. David Brinkley of NBC, Bill Cook and Jerry Lubino of Newsweek, and Daryl Lembko of the Los Angeles Times were among the media celebrities.

Bankers flew in from the east and west coasts. They accompanied their oilmen-customers so as to be ready to extend additional credit if the bidding went beyond expectations. Each prospective bidder behaved as though he was hell bent on winning whatever tracts he bid on.

Rumors ran rampant, of course, because no one was talking about how high he might bid. Some went to extremes to guard their secret, such as the 20 executives operating as a consortium. They flew in that morning from Calgary, Alberta, after spending the previous five days riding on a special Canadian National Railway train, with communications with the rest of the world cut off while they shuttled the 190 miles back and forth between Calgary and Edmonton while they worked out their final bids. "We thought it was as secure a place for our meetings as we could find," explained one member.

Hotel rooms in Anchorage were at a premium. Some executives slept in their company jets that were chock-a-block at Anchorage International Airport about two miles from downtown. A clerk at the Travelers Inn reported that "some guy with a southern accent called and said if we didn't have any rooms, he would buy the place."

On the night before the sale, Gov. Keith Miller went on television

196 | CHAPTER FOURTEEN

exulting, "We are on the eve of the greatest day our state has ever known. Tomorrow we will reach out to claim our birthright. We will rendezvous with our dreams."

It was quite a rendezvous. Seating was on a first-come, first-served basis. Some company representatives were up most of the night, standing in line to get seats for their company execs. When the doors opened there was a rush for seats. The auditorium was abuzz with low-voiced talking as all awaited the start of the big event.

A hush fell over the hall when a big, heavy-set character in flowing robes with a jubbah and all the fixings, even including colored glasses, strode down the aisle and took a seat down front. He was alone. He talked to no one and no one talked to him. He just sat still and waited, like the others. Who was he? Why was he there? He could have been Crown Prince Saud of Saudi Arabia.

The presence of that character electrified the crowd. Were Americans going to be bidding against Arabs for the Alaska leases? Bidding was posted to start at 10:30 a.m. Shortly before that time the big man with his flowing robes stood up, strode up the aisle and out of the auditorium without saying a word to anyone. One Alaskan reported he was fingering a big cigar as he left, as though he may be going outside the building for a smoke.

It was never explained publicly, as far as I know, who did it or why. Many years later (in 1995) I was recalling those exciting old days with Mitch Abood, an Anchorage resident of longstanding well-known as a former one-term legislator and actor. Mitch says he is half Arab and half Irish. Taking a wild shot in the dark I asked him if he was the guy who made that spectacular entranced into the auditorium on the day of the auction and he replied with a simple, "Yes." I asked who put him up to it and he said nobody. By further questioning I learned he did it "just for fun" and he hoped he "inspired" the oilmen to raise the level of their bidding "to keep that Arab of it."

I asked him what happened after he left. He said nothing. "I got into my car, lit my cigar and drove home."

At 10.30 a.m. an uncharacteristically grim Tom Kelly, the 37-year-old Alaska Commissioner of Natural Resources, stepped up to the podium at the Sydney Laurence Auditorium and began the proceedings.

The singing of the Alaska state song opened the ceremonies and as soon as the notes faded, Kelly reached into a box, which had been closely guarded by state troopers, and began reading bids over a loudspeaker. Jubilant spectators rocked the packed house with cheers every time one bid topped another. Clerks posted the latest numbers on the wall charts.

The Times staff had set up tables in the wings of the stage with four direct phone lines so they could relay the news of Alaska's accumulating wealth to the public as fast as the front page could be re-plated. We put out four special editions that day. The banner on the first led with the figure, "$200,000," across the top of the page. The amounts grew with each successive edition.

The oil lease sale yielded $900,220,590, the highest total ever realized in the United States. For Alaska, with an annual operating budget then averaging about $135 million, it meant a windfall of dizzying proportions.

The next day we carried a picture of the state's chartered 707 jet flying over the Chugach Mountains carrying the state's treasure-trove—the 20 per cent deposit required with bids—to deliver the checks to the banks they were drawn on as quickly as possible because "we'll be drawing $207,000 a day in interest and we can't afford to have delays." That plane flew direct to the airports closest to the banks on which the checks were drawn to avoid the delays inherent in having them go through bank clearing houses.

However, no one seemed willing to let that money sit in the bank. Alaskans came up with a variety of ideas on what to do with it. Some suggested it be split evenly among all Alaskans before hungering government officials got their hands on it. Others wanted a special legislative session called.

My newspaper adopted an editorial stance that we treat this bonanza as the last money we are going to get, not the first. We simply sold a right to look for oil in the ground, and that is not a recurring thing. It was a capital asset we sold and we should invest it, not live it up. We even urged the state to keep the money on deposit as a permanent fund.

Willie Hensley and other rising voices in the newly organized Alaska Federation of Natives argued that you can't save all your money when you have families in the villages living with leaking roofs and honeybucket waste systems. And, of course, their case was bolstered by the well-known fact that epidemics had been wiping out people in Alaska's primitive settlements with alarming frequency.

The decision landed in the lap of Governor Miller, who had moved into the chief executive's chair when Governor Hickel went to Washington, D.C., to be Secretary of the Interior in the Nixon administration in January 1969. Miller was a youthful homesteader from Talkeetna who was elected lieutenant governor as Wally Hickel's running mate. Miller had virtually no administrative experience.

Under Miller's regime the state's first fiscal policy on how to handle oil income took shape, probably more by default than decision: "When you get it, spend it." Everyone knew what the state should do, and everyone seemed to get Miller's ear on how to spend it but not how to save it.

Governor Miller allowed his political contemporaries and the state bureaucracy to fatten up the state payrolls with political pals. Under him the state budget was doubled in one year. The legislature, which was Democratic, stepped in and showed no hesitancy about increasing expenditures on every hand. The $900 million seemed to vanish almost with the suddenness that it arrived.

Our euphoria evaporated in the early 1970s. The state's windfall from the lease sales was gone and there was no revenue to replace it in the state treasury. Our state was left with its stables full of bureaucrats who required huge payrolls to support. Before enjoying royalty revenues, a trans-Alaska pipeline would have to be built to make the oil accessible for marketing. The oil companies were ready and willing to start immediately. The pipeline would be the biggest undertaking by private enterprise in the history of mankind. Authorities said that the other big projects in history, such as the pyramids and Solomon's Temple, were public works projects done by the rulling powers of that day, often using slave labor.

The state was in a bad fix. We felt that we were demonstrating the truth of the axiom that nothing is as endurable as a political entity. We created an endurable political monster when we expanded the agencies. Regardless of shrinkage in state income, the agencies weren't going to shrink.

Two new issues brought the pipeline construction project to a standstill. Alaska Natives initiated demands for settlement of aboriginal land claims against the federal government and national conservation groups seized upon the provisions of the newly enacted National Environmental Protection Act to challenge construction of the pipeline. Both groups tied up the project in the courts.

The issue of aboriginal rights to land originated when Alaska was purchased from Russia in 1867. However, the nagging problem did not come to a head until Alaska became a state in 1959. Congress gave Alaska the right to select 103 million acres but barred it from taking land to which Eskimos, Indians and Aleuts had historic claims. As soon as the state selected some land and started selling leases to oil companies, Natives complained to the federal government that the state was leasing out their land.

In 1966, Secretary of Interior Stewart Udall imposed a freeze on the transfer of federal lands to the state and barred it from further leasing until Native land claims were settled. That threw the entire state into turmoil. The state went to court to try to lift the freeze. Sen. Gruening called for a congressional hearing on a myriad of plans to pay off the Natives. My newspaper found it a hot issue to report, one of the most protracted issues and most complex for people to understand.

The Natives won amazing support nationwide from Indian support groups and others. There was reason to suspect that the Indian groups in Alaska were coached on their rights by bright Vista volunteers sent to Alaska during President Johnson's War on Poverty. The New York Times reflected a strong prevailing public attitude when it said editorially, "Legally and morally, the Eskimos, Indians, and Aleuts of Alaska can claim 90 percent of that state's land."

Subsequently, the Natives laid claim to 300,000 square miles of

Alaska, most of the useful land in the state not covered by glaciers or rugged mountains. Any reasonable person knew there was no way Natives could document such an outrageous claim.

Bills were given prolonged scrutiny in the committees of Congress. There were public hearings and amendments that slowed progress. The number of acres of land to be turned over to the Natives, and the provisions to safeguard its ownership by them, were constantly under fire and change. In the beginning it was proposed to allot four million acres to the Natives. This was raised to eight million and soon after Hickel became secretary of the Interior it was raised to forty million acres.

Land claim issues became emotional and divisive among Alaskans. There were those who felt the federal government held no liability toward the Natives. And there were others who took the opposite stand. My newspaper found the issues too complex in their historic and legal aspects. Lawyers schooled in legal interpretation disagreed in their views.

Since the Times had no legal expert in its establishment, I felt it had no leadership to offer in that area and suggested our editorials deal only with those issued we might understand. Generally, the Times favored enactment because whatever the federal government gave to the Natives in settlement would be good for the Natives and good for Alaska. We cheered when the figures were increased and lamented, with the Natives, when the figures were reduced during the legislative process.

When the newspaper discovered Congress had a provision in the bill to grant to the Natives almost $1 billion in cash and that half of that $1 billion would have to be paid by the State of Alaska from its oil royalties, the Times took exception, not to the settlement but to that provision. Never in history had a state been compelled to pay part of an aboriginal obligation owed by the federal government. Give them a billion if that's what is owed them but not one cent out of Alaska's pocket, we argued.

Some Natives interpreted that stand as opposition to enactment and said the newspaper was out to kill the land claims settlement. The more radical leaders were bitter. John Upickson of Barrow frequently called me from anywhere he was (he traveled a lot) at midnight or later to tell me in a very deep, slow voice, "Get off my land!" He would get me out of bed to hear that and kept repeating the message, over and over. I told him, "I'm not on your land, John. I bought and paid for it. Be reasonable, we're not working against you." He wouldn't listen. I told him, "Okay, I got your message. Anything more?" And I got more of the same thing—"get off my land." He knew how to get my goat.

Charles Edwardsen, a hard-drinking Eskimo hell-raiser from Barrow, used to publicly advocate violence to take back the land. My relationships with him were strained but strictly correct. We had many friends in common. We were partners in working for statehood. But he was too radical for me. Yet he frequently invited me to Barrow to be his guest on a

200 | CHAPTER FOURTEEN

whale hunt. I would have liked that experience but I wasn't at ease with him. In fact, I wasn't at ease any time I was within 10 feet of him.

One day during the period when emotions were running high on the land claims issue in Congress, I heard that Edwardsen had "a contract" out on me. I came across him demonstrating in town and I asked him if that was true.

"Sure, I got a contract out on you," Edwardsen replied.

I asked him why he invited me on a whale hunt and suggested, "Is it to get me out on the Arctic Ocean ice all alone with you?" He smiled and said, "It would be fun, wouldn't it?" To the credit of Willie Hensley and the other Natives pushing for an equitable settlement, they distanced themselves from the Edwardsen brand of recklessness.

In 1971, Congress, under pressure to clear a right of way for the pipeline, passed the Alaska Native Land Claims Settlement Act. It gave the Natives the right to select 44 million acres of land and a cash settlement of $962 million, the largest ever awarded to resolve aboriginal disputes. The law provided for deducting $500 million of it from Alaska oil royalty payments. That lifted the land freeze, but it did not settle the pipeline environmental issues..

By this time, 14 years after the Kenai Peninsula began producing oil, the national conservation organizations had "discovered gold" in Alaska. They found that frightening letters warning their members and supporters about the impending destruction of the Alaska wilderness, were their most lucrative tool in raising money and enlisting new members. No matter how ridiculous their claims might be, their warnings paid off big.

The new environmental protection legislation gave conservation groups a basis for opposing the idea of building a trans-Alaska pipeline that would enable production of the Prudhoe Bay oil. They made the battle of national significance. It is difficult to exaggerate the dread and sense of crisis that they created in the nation if the pipeline were built.

On Feb. 17, 1971, critical hearings on the proposed Trans-Alaska Pipeline opened in Washington under auspices of the Department of Interior. Not surprisingly, the big gun leading the opposition was former Interior Secretary Udall, now speaking as a member of the National Wilderness Society. He charged the Interior department's environmental impact assessment of the pipeline was flawed and that it seemed to have been conducted from the foregone conclusion that the pipeline must be built. He called for a new study in which "no one wears blinders."

While speakers carrying the banners of environmental groups had been expected, I was appalled by the number of oddballs——mad housewives, birdwatchers, crackpot scientists among them—from all over who came to Washington to testify against disturbing any part of the 800-mile route from Prudhoe Bay to Valdez. By the time some 100 witnesses had tracked their way before the microphone, the record was filled with predictions of dire events that could occur if the pipeline were built.

Consider a few of them:

—A large oil spill in the Arctic might result in the absorption of enough heat from the sun to initiate a melting of the polar ice cap, causing the sea level to rise so that coastal cities would be drowned," the consequences of which are too horrible to contemplate."

—Wilderness animals like caribou are dependent upon "the maintenance of climax or near climax conditions such as tundra biome. The destruction of this system and its balance would create serious conditions for the animals, possible extinction."

—The extremely loose character of Alaska soil and the frequency of earthquakes would make the pipeline susceptible to leaks and ruptures … the serious changes in the character of the country could gravely alter the pattern and populations of wildlife upon which many of the native Eskimos and Indians depend for food and shelter.

—Helicopters (monitoring the pipeline) would panic mountain sheep, making lambs very vulnerable.

Consider how these predictions of horror look at this writing, after the pipeline has been delivering oil to Valdez for 18 years:

—There has been no oil spill of any consequence along the Arctic pipeline. Leakage is probably less than you would find on the refueling platform of a military base.

—The pipeline is holding up very well on Alaska's loose and unpredictable permafrost soils. It is regarded as an engineering marvel and has become a tourist attraction,.

—Caribou populations have thrived and multiplied and are at record highs. Mountain sheep just keep munching when a helicopter passes.

—And Natives on the North Slope are enthusiastic backers of the oil rigs in their backyard. Oil has given them their first good-paying jobs and many a village's modern amenities are financed by property taxes on the oil companies.

The Anchorage Times refuted the claims of the conservation agencies repeatedly and constantly over the years. We had a long list of claims and fantasies that had already been disproved.

They said drilling on the Kenai Peninsula was destroying the moose. It didn't. The moose almost doubled in numbers.

They said the wilderness characteristics would be lost to mankind. They weren't. Canoe trails developed in the oil area opened the way for people to enjoy the great outdoors.

They said offshore drilling in Cook Inlet would destroy the salmon runs. It didn't. Since offshore oil production started the runs have set new records for size and commercial value.

202 | CHAPTER FOURTEEN

They said tidal currents and winter ice would destroy the platforms, causing oil spillage that would pollute Cook Inlet. Nothing like that has happened. Oil production has continued almost 40 years

We branded the Washington testimony of the conservationists as Chicken Little crying, "The sky is falling! This was the day for the preservationists," we said editorially. "They made the most of it in their own fanatical fashion which boils down to one thing—they don't want Alaska to have the right to develop its own resources ... The tragic part of all this is that Alaskans—if these national efforts are successful and the pipeline development is further delayed and delayed—are the ones who will pay the terrible price ... Alaskans will be driven to bankruptcy by people who live in their own ecological squalor elsewhere—who perhaps have never even seen the state in which we live."

For five long years pipeline construction was stymied while environmentalists and their lawyers argued against it. They told the court the pipeline, much of which would be above the frozen ground, would be a barrier that would stop the annual migrations of caribou herds and upset the lifestyles of Eskimos across the top of the world. They claimed excavations for the pipe would open the way for surface erosion which would destroy the fragile tundra. Even haul roads and work roads used in building it would permanently scar the virgin surface of the world's last great wilderness.

And, indeed, the pipeline was delayed. Those Interior department hearings were only a preliminary to a long congressional fight. And Alaskans did pay a heavy price. The cold language of court records reveals the dimension of bankruptcies, but the impact on humans, particularly small businessmen and budding entrepreneurs, can never be fully measured.

As a newspaper publisher I did business with virtually every business enterprise that had goods or service to market. Most of my business with them was on credit and when they were in trouble I knew that I was too. Consequently, I had first hand experience with many ramifications of the pipeline dilemma.

One of my long-standing customers with a solid gold credit record was an elderly man who made his fortune in his lumberyard. He was about to sell his yard and retire when the pipeline project loomed on the horizon. This man, well-known as a man of great integrity, was inspired by the opportunities he saw in the offing. He envisioned a great need for wooden cradles to hold the 48-inch pipe (which Japan was manufacturing). He invested his life savings in a state-of-the art plant to make 48-inch cradles. He planned it up so he could produce them faster and cheaper than any possible competitor.

The conservation agencies and their court injunctions did him in. He spent his last years watching his business go down the drain. For the first time, he had to sell his assets to pay for his expensive new machinery for which there was no customer.

Another sad story was that of a young man in his prime years who had built a healthy business selling and servicing sportsmen's boats and everything that goes with them. He had the vision to realize pipeline contractors operating in the remote wilderness would need small power generators for their installations across 800 miles of wilderness. He went Outside to line up franchises for the best lines of portable generators and other gear. He invested heavily to inventory generators, mortgaged everything he owned. He had hundreds of these generators sold and even delivered to contractors who were signing up contracts for pipeline construction.

The court injunctions forbidding pipeline work did him in. His customers who had bought the generators returned them because they couldn't pay for them. They shipped them back to his yards on International Airport Boulevard. The young man had no income to pay his bankers who financed him in buying the generators from the manufacturers. He was in deep trouble.

He came to me with a pitiful story. He owed me a big advertising bill because he was a big advertiser. He asked me to help him find a way to continue his daily advertising for his boat business while he worked out the problem with the generators. He needed to advertise to keep the Midnight Sun Boat Co. going.

I worked with him and we set up two separate accounts. One would be the current account for the ongoing boat business, which he would pay monthly and keep current. The other account was the old debt which he was to pay off whenever he could. I became his partner, of sorts, in this venture and found him a good partner. He did everything he said he would do and we both ended up healthy and happy. I had similar problems with other customers and resolved them with similar agreements.

I asked the boat company man what he did about his bankers who were hot after him. To my surprise he said they treated him much the same way I did—with two accounts, one to keep current and the other to pay off sometime. I think it is safe to say much of the entire Anchorage economy was affected by that pipeline litigation.

The oil companies also tried to help the contractors. They didn't want their subs going broke because of the lawsuits. They wanted them to be on the North Slope ready to go when the time came and so they advanced money on a scale I thought was extremely generous. To bail out a contractor, they were known to have purchased heavy equipment outright and held it as their own for the duration of the court action. Millions and millions of dollars of machinery and materials just sat in open fields for as long as five years, as did the pipe itself which was shipped to Valdez from steel mills in Japan.

Neither oil company pressure on Congress nor a letup in the environmental campaign cleared the way for the pipeline. Help came from a

204 | CHAPTER FOURTEEN

surprising place—from Persia, just about the opposite side of the earth. The Arab oil moguls, unintentionally and unwittingly, came to the assistance of Alaska by ordering an embargo in 1973 that halted oil shipments to the United States, purportedly in retaliation for U.S. support of Israel. King Saud turned off the valves and shut off the flow of crude oil to the United States.

Shortages hit the refineries almost immediately. The supply of gasoline was cut down to a trickle. There was general consternation among motorists who depended upon their cars for their livelihoods. Newspapers and TV shows had pictures of long lines of cars awaiting service at gas stations. The public, well-known to be short on patience, was soon demanding that Congress do something about the nation's over dependence on foreign oil supplies.

Congress suddenly moved at a crisis pace. Quick action came on a bill that lifted the pipeline construction issue out of the courts and, indeed, forbid the courts from butting in on it.

In the process, Alaskans were amused by the jockeying of its two U.S. senators whose rivalry sometimes bordered on contempt. Ted Stevens, the Republican, was then an abrasive young lawyer. Mike Gravel, the Democrat, was a maverick always looking for one-upmanship. Both senators backed a bill authored by Sen. Henry Jackson which stated that the Department of Interior was in compliance with EPA requirements and was free to award the permit to build.

Apparently without consulting Jackson, Gravel managed to tack on an amendment closing the door on the possibility, or perhaps I should say the probability, of further court challenges and consequent delays by the conservation groups. Stevens is said to have exploded, contending that it would alienate enough votes to wreck the bill's chances of passage. And it nearly did. The Senate voted 49-49 and only a tie-breaking vote by Vice President Spiro Agnew saved it. Gravel's end run grates Stevens to this day.

The next three years—1974-77—were in many ways, as hectic and uncomfortable as the war years when Alaska was an active front. Every facility in Alaska, whether public or private, was overloaded with demands to produce or accommodate more than it was designed for. There was an influx of thousands of workmen in search of jobs. The project had 25,000 on its payrolls at the peak. To maintain that level it was necessary to maintain a flow of more thousands to replace dropouts.

The state's infrastructure was sufficient to support a normal population of perhaps 100,000 but not the needs of the biggest construction project ever undertaken by private enterprise. The $9 billion project equaled defense construction in this state during and after World War II. Several books have been written about this engineering feat and its impact on Valdez and Fairbanks, the key supply centers along the route. A separate book could have been written on what happened in Anchorage.

Anchorage was the headquarters city for the oil companies in Alaska and the impact of the huge project was felt throughout the city although the center of action for pipeline construction was Valdez, about 125 miles east of Anchorage.

About 15,000 people arrived in Anchorage during 1974-75. Many came looking for opportunity to start life over and cash in on our booming frontier. Prices for homes tripled and quadrupled. Finding a house or apartment for rent was about as difficult as finding gold nuggets on Fourth Avenue.

Construction contracts called for workers to live in company camps along the route of the pipeline, far from the amenities of urban lifestyles. The project was divided into five divisions each with a general contractor who had subcontractors under him.

The financial burden was so huge no one bank could handle it. A string of the nation's biggest banks became involved. Before they would participate they required guarantees from the oil companies that construction would be completed by a certain date and the flow of oil would begin immediately, thus assuring revenue to meet the loan obligations.

In order to guarantee the completion date, the oil companies needed a "no strike" clause in their contract with the Alaska Teamsters Union which would control most of the workers. And to get that from the tough-minded Jesse Carr, the teamster boss, was not easy. Oil officials told me they got the "no strike" clause in a contract providing the prevailing wages in the trade, but the working conditions ran the total cost sky high.

Contractors worked their crews around the clock, two 12-hour shifts seven days a week. The first 40 hours were at the regular hourly scale, and all the rest was at overtime rates. Consequently, some fantastic earnings by workmen became the talk of the day. There were electricians who made up to $4,000 a week and maybe more. Unskilled workers came back from a stretch on the pipeline with a nest egg that would put them through college. But they worked hard for the money, in temperatures often more than 60 degrees below zero with the chill factor perhaps 90 below in a land where winter had no sunshine.

Faced with sudden new wealth, Alaska again debated how best to use it. Again it pitted the savers against the spenders. By this time the people recognized their legislature as a part of the problem and not necessarily helpful in the solution. The quick disappearance of that first $900 million from the oil lease sales had not been forgotten. Alaskans had become well acquainted with the wisdom of economic leaders and literary axioms, such as Parkinson's law: Spending increases commensurate with the supply of money to spend. The deprecating remarks and joking about politics and politicians led to a public search for a way to keep public funds out of the hands of the legislature. This led to plans for a fund set aside from oil revenues that could be spent only by a vote of the people.

206 | CHAPTER FOURTEEN

Fortunately, we reached a crucial decision in the calm before the oil money began to flow. In 1976, voters approved an amendment to the state constitution establishing the Permanent Fund. This mandated that the state deposit 25 percent of the oil royalties in a fund for the sole purpose of "income producing investments."

Gov. Jay Hammond and legislative leaders backed the measure. In light of the free-for-all to grab the money that occurred later, I often wonder whether such a consensus could have been possible had the oil money actually been within reach of their fingers at the time.

Subsequent legislation in 1980 created the Permanent Fund Corporation to manage the money as a savings account with the provision that only the earnings, not the principal, can be distributed. The fund has grown to $15 billion at this writing and to the astonishment of many Outsiders, it sends dividend checks of more than $900 each year to every Alaskan who has lived here for at least a year.

I believe that is the last battle the savers won since the oil money gusher began. The state did try to search for guidelines on how to spend its oil riches but only came up with costly but worthless reports.

At the price of $160,000, the Brookings Institution of Washington, D.C., staged a series of seminars here in 1969 involving 115 leading Alaskans to search for an appropriate fiscal policy for our new era. I participated but soon found that those great brains from the liberal establishment in Washington had one theme in mind—resist development and keep the environment clean. The framers of our excellent constitution set forth something more than that for Alaska.

Next, the executive branch financed its own think tank, hiring Stanford Research Institute of Menlo Park, Calif., at a $179,000 fee. Their economists traveled the state and concluded we ought to spend the money on industrial development, transportation and community development.

Both economic reports ended up in the dust bins in Juneau. Instead, governor and legislators simply went on a pork barrel spending frenzy. Oil prices quadrupled between 1979 and 1982, thanks to the Iranian revolution and OPEC production restraints. The $700 million a year in oil revenues that had been anticipated when Prudhoe oil first began to flow now surged into the billions, hitting a high of more than $4 billion by 1982.

The state had more money than it ever imagined. Even after funding bloated budgets, there was plenty extra to divvy up. Lobbyists swarmed into Juneau, not only from the private sector but also from municipalities and school districts. State and local government employees hired their own people to work the legislature for a share of the largesse.

"Legislators acted like drunken sailors, guzzling everything in sight," is the way one historian records this era. Editorials urging restraint made no impact. If a legislator tried to balk at the spending, someone else would sweep up the money he tried to save. These were the years that we lost sight of economic realities and we did not really sober up until the mid-1980s when the price of oil went down as suddenly as it came up and someone began to notice that production at Prudhoe would soon start declining.

Governor Hammond reigned in Juneau during the eight years—1976-84—when someone should have applied the brakes. He was a charming fellow, a Hollywood version of an Alaskan—bush pilot, hunting guide, wolf trapper, fisherman. He had lived in a log cabin and chopped wood. But I always suspected he didn't know what an In and Out basket was because that is the way he ran the state.

Hammond had been a mediocre legislator who used to sit in the background and write poetry. Bill Tobin, the Anchorage Times editor and columnist, would pick up his poetry and witty remarks and run them in his column. That brought Hammond notoriety around the state. He was also one of the legislators who opposed the pipeline and favored the overland route to Canada, which would have put the pipeline right across the Arctic National Wildlife Refuge (ANWR), the wilderness area that the federal government today is trying to protect.

Glamorous as he was, he was no leader. When the oil money spending frenzy started, he was helplessly swept up in the tide and even made a deal with legislators for an equal share of the bounty to finance his own boondoggle projects. The botched $100,000,000 agricultural plan to make Alaska the dairy state and bread basket of the far north is one of his legacies.

The remarkable thing about this period of unsustainable spending is that no real villains stand out. Every region seemed to get a piece of the action. The Institute for Social and Economic Research at the UAA estimates that through 1990, the state took in $33.2 billion in oil revenues since oil started flowing out of Prudhoe. They did spend $27 billion of that, but surprisingly $6.2 billion had been saved. Perhaps more surprising, no single public figure who had a hand in the spending pocketed enough for himself to invite a criminal investigation.

Pipeline construction just north of Livengood about 12 miles. Photo by Steve McClutcheon/Alaska Pictorial Service

Laying trans Alaska Oil pipe line between Glenn Allen and Valdez. Photo by Steve McClutcheon/Alaska Pictorial Service

Construction of the Trans Alaska Oil Pipeline went on winter summer. Photo by Steve McClutcheon/Alaska Pictorial Service

210 | CHAPTER FOURTEEN

Early day Prudhoe Bay drilling rig – this wildcat turned into a production well.

Little "Patti" could drive any of the heavy equipment in the Pipeline Camps: Mostly she operated a variety of types and sizes of fork lifts. Photo by Steve McClutcheon/Alaska Pictorial Service/Sept. 29, 1974

CHAPTER FOURTEEN

Valdez Tanker Terminal site – only some brushing or site clearance had begun. Insert: Oil terminal for Prudhoe Bay crude at Valdez. PhotoS by Steve McClutcheon/Alaska Pictorial Service

FILTHY RICH | 213

Pipeline construction just north of Livengood about 12 miles. Photo by Steve McClutcheon/Alaska Pictorial Service

Drilling in the Prudhoe Bay Oil Fields – Permafrost and Tundra Company. Photo by Steve McClutcheon/Alaska Pictorial Service

— CHAPTER FIFTEEN —

Capital Move

Alaskans distinguished themselves as first class American citizens as soon as President Eisenhower proclaimed statehood in 1959. They did what so many U.S. senators, who opposed statehood, had told them they didn't have the know-how to do. They created a new state government en toto, and they did it surprisingly fast.

This is remarkable because Alaskans had lived so long as "political eunuchs" under rule from Washington, D.C. They had never learned the art of consensus. Their politics had become divisive and unruly, motivated essentially by sectional interests.

But the responsibilities that came with statehood seemed to give Alaskans a spiritual lift, a desire to pull together in the common interest of building a new state. For the first time they felt the pride of being fullfledged Americans. No longer would they be called second class citizens because they had no vote for president or had no voting representation in Congress. They were liberated from the bondage of insensitive "carpetbag bureaucrats" sent by distant Washington, D.C., to manage Alaska's precious resources.

Under territorial status, Alaskans supplied leaders only for such public jobs as city mayor and councilmen and the good people who ran their tiny communities. Now Alaska could elect its own governor and legislators, select and appoint its own judges and staff its state agencies with true Alaskans, chosen by Alaskans and responsible to Alaskans.

The legislature set the pace for transition. In the space of 85 days, it enacted bills providing for the creation and operation of the three branches of government, every department and virtually every agency that would run the new state. And it did so with a minimum of argument.

This monumental achievement had been made easier by the fact that the state constitution had been written five years before and had been under study since. But not all circumstances made it easy. Health problems put Bill Egan, the first elected governor, into a hospital in Seattle and deprived the new state of his services when they were needed most.

The state, in effect, staged a bloodless revolution, throwing out the defunct territorial regime and replacing it with one of the nation's most modern state governments. Just about all old institutions were terminated.

CAPTIAL MOVE | 215

Congress did help by drafting the Alaska Statehood Act so as to provide a soft landing for the newborn state. It appropriated $20 million as seed money for the state treasury, sparing Alaska financial problems before its revenue machinery could start generating.

Congress also provided that the court system and law enforcement under the U.S. Justice Department would continue until the new state courts could take over. Federal statutes remained in force until the state legislature enacted new state laws.

However, while Alaskans did so well in agreeing on basic principles for building their new state government, one vexing problem threatened swift transition. They found it impossible to agree on the location of the state capital.

Finding a permanent site for the capital is an issue that has haunted Alaska ever since it became a U.S. territory. When Alaska was purchased from Russia in 1867, the capital was in Sitka. The Russians had moved it there from Kodiak to keep it in the mainstream of travel and central to their activities. The U.S. Congress, not desirous of spending money, left the capital at Sitka.

Many apocryphal stories circulate about the next development, but this much is certain: In 1880, two boozing prospectors—Joe Juneau and Richard Harris—discovered gold in Gold Creek on the Gastineau Channel in Alaska's panhandle. This discovery attracted hundreds of adventurous gold seekers. As claims were staked over a wide area, a townsite was laid out and the 1890 census reported a population of 3,211. This new town became Juneau.

Enterprising miners and businessmen who moved in were enthusiastic boosters for their new community. They passed the hat and secretly sent a representative to Washington to urge Congress to move the capital to Juneau. This new mining town was on the mainstream of steamship traffic while Sitka was too remote, inaccessible and inconvenient, Congress was told.

Juneau tried to keep its capital-grabbing ambitions secret so that no other community might become a competitor. Therefore, members of Congress heard only the Juneau story and tended to agree. Only when they asked for the views of the incumbent territorial governor, John G. Brady, did they get an earful of objections.

Brady was firmly established in Sitka, had his friends there and was comfortable in his quarters and lifestyle. He protested the move, arguing that Juneau, built on a hillside at the edge of an ocean channel, had no decent building for the capital nor did it have the land to build one.

At the same time, the record shows some in Congress developed reservations about the move. They envisioned that development, now stirring in the southeast, was only a dribble of what was yet to come and that in future years greater development would be in western Alaska, and the permanent capital should be there.

In the end, Congress thought it found a way to please everyone. In 1900, it enacted a law declaring Juneau to be the temporary capital and added a provision that the move from Sitka would await the day when Juneau had adequate quarters for it.

Under that provision, Governor Brady simply kept the capital in Sitka. However, those enterprising Juneau business interests organized a concerted campaign to prevent Brady's reappointment.

In 1906, they managed to oust Brady and replace him with their own man, Wilford B. Hoggatt, a nonentity whose biggest qualification seemed to be that he owned a gold mine in Juneau. "My first official act will be to move the capital to Juneau even if I have to pay the rent myself," Hoggatt vowed.

Historians say Hoggatt quietly rented two rooms in the Juneau court building, one for himself and the other for his secretary, and declared, "Now the capital is in Juneau."

His sitting in Juneau may have satisfied his backers at that time but the satisfaction didn't reach far beyond the city limits. The congressional designation of Juneau as the "temporary" site left the capital location a lively issue among western Alaska communities as they grew. Through the years there had been proposals at one time or another for moving it to almost every city of note west of Yakutat, but Alaskans never had the power to move it. As long as their land was a territory, they were subject to federal rule.

Some looked to the Alaska Constitutional Convention in 1955 to address the lingering discontent. However, recognizing the potential for paralysis, the convention sidestepped the capital location issue by applying the art of imprecision. A clause was inserted designating Juneau to be the capital, but the clause was inserted into the list of "transitional" measures whose stated purpose was to assure a smooth transition from territorial to state government.

That action ended a debate that had the makings of a major disaster. Keeping Alaskans in the same room to draft a good constitution was the main goal, and it wasn't always easy. When the capital designation was included as a transitional measure, both sides claimed victory. Juneau was to keep the capital while Alaskans in other areas believed they could move it if and when they wished.

By the time of statehood in 1959, the Anchorage Times had become the major daily newspaper in Alaska. Oil had been struck in Cook Inlet and tremendous growth for mainland communities on the railbelt was in all forecasts for Alaska. I pondered, privately at first, whether the time had come for the paper to be doing something about resolving permanent status for Alaska's capital.

Residents of western Alaska certainly were talking a good case. Juneau was too isolated from the mass of the population. Eighty-five per cent of Alaskans lived between Fairbanks and the Kenai Peninsula while only 15 per cent lived in southeastern Alaska where Juneau was sequestered.

In western Alaska, the main communities were accessible by roads. In the panhandle, no roads connected to the mainland, and only the foolhardy would consider forging a highway across the mountainous terrain. Travel was mostly by boat. Aircraft were useful in good weather but there was so much fog that it was said pilots flew only at low tide so as to have three feet more ceiling.

The issue became the subject of an intense in-house debate at the Anchorage Times. It happened that I recently had hired a new executive editor, the late Bob Kederick. He came to us from the news staff of the Juneau Empire, imbued with what I called the "Juneau syndrome." Kederick had all of the arguments for not moving the capital.

Up to now I had no special emotional attachment to the idea, but I played the role of the devil's advocate to draw Kederick out. He also drew me out, and each of us kept digging for facts to bolster our positions.

I pointed out to him that the capital city in any state is a state facility and must serve all the people. Thirty-five U.S. states had moved their capitals, many of them several times, before finding a satisfactory permanent location, usually near the midpoint of the state. Throughout history, the common reason for moving the capital was to make it more accessible to the mass of the people.

A glance at the map of the Lower 48 will show that most state capitals are near the center of the state and equally accessible to all citizens. Juneau is the opposite. It is far from the people and costly in time and money to reach by land, sea or air.

Surrounded by glaciers, mountains, and fjords, Juneau is so isolated, I argued, that neither state executives nor legislators can keep in touch with what their constituents want. And think of the money the state wastes in paying the costs of tickets and travel time for its administrators to go back and forth across the Gulf of Alaska. For example, the Alaska Road Commission had headquarters in Juneau yet the nearest road under its jurisdiction was 500 or more miles away. School officials, also headquartered in Juneau, had to travel those same 500 miles across the gulf before reaching most of the schools they administered.

I knew first hand that travel to Juneau by air was hazardous and also unnecessarily costly. Anchorage was the collection point for travelers to Juneau from interior cities and villages. When planes left Anchorage for Juneau, passengers rarely knew for sure where they might land. The civil air route stretched along the 500-mile coast of the Gulf of Alaska, a stormy harborless coastline that was mostly wilderness. It was occupied by more glaciers than people, including one glacier that was larger than the state of Rhode Island.

The prevailing weather was rain and fog. The planes let down in the area of Icy Straits, near Glacier Bay National Park. Directed by radar, they had to find their way down among the jagged peaks of the mile-high or higher mountains and, if they made the proper turns at the proper time, they could land on the Juneau runway on the shore of Gastineau Channel.

They say a commercial airline pilot who had flown in and out of Juneau for years, always on instruments, approached the area on a clear day when visibility was unlimited. He saw, for the first time, the hazardous mountain peaks. He was so frightened that when he ended his flight in Seattle he put in for transfer to another route and swore he would never fly into Juneau again. (His fear was, perhaps, prophetic. Years later in 1971, the worst airplane accident in Alaska's history occurred on the approach to Juneau. An Alaska Airlines 727 hit a mountain and all 111 passengers and crew were killed.)

The common practice was for planes to make one or two attempts to land at Juneau and if conditions were bad, to fly on to the nearest alternate field. Passengers destined for Juneau were put up in hotels or dormitories and invited to fly back free the next day. If the airport was still closed, they would be taken to Anchorage—two days lost and still at the beginning.

Juneau's annual precipitation was often cited in feet, not inches. Low-lying clouds were frequent. Ocean-going ships sounded their fog horns and reduced speed while cautiously guessing their distance from land by counting the seconds in time lag before hearing the echo of their fog horns bouncing off the mountain sides.

My arguments began to convince me, but none swayed Kederick. He insisted that Alaskans would suffer more by moving the capital. It would hurt the businesses and homeowners in Juneau. It would be too costly to build facilities at a new location and, rather than moving, the state would do better by spending its money improving the present capital city.

After weeks of such discussions, we reached no agreement, but Kederick did concede that a capital move was a proper subject for public discussion and the Anchorage Times should use its editorial pages to start a dialog.

My first editorial opened the subject gently. It ran on March 16, 1959, just 82 days after Alaska became a state. It noted that the Russians had put the capital in Sitka and that Congress had moved it to Juneau on a temporary basis at the behest of Juneau businessmen. Now, for the first time, Alaskans had gained the right to select the location of their state capital.

Instead of taking a stand, the editorial essentially reviewed the many times over the years that Alaskans had talked about moving the capital only to be rebuffed by their guardians in Washington. "Now Alaskans can move if they really want to," I wrote. "If the state makes a study, it might point up substantial reasons for a move.

When that editorial hit Juneau, the response was immediate, violent and personal. The Juneau Empire made me out to be a greedy, selfish editor and publisher who sought to kill Juneau for the aggrandizement of Anchorage.

Little did I realize at that time that this was the opening of a Battle of Ink between the Times and the Empire and that the battle would go on for decades and lead to three statewide votes on moving the capital, including one in which the voters gave strong approval only to have their wishes thwarted by the scheming politicians in Juneau.

At first it was a lonely battle. Neither major political party wanted to become involved. Politicians in office opted for the status quo. Only people acting out of plain citizen zeal took up the cause. They made capital relocation a genuine populist movement.

Dr. Merritt P. Starr, a physician with a private practice in Anchorage, organized the first committee to support the move. He shared leadership of the cause with Morris G. Reese, owner of a grocery Neither of the men had been in the public eye as leaders, except possibly in the efforts to win statehood for Alaska.

Starr was a new personality in public affairs. He led a quiet life in Anchorage as a well-respected physician. He was born and reared in Illinois, the son of a well-to-do family prominent in Winnetka, a suburb of Chicago. He and his wife had a small circle of friends in Anchorage and enjoyed an orderly social life.

Reese was a hard-working small town grocer whose hobby was writing letters to the editor making brief, pithy one-line comments on the affairs of the day. He was delighted to have the title of co-chairman of the Capital Information Committee.

They enlisted outlying civic leaders, Kenai attorney James K. Fisher and Clarence Bailey of Palmer among them, to join the effort. With limited funds, most coming out of their own pockets, they set out to spread the message and urge residents to support a ballot petition.

Meanwhile, city council in Juneau countered by appropriating $50,000 to fight the move. That financed a campaign of fright, the favorite themes being that moving the capital would leave Juneau a ghost town, homes would be valueless and jobs would be exported to enrich the greedy merchants of Anchorage.

Our editorial urged that a study be made compiling the pros and cons for the public to use in making a good decision. Two weeks later the House approved a legislative council study of "the best location for the Alaska state capital." Rep. John , D-Anchorage, tried to calm the uproar in Juneau, saying it was unfair to Juneau to keep talking about moving but never making a decision and he expected a study would show a move to be too expensive, thus helpful to Juneau.

Rep. Earl Hillstrand, D-Anchorage, chaired the Capital Relocation Steering Committee to solicit signatures to put the question to a vote. A referendum would go on the ballot of Aug. 10, 1960, provided Hillstrand's committee could file petitions carrying 5,034 signatures, representing 10 percent of the voters in the preceding election.

The initiative proposal provided for moving the capital by Jan. 1, 1965. The governor would appoint a committee to select the new capital site somewhere in the Cook Inlet-Railbelt area. That was described variously as anywhere between Seward and Kodiak on the South and Fairbanks on the North.

While Hillstrand's committee circulated petitions, Juneau Mayor Larry Parker frantically tried to pump vigor into the anti-move fight. He announced plans to expand the city by annexing surrounding land areas and extending Juneau across both sides of Gastineau Channel. He also promised to extend the antiquated airport runway and seek a huge hydroelectric power development.

Public interest continued to build up. With Bob Kederick, our Juneau transplant now firmly on my side, we alternated writing editorials down the stretch almost daily in support of the capital movers. We tried to keep our tone on the high plane. On June 1 the lead editorial in the Anchorage Times listed some of the reasons in support of relocation. The editorial gave new grist to the mills of the proponents by simply recalling the main items mentioned in all the past years.

"Alaska learned as a territory that federal officials 5,000 miles away in Washington could not administer the affairs of the territory. History shows that Russian officials 7,000 miles away from Alaska learned the same thing. They were equally ineffective as administrators.

"By perpetuating Juneau as the capital city, Alaskans would be maintaining one of the costly barriers to good government about which they have complained for many years."

The ranks of those talking relocation were bolstered July 11 when the Times noted that Sen. Seaborne Buckalew, D-Anchorage, had taken a stand in favor of moving the capital somewhere in the area of Palmer, Wasilla or Talkeetna so as to be more accessible to the greatest number of people.

Buckalew, a lawyer, was a long-standing Democratic activist. He had been a delegate to the state constitutional convention and eventually became a state court judge, serving until his retirement. He had a big following among Democrats.

Another Democratic leader, Sen. Irene Ryan, an Anchorage civil engineer and later one of the designers of the Anchorage International Airport, announced she favored a move and noted she was fifteenth among Alaskans to sign the petition asking for a referendum vote.

In these months of feverish activities by both sides, someone tossed into the ring a report that the military was contemplating the abandonment of Whittier, a complete port with its own city as a support center on Prince William Sound. This upset the best schemes of many schemers.

If the Army quit Whittier, what would become of the fine docks and waterfront facilities? Under private ownership they could be fierce competitors to the Seward and Anchorage docks. If ownership reverted to the state, fine high-rise buildings linked by underground tunnels and heated by steam from a central power plant would provide a bonanza of excellent housing and office space. Juneau property owners would stand to lose the state as their virtual captive customer. So many Alaskans started pumping life into the idea that maybe Whittier was the ready-made solution to finding a site for a permanent capital.

However, Lt. Gov. Hugh Wade, a fierce Juneau supporter, took no great stock in these panaceas. He spent his time scrutinizing every signature on the initiative petitions, hoping he could find a basis for throwing them out. He also hounded the state attorney general for legal opinions as another possible way to block a vote.

But all of Wade's efforts to sabotage the referendum failed. The signatures were genuine. The signers were duly registered. And the attorney general told the lieutenant governor that he had no authority to ask further questions.

Excitement, however, is always at hand in Alaska, even in the dull process of collecting signatures. Filing them in Juneau turned into a breathtaking experience.

The deadline for submitting the required 5,034 signatures was the opening day of the 1960 legislature in January. It just happened that on the weekend before the Monday opening a low-lying fog set in over the fjords around Juneau and halted air transportation entirely and slowed down or stopped ocean travel.

Legislators trying to get to Juneau for the new session found themselves stranded in various southeastern Alaska towns. Their planes had to overfly Juneau because the airport was closed. The fog put the lid on travel for an unprecedented five-day period. This became big news everywhere because of the broad public interest in relocation. The fog seemed to be backing up the statements of the pro-movers—that Juneau really is too inaccessible.

During that fog "black-out" hundreds of federal and state employees went without regular pay. Their checks were issued from Juneau and held up in the backlog of mail that couldn't move. Among the payless

Anchorage Daily Times pushed hard to move the State Capital from Juneau to the Anchorage area. Photo by Steve McClutcheon/Alaska Pictorial Service

were employees of the Bureau of Land Management, Bureau of Indian Affairs and the weather bureau, three of the larger federal agencies in Alaska.

As the opening day for the new legislature approached and there was no sign of the fog lifting, Governor Egan cajoled the U.S. Coast Guard to send a cutter to the various towns along the fjords and pick up about 17 stranded legislators.

The cutter returned to Juneau carrying a larger load than expected. It also bailed out many important state figures who had been attending a Democratic convention in Ketchikan and were forced by the fog to "hang around" there for four days after it was over. Among them were Sen. William Beltz, president of the Senate, Rep. Russ Meekins of Anchorage, Rep. Harold Hanson of Cordova, James Hurley of Palmer, Rep. Grant Pearson of McKinley Park, William Erwin of Seward, and Hillstrand, chairman of the committee leading the effort for a new capital.

The cutter also brought back Bill Tobin who was then chief of the Associated Press bureau in Juneau. He had been in Ketchikan to cover the Democratic convention.

Of course the tales from these travelers about the hours and hours they sat in airplanes circling Juneau before going to an alternate field were heard over and over for many days. However, distress of the Democrats seemed to have been somewhat tempered by the privilege they had of being with Hubert Humphrey, their favorite candidate for the Democratic nomination for the next president, and his wife. They, too, were stranded for four days with nothing to do in Ketchikan. Some of them claimed Humphrey never stopped talking the entire time.

In Anchorage, the committee workers who had worked so tirelessly gathering signatures for the referendum petition were frantic because the fog prevented them from delivery to Juneau on deadline, the opening day of the new session. They didn't trust the mails and wanted to hand deliver them to the lieutenant governor.

When it appeared that the fog was going to endure another weekend, they had to resort to the mails. Because they had postmarks to show they were mailed before the deadline, they met the test. The election would go on as scheduled in August, but not before Alaska would go through seven months of one of its most tortuous, divisive battles in history.

— CHAPTER SIXTEEN —

Battle Heats Up

Relocation of the state capital by this time had taken on a life of its own. Alaskans everywhere were aware of it, and most of them were forming opinions that would be the basis for their polarizing into groups pro, con or don't care.

Feelings expressed by the people gave the impression that this time, unlike other times in Alaska history, something was going to be done about it. The only need was for a leader and an organization to give it direction.

I was amazed at what grew out of that tame editorial I wrote early in 1959. I had just intended to remind Alaskans that statehood had given them one more benefit—the power to move the capital out of Juneau if they wished. Instead of opening a dialog, that informative piece ignited a furious battle.

Dr. Starr and his volunteers, operating without funds, found themselves heading up a spirited group, anxious to push its cause. The cause took on character and permanence as it was dignified by the addition of more and more prominent personalities.

Juneau had a citizens committee called Alaskans United. It raised money to wage a costly, statewide campaign against relocation. The Juneau city council appropriated $50,000 to give to the committee as a starter. That was big money in the 1960s (the equivalent of $257,000 in 1995 dollars) and threw a fright into the ranks of those favoring relocation. How do we fight city hall?

Some four months before the referendum election, Juneau made a quick change in strategy. Until that moment the leaders, and virtually all their constituents, had opposed holding the vote. Now they switched to support it, contending that it is best for Juneau to let the vote take place.

In other words, "if you can't beat 'em, join 'em." Leaders of Alaskans United realized that the vote would be held, whether they liked it or not. Therefore, they said they would encourage a big voter turnout and wage a vigorous statewide campaign to have the proposition voted down.

The new strategy marked a big change for Alaskans United, but for few others. Individual Alaskans continued their barrage of letters to the editor in which they sounded off as they pleased, most of them favoring a move. The Capital Information Committee continued releasing statements in favor.

In Juneau, they put together teams of volunteers who would be willing to travel to other towns and make speeches against the move. In Anchorage, it was said that Alaskans United held training sessions for the speakers, emphasizing emotional aspects that would stir the sympathy of their listeners.

Skullduggery was suspected in July when Lloyd Ahvakana, an Eskimo captain in the Alaska National Guard, astonished Alaskans with a report on anti-move activities. He said that Cyrus Peck, secretary of the Alaska Native Brotherhood, had told him he had gotten money to travel to every Brotherhood camp throughout Alaska to urge members to vote "no" in the referendum in August. And he believed the money came from the people in Juneau.

A howl of protest arose from the pro-move activist groups. Even though Peck denied that he had said any such thing, the report persisted and was exaggerated as it was passed from mouth to mouth, with embellishment and colorful opinions added as it went.

A new twist was introduced when Jack Ryan, newspaperman with the Fairbanks News-Miner, announced his candidacy for Republican nomination for Congress and took a stand opposed to moving the capital. Ryan had a substantial background in opposition from his experiences in Fairbanks and with the Anchorage News before he moved to Fairbanks. He went on the hustings with his anti-Anchorage pitch against relocation but he failed to win the GOP nomination.

Heading into the election of Aug. 9, 1960, the referendum on capital relocation was dominating political discussions. Alaskans gave more attention to the issue of moving the capital than they did to the candidates who were campaigning for their votes. Emotions were running high. Arguments were heated. The issue became the hottest on the public agenda.

My newspaper gave much space to relocation. Besides editorials favoring it, the news columns carried reports on civic, social and neighborhood meetings that talked about it. We reported what people said about it, both for and against.

The Anchorage Times must have been the only medium in Alaska that made a conscious and deliberate effort to print both sides of the arguments. For one thing, we thought that was good journalism and for another, we thought it good for our circulation. We wanted our readers to depend on us for the whole story and not feel it necessary to read any other newspaper, especially the News.

The Times was credited (or blamed) for starting it all. It was forthright in its all-out editorial support and it was generous in allocating news space for reports on meetings, quoting individuals and even printing letters to the editor both for and against.

In Juneau, of course, the Times was seen as a monster and was constantly accused of slanting the news, something we never deliberately did and strived to avoid.

226 | CHAPTER SIXTEEN

Inevitably, the Battle of the Ink grew nasty. The Juneau crowd dropped its biggest bombshell when the Juneau Empire reported it would cost the state a minimum of $50,000,000 to move the capital. That struck the nerve center of every voter.

"A big lie!" we responded editorially, and we likened Juneau's campaign to the campaign of lies used by Hitler.

And they were lies. We found that $50 million cost estimate was contrived by including such nebulous items as "loss of operating efficiency during the period of transition, $2,500,000; a new jet airport, $10,000,000; cost of moving household effects of state personnel having to move from Juneau, $700,000."

We knew that words of outrage were not enough to rebut this lie. Fortunately, Dr. Starr and his committee reponded brilliantly. They managed to gather enough donations to bring in a world authority on how to select sites for state capitals.

He was Donald J. Belcher, an internationally known engineer who was famous as the key man in finding the site for Brasilia, the new capital of Brazil inaugurated in April 1960. He addressed Alaskans in many cities. He was interviewed on television talk shows. His message was that there was no justification for keeping the state capital isolated in Juneau.

He said Juneau's estimate that relocation would cost $50 million or more was out of line, and that the cost would be offset by the appreciation in the value of land surrounding the new city.

It wouldn't have to "cost a cent," he said. It was his belief that the sale of state lands around the capital "would be an aggressive economic weapon. It would bring people and money here from all over the world."

Belcher further debunked the Juneau claim that it would cost $50 million or more. 'That would be half of the cost of Brasilia, a national capital," he said. "Brasilia had no railroad, no water system, and the nearest road—a dirt one—was 26 miles away. They built a lake, a jet-age airport and a 150-mile extension of the Brazilian highway system. They also built extremely fancy and expensive buildings. And to top it off, Brasilia was built for a population of 500,000." In 1960 Alaska's total population was not yet half that.

Belcher said development of Alaska would be accelerated by relocating the seat of government.

The Anchorage News remained on the sidelines and didn't seem to know how to handle the relocation issue. It rarely agreed with the Times on any subject— be it roads, airport, statehood, aviation or whatnot. In July of 1960, with the election scheduled for Aug. 9, the News jumped into the melee with an editorial questioning the constitutionality of using the initiative and referendum procedure for moving the capital. It expressed the view that the capital location could not be changed except by constitutional amendment. That was an old argument that had been thoroughly debated and discarded long before.

A week later the News carried an editorial taking a forthright stand against a move. The gist of it was that everything was fine in Juneau and it would be needless waste to move to a new site where so much would have to be duplicated. The News obviously expected the relocation issue to simply "go away." The editorial summed it up like this: "A TV speaker in favor of the move described the matter as a 'problem.' He was inventing phrases. No problem exists. There will be plenty of them, however, if we vote to move the capital to a new location."

On July 14, Rep. Hillstrand suggested that Southeast Alaska should choose which it wanted—the capital at Juneau or a state ferry system serving the towns along fjords of the Panhandle.

He noted that legislators representing the Panhandle had proposed a $15 million state bond issue to construct a ferry system. He contended that the 15 percent of Alaskans who lived in the Panhandle shouldn't expect the 85 percent in the rest of Alaska to subsidize both the ferry system and keeping the capital in Juneau.

The long days and short nights of summer gave Alaskans plenty of time to talk and debate. Relocation was a household word. It was heard over the back fences, on playgrounds as well as in the fancy halls of formal social occasions. Everybody with an idea got into the act. That included almost every Alaskan, young and old. Even comedians, including Rep. Bob McComb, a legislator from a tiny town named Chicken deep in the wilderness near the Canadian border.

The Associated Press carried a story quoting him as saying if the voters decide to move it, "Chicken is where it should come to roost. There is plenty of space; they would not feel so cooped up."

Heinie Snider of Wasilla launched his own campaign for relocation by offering to sell "50 or more acres" of his land to the state for $1 to use as a capital site. He described the land as "one-quarter of a mile from Wasilla and the Alaska Railroad station, on the Big Lake-Talkeena-Fairbanks-McKinley Route."

In a letter to the editor that was published in the Anchorage Times Snider said this "unsurveyed land is one mile long and contains from 50 to 60 acres, joining the airstrip 10-acres previously donated to the territory by the undersigned."

The Alaska Junior Chamber of Commerce provided the platform for the first Juneau speaker in Anchorage. Bob Boochever, prominent as a practicing lawyer, later a Justice in the Alaska Supreme Court and more recently a judge in the U.S. Ninth Circuit Court of Appeals, was the volunteer from Juneau. He appeared in debate with Rep. Hillstrand.

The Juneau speakers gave emotional appeals predicting the ruination of their hometown and discombobulation of hundreds and perhaps thousands of families, many of whom stood to lose their lifetime savings because of the inevitable devaluation of Juneau real estate and more particularly, the individual family homes.

228 | CHAPTER SIXTEEN

This story, with variations, was repeated over and over in many cities and villages as the Juneauites pursued their campaign to kill the move. Even though there was no factual basis to support their claims their pitiful story impressed many. Nobody desires to hurt a neighbor as they said the move would. Besides emotions, the opponents repeated their claims that the idea of moving the capital was based on the greedy, selfish aspirations of Anchorage businessmen.

These claims were denied constantly by proponents who explained many times that the capital move was not an "overnight" deal. They said capitals serve their states for generations and are not built overnight. The Alaska capital could be moved gradually, so as to minimize the economic or social impacts on Juneau residents.

Newspapers ran hundreds of letters to the editor giving the views of men, women and youngsters in all walks of life and every corner of Alaska. Headlines on the stories of the day described the debates as "boiling."

A survey of candidates late in July showed a majority of those in the Anchorage area were in favor of the move. The Anchorage Times found that of 24 candidates running, 17 were in favor, one was against, one gave "no comment" and one "don't care." The other four said it was for the voters to decide, not the candidates.

Excitement ran higher and higher as election day approached. Just two days before the vote Steve McCutcheon, chairman of the Southcentral Democratic Committee, tossed a new bombshell into the melee by suggesting that Ladd Air Force Base at Fairbanks be acquired as the new capital site. He said the Air Force wanted to deactivate it and the state might well purchase it for $1.

McCutcheon noted that Ladd Field is accessible by air, highway and railroad. "There is a jet-length concrete runway with ample foul weather landing aids," and buildings and infrastructure "more than we could expect to get in a new capital, or old, in 50 years."

McCutcheon was a man of stature among Alaska Democrats. His father served in the legislature as did Steve's brother, Stanley. Steve also was a former legislator and delegate to the constitutional convention, making him one of the state's founding fathers.

McCutcheon's suggestion was too late in the campaign to get much attention. The Air Force turned Ladd Field over to the Army, which operated it for many years as Fort Wainwright.

Joseph Nissler, a Fairbanks businessman, said he was starting a committee to move the state capital to Hawaii. "As long as people want to move it, let's make the move worthwhile," he said.

On election day almost 40,000 voters went to the polls. The referendum lost statewide by 5,107 votes.

In Anchorage it prevailed with a five-to-one vote in favor. But in Southeastern Alaska voters were 30 to 1 opposed. Fairbanks showed

4,445 against and 1,936 for. Northwest Alaska, including Nome and Interior villages, voted 770 against and 273 for.

Celebrations were in order in Juneau where the leaders thought the monster had been killed and buried for good. In Anchorage, however, there was no such feeling. Dr. Starr said the election was so close that he would continue his committee and initiate another vote.

The Associated Press summed up the campaign by describing it as the bitterest in the state's history. It crossed party lines, broke up neighborhoods and strained friendships.

Official announcements from the governor and other high officials urged the people to end the debate and relax now that the election was over and the people had made their decision. Ten days after the plea for harmony, state officials stirred up a new rumpus by calling for bids on $194,000 in contracts to update the worn-out elevated system, replace old electric wiring and fix up the boilers. It brought an immediate response from Western Alaska that the action debunked the Juneau claims, before the election, that it would cost nothing to keep the capital in Juneau, that the buildings there were in good shape.

The Anchorage News carried an editorial suggesting that now the election is over it is time to launch a study of the pros and cons of relocation.

Juneau city officials planned municipal improvements now that they were sure their city would remain the capital. They announced plans for new buildings, highway improvements and such. One developer talked about building a new residential area. Others talked about annexation to make the townsite bigger.

But in Anchorage, the capital move was still very much alive. Election returns showed strong support for the move, the way the pro-movers interpreted them. The opposition was strong only in areas where the Anchorage Times had few readers, they said. Therefore, if we can get another referendum, all we have to do is convince half of those 5,107 voters to switch.

"And that ought to be easy because those voters were deprived of the arguments favoring a move," they said. The next campaign would get the story to more places, especially Fairbanks.

The Anchorage Times reported these interpretations and told of the plans to initiate another referendum.

Bob Kederick wrote in his column that a lady called him to ask how long it would take to bring about another vote. "I told her I didn't know, exactly," he wrote, "but I was reasonably certain it would take at least a half an hour, long enough for a couple of cups of coffee and another look at the favorable returns from Southcentral Alaska. Maybe it would take only 20 minutes, I suggested."

Throughout Alaska the war of words continued. Rep. Bruce Kendall, R-Anchorage, said the election returns were a "mandate" to the state to take action. He explained, "When the most populated areas of the state—Anchorage, the Matanuska Valley, Chugiak and the Kenai Peninsula—vote five to one to move the capital, they (Juneau) must realize they can't tell them to forget about it."

The Ketchikan Daily News suggested dividing the state in two. So did the Sitka newspaper. That was an old idea that had been suggested many times in history. In 1923 it found its way into a bill in the legislature and drew a tie vote in the House. This time it didn't draw at all outside of Ketchikan.

By Nov. 2 the Capital Information Committee unveiled its new petition, which was drafted in cooperation with the Fairbanks Capital Building committee. The new petition sought to eliminate Anchorage from the debate by providing the new capital could not be within 30 miles of either Fairbanks or Anchorage. It was hoped this would cut out the possibility of Alaskans United making the big city the whipping boy.

The initiative, if enacted, would provide for the governor to appoint a commission to select three potential capital sites, each with at least eight sections of state-owned land, and the people would select one of the three by vote in the November 1964 election and the actual transfer could start by June 1, 1968.

October 1960 was a mighty busy month on many fronts. The filing of the documents for the new initiative triggered reactions on every hand. In Western Alaska, civic and political groups were quick to announce their support. State and civic officials in Juneau were equally quick to deplore the action. Of course, there was a general response of "Ho, hum, here we go again," among those who didn't care.

The Times naturally welcomed the new attempt and we took the opportunity to document the hypocrisy of our Juneau opponents by citing a couple of state actions as new proof of proponents' claims that relocation was essential for efficient and effective state government.

One was a decision to move headquarters of the Alaska Civil Defense agency from Juneau to Fairbanks. Governor Egan, an anti-move stalwart, said the agency would be moved to the railbelt area "where the major portion of the state population is located." The Times applauded the move, saying, "Recent Civil Defense practice alerts were badly messed up for lack of communication and coordination. In Anchorage, qualified volunteer workers resigned in disgust for failure of the state program to provide adequate leadership and coordination."

Egan again made himself the target for comment by announcing he was opening an office in Anchorage "so he can be closer to the people." The Times commented that "by opposing the plan to bring the state capital closer to the people, the governor seeks to deprive the rest of the state government the close contact he seeks for himself.'

Public debates and arguments continued through the winter and by spring several new factors were tossed into the ring to heat it up further.

The legislature became entangled in arguments for and against a bill to authorize the state to enter long-term leases for office space in privately owned buildings in Juneau.

Then came word that private developers were contemplating a high rise office building on Douglas Island, across the channel from Juneau for lack of a suitable site in the capital city. Federal builders were planning a $13,130,000 office building and already $1 million had been obligated to purchase land—the highest price ever paid on a building site anywhere in Alaska.

Sectional arguments grew sharper as more and more Alaskans became polarized in their views. Western Alaskans were prone to interpret actions taken in Juneau as inferior to those that could have been taken if the capital were closer to the people. The almost universal support for relocation among Western Alaskans brought bitter emotional responses from Juneauites.

In February 1962, the issue was taken to the Superior Court in an effort to deny it a place on the ballot. The suit had 23 Juneau plaintiffs, including 12 legislators. Judge James von der Heydt, who later became a federal district judge, granted the injunction and the case went on appeal to the State Supreme Court. It was pending there for four months, during which time Alaskans generally bad-mouthed each other.

Carl Berato, a retired Anchorage jeweler, made himself a hero in the eyes of his neighbors by offering to give the state 100 acres of cleared land between Wasilla and Big Lake if the state would build the capital on it.

On Aug. 16, 1962, the Supreme Court upheld the legality of moving the capital by the initiative and referendum process. It was a split decision with Chief Justice Buell A. Nesbett of Anchorage, and Justice John H. Dimond of Juneau supporting it, and the third justice, Harry O. Arend of Fairbanks, opposed.

That decision ordered the vote to be on the ballot in the November general election. Reactions to the court's ruling followed sectional lines, the same as the pro and con arguments. Rep. William Sanders, a Republican legislator and practicing attorney in Anchorage, said the majority "interprets the constitution fairly and accurately," and, he added, the opinion shows "extreme courage on the part of the majority because they are well aware of the possibility of repercussions."

He was right about the repercussions. Justice Dimond and his family paid dearly for having ruled in favor of the referendum procedure. It was said that he was virtually ostracized by his social groups in Juneau. His children were tormented at school as other youngsters looked on them with derision because of what their dad had done. Mrs. Dimond, too, suffered along with the family.

Justice Dimond was the son of Anthony J. Dimond, one of the greats among Alaska's public servants. The elder Dimond, originally a gold miner in the Valdez area, became a lawyer, served in the legislature and

232 | CHAPTER SIXTEEN

was Alaska's delegate to Congress from 1933-44 and U.S. District Court judge based in Anchorage from 1945-52. He was beloved in Alaska and his son, John, had the attributes of a distinguished successor in public service. But the repercussion from the relocation decision did him in. John Dimond's health failed. He resigned as justice in 1971 and ended his life in quiet seclusion.

Ostracism in varying degrees of severity was noticed by many Anchorage residents who had occasion to visit Juneau. Legislators from Anchorage reported that they were frequently left sitting in a restaurant with no food, served only after others had been served. In bars, they were the last customers to be served. They found themselves at the bottom of the list when apartments were in short supply.

With the election set for Nov. 6, the battle lines drew tighter and emotions were aroused. The relocation issue brought out the worst aspects of Alaskans' sectional bias. Political parties were under strain as their members split. Families felt the same strain, as did neighborhoods and entire communities.

The Times featured a story on how Texas swapped 3,000,000 acres of vacant land to a contractor to pay him for building the state capitol at Austin which, the governor's office said, was the only "structure of such magnitude, beauty and type that had ever been built with like dispatch, economy and cooperation of those in charge."

Alaskans took up the cudgels to do the same thing in their state, where they were rich in land but poor in dollars. Opponents, however, took dimmer views. The Ketchikan News, upon hearing that a contractor had made an offer to do an Alaska capitol, said it would be scandalous and likened it to Teapot Dome with no further explanation.

Rep. Ron Rettig, R-Anchorage, a public accountant, came out with figures showing how the new capital could be financed from the sale of land around the new city. These facts and figures were used by speakers who were available to civic group meetings upon invitation.

In Juneau, Alaskans United proposed a one-mill tax on property within the city to raise a fund for financing the campaign to keep the capital in Juneau. They also suggested an equal voluntary payment by property owners in Douglas and the Juneau School District, and that all non-property owners should contribute the equivalent to two hours pay.

By Oct. 1 it was obvious that the people of the state were lined up for a vigorous campaign to win votes in the November election. Alaskans United had a big treasury to finance sending their speakers far and wide. The Anchorage committee had no such support and depended on money-raisers held in homes of volunteer workers.

H. M. Pentecost, who had recently quit his job as state planning director after six years of service, described Juneau as "Kind of a lost Colony of Atlantis—an almost unreal city shrouded in the mists and reached only after an uncertain journey."

Juneau speakers were repeating what Western Alaskans had dubbed their "Big Lie"—placing the cost of the new capital anywhere between $150 million and $350 million.

Alaska Methodist University students who were assigned the negative side in a school debate on relocation found themselves so hard-put to dig up facts to support keeping Juneau as the capital, that they argued having so many people close to the legislators would bother the lawmakers. Their side lost.

And, it seemed, every time Alaskans got wound up in their intramural battle, the fog moved in on Juneau, stopping transportation and providing a new topic to talk about. It happened again in 1962 just in time to jeopardize the annual Alaska Day ceremony commemorating the transfer of Alaska ownership from Russia to America in 1867.

The Army always led these ceremonies and in 1962 the band was stuck in Juneau, the color guard was stranded in Whitehorse and three generals were somewhere among the fjords trying to get to Sitka. In other years, the Coast Guard had moved the personnel through the fog by ship, but this year it had no ship available.

The Anchorage chapter of the American Society of Professional Engineers debunked a report issued by the Juneau chapter saying that the move would cost $262 million.

Robert N. Hoffman, local president, said that his chapter declined to agree that the Juneau document was an "objective, unemotional" study and suggested 12 additional factors that should have been considered.

A New York bond house became involved. It was quoted as agreeing with Juneau leaders that the capital issue would ruin the credit of the state government. And, at the behest of Western Alaska cities, subsequently said it was "tricked" into saying that.

Each incident incited activist Alaskans to come up with comments, raising the temperature of everybody concerned.

Election day was Nov. 6 and a new thunderbolt hit on the first day of the new month. The Federal Aviation agency in Washington, D.C., held a hearing on Juneau's problems with air service. Juneau city leaders were embarrassed to discover that they were riding horses in opposite directions. In Washington they were saying that flying is so difficult between Juneau and Fairbanks that the capital city needs the small planes of Wien Airlines on that route instead of the jets of Pan American. To prove their case witnesses from Juneau and high officials of the airline testified about the difficulties of travel in that area.

These statements, of course, didn't conform with the story they were telling in Alaska—that Juneau is totally accessible and airplane landings are on schedule 98 percent of the time.

Twenty-four of the 28 candidates on the ballot in the November election were on record as favoring relocation. The pro-movers were optimistic that they were going to win this time.

234 | CHAPTER SIXTEEN

On election day, the proposition failed by 2,443 votes, about half as many as in the first election. Voters of the Panhandle, which includes Juneau, were 19 to 1 against the move. Voters in Anchorage were four to 1 in favor.

Once again, an election and a decision at the polls did not kill the idea of moving the capital away from Juneau. Alaskans remained divided and immediately started talking about the "next time."

Only 20 days after the election, Senator Gruening, former territorial governor and dedicated supporter of Juneau, presented his ideas on what should be done to retain the capital in Juneau.

His pitch was to make the city more attractive but his prescription, given in a speech before the Chamber of Commerce, listed one item of beautification and three items of politics.

Gruening devoted much of his speech to blaming Bob Atwood for conceiving the idea of moving the capital, promoting it and perpetuating it. His remedy, to "keep the capital in Juneau forever" was to

1. Unify the area into one political entity to end what he called "micro-sectionalism."

2. Change state law so as to prevent the use of the Initiative and Referendum clause so often or by requiring more signatures on the petition.

3. Close the garbage dump at the "front door" of the city, in Gastineau channel where the cruise ships arrive.

4. Get more subscribers to help the Juneau Empire and the Anchorage Daily News, the two newspapers opposed to relocation.

As a longtime friend and supporter of Greuning, I was disappointed and hurt. But not deterred. That narrow defeat convinced me that the next battle could be won. The capital move issue shifted to the back burner for a few years but it was never far from my mind. I felt sure we could win with the next effort.

236 | CHAPTER SIXTEEN

— CHAPTER SEVENTEEN —

Victory Without Reward

The way Alaska civic leaders regrouped and rallied after that second setback to move the capital said much about the new vitality energizing the state as we moved into the mid-1960s. Plans for a new campaign and a third referendum vote were announced almost immediately. Public confidence was high and a new capital was foremost among the dramatic improvements many envisioned for Alaska because a brilliant future loomed on the horizon.

Oil in commercial quantities discovered in 1957 on the Kenai Peninsula had triggered the nation's biggest rush for oil leases. Most of the major oil companies as well as many independents sent geological expeditions and leasing agents in a spare-no-expense race to position themselves in the Alaska oil boom that now looked inevitable.

Alaskans, used to a boom or bust economy, were excited by the prospect of new wealth flowing into their treasury on a stable basis. Swanson River wells on the Kenai Peninsula started production in 1960 and in the next five years three more fields had been discovered nearby in the land under the waters of Cook Inlet.

The influx of oil and construction workers made business hum. In Anchorage and all along the railbelt from Seward to Fairbanks the impact of the oil excitement was felt first hand. Alaskans were finding Texas oil-men upbeat and friendly neighbors, casually insensitive to our so-called hardships——the distance away from their roots, the harsh climate, the risk of bear encounters, and other horrors usually highlighted by Outside reporters. They came to develop an oil industry in Alaska and nothing seemed to deter them.

We described arriving Texans as "instant Alaskans" because of their demeanor and attitude. When they would return to Alaska after a visit "back home in Texas" they regaled Alaskans with reports on "what I told them about how big my Alaska is compared to their tiny state." They started the Alaska-Texas rivalry that continues even today.

This was an exciting period in other parts of the world, too. The U-2 spy plane was shot down over Soviet Russia. The Soviets launched the world's first satellite, Sputnik. A U.S. submarine made an underwater launch of a Polaris missile. John Kennedy was elected president and announced America would land a man on the moon in "this decade." U.S. troops on a training mission in Vietnam had been ordered to shoot back if they were fired upon.

These world events affected the military in Alaska. We were all concerned when two Soviet reconnaissance bombers flew over Alaska in 1963, causing the U.S. to file a formal protest to Russia.

Relocation of the capital took a back seat for public attention during these years of oil excitement and escalation of the Cold War. It was in March 1969 that Sen. Vance Phillips, R-Anchorage, rekindled the issue by filing a bill that would move the capital to the Big Lake/Wasilla area. It was greeted with a noisy din in Juneau, but the rest of Alaska was still not quite ready to push the issue.

To its credit, Juneau tried hard in this interim to improve its image. They cleaned up the Gastineau dump and organized civic committees to make the city more attractive. However, they stopped short of implementing an important change that Gruening had urged to blunt further attempts to dislodge the capital. In the summer of 1969, after Sen. Phillips revived the move issue, Juneau voters went to the polls and defeated unification with the adjoining city of Douglas. This was a setback to shoring up Juneau's defenses since passage would have quieted claims that the capital city had no place to expand. (The merger did occur in 1970.)

On June 7, 1969, Anchorage Times editor Bill Tobin publicly noted a continual buildup of interest in moving the capital. In his weekly column, "Saturday Sundry," he wrote, "Soon it seems certain we will be swept up once more in conflict not yet settled in a movement twice put down but never conquered. The flags are up, the fever spreading and the cry of 'Move the Capital' is heard across the land … the tide now runs strongly in another direction. The pull is west of Yakutat, wherever that may be, as the population swells along the railbelt and the oil gushes from the sands beneath the North Slope permafrost."

He was right. For the next five years Alaskans were to go though a new series of capital move battles. The issue would flare anew despite the considerable anxieties in those early 1970s. Alaskans worried that the trans-Alaska oil pipeline might never be built because environmental groups declared it so hazardous. The oil wealth that was to propel the renaissance of Alaska was not coming as quickly as we anticipated.

Alaska, a baby state, was in the anomalous position of having ownership to the largest oil field in North America, but without that 800-mile pipeline to Prudhoe Bay, it could not sell a barrel of it. Environmental groups blocked construction for five years under court injunction. Only after the Arab oil embargo created gas lines across the nation did Congress enact a bill allowing the pipeline project to proceed. Even so, it barely passed the Senate where Vice President Agnew had to step forth and cast the tie-breaking vote in 1973. (Just in time, because Agnew left office in disgrace soon after for accepting bribes while governor of Maryland.)

As Tobin noted, a string of events constantly added tinder to the fire simmering since the last capital move vote. For example, in August 1970, the state held a routine land sale at Palmer that brought it $614,200 for 65 lots that the state appraised as worth only $225,970.

Such a return set the mathematicians to work calculating the value of wilderness land around the site of a new capital in any of the several places in western Alaska where the state was a big landowner. Projections from that Palmer area sale gave credence to the argument espoused by capital movers that the revenue from those perimeter real estate sales could largely offset the cost of building a new capital.

Then, on Sept. 8, 1971, a tragic accident dramatized anew the perils of traveling to Juneau. Alaskans were appalled when an Alaska Airlines transport plane en route from Anchorage crashed into the mountains while approaching the Juneau airport, killing all 111 on board.

Most of the dead had friends and relatives throughout the state. It was as though a pall of grief had befallen us. Naturally, there was a feeling of guilt for turning down past plans for moving the capital. Few of the victims would have been on that plane had they not had reasons to go to the capital. The common reason was state business.

The inaccessibility of Juneau became a factor again in February 1972 when the Juneau airport was closed by weather and travel patterns were again upset. A foot of snow fell over the same weekend that Alaska Airlines planned ceremonies to mark its debut as the sole air carrier on the state's busiest air route serving Anchorage, Juneau and Seattle. Most of the legislators who were to participate were stuck in Anchorage. Sen. Ted Stevens, the main speaker, was on a flight that overflew Juneau because of the storm and landed in Anchorage, 500 miles away. Newspaper reporters had a great day writing about it.

An initiative to renew the relocation battle was successfully proposed in 1971 but never appeared on the ballot. Two years later, identical bills to move the capital were introduced in both houses, specifying that the seat of government be located somewhere between Fairbanks and Seward.

It was clear that public sentiment for another election test was growing, but a serious third campaign did not coalesce until Frank Harris stepped in early in1974. An Anchorage business owner, Harris had been a legislator and later became chairman of the Southcentral Republican Committee. He was quick to see that if another relocation election was to be staged, he was the logical one to be the leader. He resigned from his Republican Party job and went into the new job with enthusiasm and lots of know-how.

Harris had many things going for him. An unnamed company offered to build the new capitol building and take payment in the form of land ownership. That was a mighty enticing offer in a state that owned land galore but had little money. The offer was the subject of discussion throughout Alaska. We pointed out that Texas paid for its capitol with land.

City planners and local architects started to become involved. They injected new considerations, such as what kind of a city to build in the wilderness. They expounded upon the advantages and disadvantages of the lineal city, the radial city and the vector city. As Alaskans talked to each other, those words became commonplace in local conversations.

As usual, we had typical Alaskan distractions. Capital move fever inspired Albro Gregory to put his oar in. He was editor of the Nome Nugget and had his office 500 miles away on the Bering Sea, opposite Siberia. He found it lonesome out there and difficult to keep Nome tuned in on modern developments. So he suggested Nome as a possible capital city.

He said that Nome would be an excellent capital because it is so remote that the legislators on the job would not be harassed by constituents. He said lawmakers could take their time and do a lot of thinking about good laws. And they could put their feet on the desk without being seen, and they could even blow off steam in the local bars without repercussions.

He won noisy support from those who wanted to send the legislators to Nome to get rid of them.

Sensing the public pulse, more legislators began to show interest in the controversy. Debates on the floor of both houses broke out frequently. They watched with interest as Harris and his committee planned a two-step referendum schedule that, if successful, would provide for an orderly transition to a new capital site by 1980.

The next vote would be held in 1974, but would not pose a direct question. Instead, it would ask the voters to authorize the governor to name a commission to select three potential sites suitable for a new capital city, each to include at least 100 square miles of state-owned land, not closer than 30 miles from Anchorage or Fairbanks, near the highway system, the Alaska Railroad and capable of having an airport for 24-hour air service. After the three sites were selected, there would be a vote in 1976 on a constitutional amendment that would designate the winning site.

Meanwhile, Juneau leaders were busy planning new strategy to thwart the move. Sen. Bill Ray, D-Juneau, their point man, said he would push through the legislature a law providing $100 million dollars in reparations for residents who could prove they suffered an economic loss if the capital were moved. To pay the reparations, he suggested a $25 per capita tax on all Alaskans to create a fund to be paid out by a three-member board.

To the delight of many, Rep. Hillstrand countered by introducing a bill to pay reparations to the people of Sitka for economic losses from the removal of the capital from Sitka in 1906.

Voting on the next referendum was scheduled for August 1974. Suddenly, the legislature decided it ought to provide facts to guide the

240 | CHAPTER SEVENTEEN

public. It appropriated $100,000 to fund an independent study to determine if it was a feasible project economically for the state to undertake. Governor Egan promptly contracted with a Seattle firm, the consulting division of Boeing Computer Services, to do the job.

While Boeing did its study, the Alaska Division of Land revealed that there were more than 20 parcels of land that met the requirements of the referendum. Maps were distributed widely showing 100-square-mile blocks of vacant land owned by the state and located between Anchorage and Fairbanks.

The Boeing report was originally scheduled to be released at a press conference in Anchorage but that plan was mysteriously canceled. No reason was given to the public. This action was like waving a red flag indicating the possibility of hanky-panky among the political hierarchy at Juneau, which was known to be solidly opposed to relocation.

Rumors spread that the report concluded it would cost more to keep the capital in Juneau than to move it and the political bosses were trying to cover that up. Further, rumors had it that a move would involve only five and one-half square miles, or 3,500 acres, for the government complex and the rest of the 100-square miles could be sold for private development. There would be no need to move more than a mere minimum number of employees and few, if any, judicial workers.

With the Aug. 27 election barely three weeks away, we unleashed a series of editorials denouncing the delay in releasing the report as a "coverup" and blaming Egan, whom I long respected. One editorial on Aug. 6 was titled "Dirty Tricks in Juneau." These events came close on the heels of the Nixon Watergate scandals, so everyone was aware of coverups.

As details of the report leaked out, there were added accusations of tampering. This time Rep. Tom Fink, R-Anchorage, speaker of the House of Representatives (and later mayor of Anchorage), hurled charges of dishonesty. Legislators called for public hearings on the Boeing report. Egan denied he was covering it up. He said all he wanted was an orderly presentation of the report so it would have a good understanding.

After 11 days of speculation, accusations and denials, the Capital Relocation Committee acquired a copy of the report and reproduced it. The committee had 5,000 copies printed, 3,000 for distribution in Anchorage and 2,000 for Fairbanks. The Anchorage Times published much of its contents as news matter, including charts and graphs.

Following unauthorized publication of the report by the Committee, the Boeing study was finally presented to Alaskans by an official team of Boeing engineers. They traveled from town to town holding press conferences and fielding questions. They had a difficult time explaining the delay in making the report public. After all, they were just hired hands from Seattle sent here to do a job and they found themselves involved in the enigma of Alaska politics, which was not a part of the job description.

VICTORY WITHOUT REWARD | 241

A significant finding in the report noted that if the capital remained in Juneau, a new city would have to be built in the area of Mendenhall Glacier, 10 miles from downtown Juneau to accommodate the growing population.

Just a week before the election, we featured page 79 of the report, which we deemed the most significant. It read: "... the cost of keeping the state government in Juneau through 1990 will be $225.9 million and the cost of a new capital city in the area of Wasilla, Palmer or Anchorage can be as low as $109.7 million." It also stated that by 1986 the state will have a surplus in the treasury of $3.8 billion if the capital is left at Juneau, and $3.75 billion if it is moved, and then added the comment, "There is little hardship to be found in such figures."

By election day, Aug. 27, 1974, voters had to decide in an environment of suspicion and distrust. The suspicions and rumors overshadowed the natural emotional concerns of many who once hesitated to vote for the move for fear it would hurt their neighbors and friends in Juneau. This time, they voted to relocate and construct the capital by a convincing margin of 46,659 for and 35,683 against

This was a landmark moment in the state's history, the first time the people agreed that they wanted the capital somewhere other than Juneau. It was a triumph for those volunteer civic workers who made it their cause, some of them working on the issue ever since 1959 when Alaska became a state.

It was also a vindication of the vision of Congress when at the turn of the century it debated moving the capital to Juneau and decreed it should be only a temporary home because the future would be in the west. Western Alaska did become the enter of commerce and population and it was only natural to relocate the capital there.

Celebrations were everywhere. Our editorials spoke of "Great Days Ahead," citing the exciting events yet to come with the planning of the new city, its construction and finally its occupation. Alaska would have the newest capital city in the nation and perhaps the last one to be built in American history.

The rejoicing was short-lived. That November, Jay Hammond was elected governor. He was probably the worst thing that could have happened at that time. Hammond was adamantly opposed to relocation and it was up to him to pick the Capital Site Planning Committee, which would propose the three new sites. He promptly packed it with members known to be opposed to any relocation.

One appointee, Bill Corbus of Juneau, commented on a TV program that serving on that commission was like being assigned to "plan your own funeral."

The governor gave the chairmanship to Willie Hensley, an Eskimo who shot into prominence as a leader during the lobbying efforts preceding the Native Land Claims settlement five years before. He was consistently opposed to moving the capital, arguing that the money to be derived from oil production should be used to rehabilitate the primitive bush villages where his people lived rather than building new state edifices.

As chairman, Hensley pledged to be impartial, whatever that might mean. But his committee had a bad start. He immediately was deadlocked with the legislature over funding of his group. He sought $1.5 million but the legislative leaders said $250,000.

Exasperated by the delays and the continuous political posturing, my newspaper commented editorially that any barefoot boy of reasonable intelligence could pick a townsite, or even three sites from western Alaska's wide open spaces, as the committee is directed to do. We urged the committee to get on with the selection of land instead of dreaming of big money and magnificent schemes for spending it.

Hammond's subtle attempt at sabotage was hard enough to take, but a series of unbelievable events was still to come. Juneau asked the legislature to appropriate $195 million to indemnify the property owners. Our editorials pointed out that they were asking for more than the assessed value of their entire town, which was $185.9 million.

Frightening the public with the specter of tremendous costs to move the capital worked before, and now Juneau hired DeVries Associates of Wrightville Beach, N. C., to come up with new schemes to fan those fears. The staggering demand for indemnifying Juneau residents would be but the first.

On Dec. 6, 1975, the Capital Site Selection Committee finished its job and proposed three sites, as mandated: 1. Willow south. 2. Larson Lake. 3. Mount Yenlo. Voters would pick the winning site in the general election the next November.

In the months leading up to that election, Juneau unleased a variety of diversionary tactics. No sane discussion of capital relocation costs at either of the three sites was possible. The Juneau crowd went overboard in trying to confuse the issue. They claimed taxpayers would be faced with huge bond issues which they calculated by lumping private and public cost sectors together, making it impossible to break down just what a move to either site would cost the taxpayer. We denounced these "scare tactics" editorially, but fair play was not in Juneau's itinerary before, now, or later.

On Nov. 2, 1976, voters chose Willow as the new site by a strong majority of 56,219 votes. Larson Lake came in second with 33,170 and Mount Yenlo received 16,169. Construction fever and land speculation spread like wildfire across the Mat-Su Valley.

It was up to the legislature convening in 1977 to provide for planning and construction of the new capital. By now, oil revenues were pouring into the state treasury and Alaska had a golden opportunity, plus the means, to invest in a capital complex that could be the pride of the nation.

As the legislature went to work, a series of hearings were held ostensibly to receive public input on building the new capital city in Willow. The people testifying in Anchorage had a unified message. "Get the move on," they urged. However, as the legislative session moved towards its final days, it became clear legislators were heeding a different message, one orchestrated by those committed to sabotage the will of the people.

Juneau legislators pushed through a law requiring the Capital Site Planning Commission to design and estimate costs for building a new capital city of 30,000 population. This was six times the population of Juneau and obviously much larger than the state would need.

"The weird process of lawmaking reached a new low," we stated in an editorial May 24. "The objective, of course, is to develop outrageous cost figures to bamboozle Alaskans."

The prevailing political situation was, indeed, peculiar. The people of the state thought they had made the decision to move the capital and assumed their feet were firmly implanted on the road to relocation. But the political establishment, in both the legislative and executive departments, were still adamantly opposed. Regardless of the vote of the people, they were out to prevent a move.

Juneau political powers heeded the advice of their hired gun, the DeVries group, and succeeded in an effective way to come up with a scheme to run the estimates for new capital construction so sky high that no Alaskan would support it.

When move supporters cried "foul," the Juneau crowd brazenly turned for help to their friendly state attorney general, Av Gross. Yes, he ruled, the statute set forth that it must provide for a population of 30,000. When move supporters asked for an opinion on the legality of reducing the population figure to 5,000 or even 10,000, the attorney general ruled against it, basing his opinion on "the consensus of the attorneys in the Attorney General's office." That is worthy of a place in a Gilbert & Sullivan comic opera.

Somehow those Juneau politicians made that ruling stick and the capital planning proceeded from there on an outrageous course. With 23 of the nation's major specialist consultants under contract, the commission submitted a plan reeking with extravagance. A state bond issue of $966 million was proposed to pay for the construction of 2,200,000 square feet of office space to be occupied by 8,700 state workers. The existing capital complex at Juneau had only 500,000 square feet of offices and 2,700 employees.

To complicate the picture further, perhaps as the final nail in the coffin of Alaskans' hope for a new capital, the legislature passed a special law requiring voter approval of "all bondable costs" before any money could be spent on building. The attorney general immediately interpreted that to include all private as well as public construction.

Thus it came about that Alaskans, if they wanted their new capital city, would have to build it several times bigger than needed, and also be compelled to admit public liability for the cost of private building as well as for public agencies.

Nobody of good conscience could vote for a deal like that. Even we could not support it. The Juneau schemers had the project as dead as a doornail even before the election on Nov. 7,1978. The $966 million bond issue was defeated, 88,783 to 31,491. The companion requirement for a voter approval of all bondable costs passed 69,414 to 55,253.

And again, in 1982, voters once more were given a poor choice and were compelled to vote against a $2.84 billion bond issue to build the new city. This time the vote was 102,083 to 91,249.

Even after these disenchanting experiences, Alaskans showed no diminution of enthusiasm for moving the capital. They had shown at the polls that a majority wanted the move, yet the powers that be in Juneau manipulated and schemed successfully to thwart the will of the people.

These untoward experiences are sometimes cited as demonstrating the need for a move. Political leaders meet for official sessions sequestered at the foot of a steep mountain slope in a deep fjord at least 500 miles away from the mass of their constituents and, in their isolation, they lose touch with the real world they represent.

There have been proposals in almost every new legislative session, but they haven't gone forward. In 1994, Rep. Pat Carney, D-Wasilla, won enactment of a bill to move the capital to his hometown. It lost at the polls, 91,915 against and 80,623 for.

The issue seems to have a long life into the future. Will the state capital ever be moved away from Juneau? The facts give overwhelming support to the rationale that it will. Past experiences have told us repeatedly that the issue can be brushed aside by politicians but it never goes away.

The benefits that would accrue to Alaskans would be numerous and immediate. But there are trends in present day developments that could mitigate against a move. Modern day communications have made a big difference from early years. Juneau has come a long way in trying to become a part of Alaska instead of an extension of Seattle. Eliminating the time zone differences between Southeastern and Southwestern Alaska was a giant step.

The biggest obstacle to be overcome, however, has not been touched through the years. It is the isolation of the administration from the people it serves. They have never found a way to govern all of Alaska effectively. Legislators, especially, suffer from lack of accessibility with their constituents.

The court system sequesters jurors to prevent contacts with others. We sequester legislators whose success depends on contacts with their constituents. And year after year their performance falls short of expectations.

Juneau political leaders have retained the capital despite the wishes of the majority of the people. It is obviously wrong that they should, but they have done it by deftly playing on their neighbors' emotions, manipulating the political process and perhaps bending a few laws for their own advantage. They have proven themselves masters of dirty tricks and the use of the big lie technique as taught by Hitler. Perhaps most impressive, they have become so convinced that Juneau would die without the capital, that they are willing and ready to use any and all means to retain it in their city.

Today, Juneau has substantial political power, private wealth and strong selfish motivation to fight to keep the capital. Pro-movers have none of that kind of support. The motivating factor for a move is simply better government. Most workers are volunteers. What funds are raised are modest gifts from "do-gooders."

I would predict that the capital will remain in Juneau until the day comes when Alaskans are so fed up with the shortcomings of their representatives that they will take the bull by the horns and move it.

And that day now and then appears to be on the horizon.

— CHAPTER EIGHTEEN —

Newpaper War

On Jan. 27, 1939, a headline on the front page of the Anchorage Daily Times announced, "Cordova Man Joins Times Staff." The story reported that we had hired Norman C. Brown, editor of the Cordova Daily Times for the past five years, to become managing editor to take over the actual work in connection with publication "and leave the editor-in-chief free to attend to other matters."

Brown, a quiet, conservative young man, moved here with his wife and infant daughter. He had no crusading zeal or ambition to disturb the status quo. But as the son of a commercial printer, he had skills that were a big help to me. He could take over much of the routine of putting out the paper while freeing me to hammer out editorials and poke around in civic affairs. "The Daily Times grows as Anchorage grows," I proudly wrote noting that our circulation had passed 2,000 and we could now afford a second man in the newsroom.

I found Brown to be a good friend and co-worker. We were compatible and got along well. I never thought of him as a potential competitor. The competition I was concerned with was KFQD, the local radio station. My friends told me that if I could get the radio to quit reading my newspaper over the air, circulation would increase.

However, in 1939 Anchorage was still a small town of about 3,400 people and it would be ridiculous to have the one newspaper and one radio station fighting. Such a fight would certainly split the town, perhaps right down the middle.

The radio station was largely a one-man operation, with Ken Laughlin doing everything. Ken's voice was heard on the air throughout the broadcast hours. He had no backup services to help him. He improvised every day, trying to find something interesting to put on the air. He arranged with schoolteachers to bring in their most talented students to sing or play instruments. He put on the air every choral group from schools, clubs, churches or wherever. I know, first hand, because I was often in the chorus or quartet that was drafted to perform.

He was the darling of every mother who hoped to hear her Sweet Pea perform. Actually he must have been one of the most popular men in town because he was so nice to everybody. He had to be nice because he depended on everybody to help him keep that station on the air.

Rather than fight with him for reading my news, I chose to be one of

NEWSPAPER WAR | 247

his helpers. I gave him a news report to be broadcast in the early after-noon each day. It gave a brief summary of the top stories that would be in that evening's paper. He was delighted to have it. He needed all the help he could get, especially free help like mine.

I was happy, too, because so many people who heard the news broad-cast couldn't wait to read it when they got home from work. They bought an extra copy on the street before they went home. Our circulation increased. Readers told me they had to buy the extra copy because they weren't sure what they had heard on the radio and couldn't wait to check it out.

Under these circumstances, my relationships with Laughlin were always friendly, even though we were competitors for the few dollars the merchants could spend on advertising.

As Anchorage prospered, so did the radio station and my newspaper. There came the day when Bill Wagner, owner of KFQD, planned to trans-fer Ken to his Seattle office. Ken refused to leave Anchorage and sudden-ly faced unemployment. I hired him as advertising manager for the Times. He did well for us for 20 years.

As the end of World War II was nearing, Norm Brown became an eager partner with me in planning post-war improvements for our news-paper. We were anticipating the end of wartime shortages. We had out-grown the capacity of our press, our building and our staff. We simply needed more of everything.

One of the first things we planned to do was to resume publishing the Anchorage Weekly Times, which we had suspended for the duration due to the shortage of newsprint. We planned to make it much more of a lively paper than it had been before the war. Together we selected fea-tures, formats and worked out production schedules.

However, before the first issue could be published, Brown resigned. To my surprise, he said he was leaving to start his own paper. On Jan. 13, 1946, a month before we were to launch our new weekly, he came out with his weekly paper titled "Anchorage News." Inside, it had most of the features we had talked about. He took the format we had planned together and adopted it as his own. That left me back on square one in the game of planning. I didn't want my Weekly to look like an imitator of his so I had to come up with something dramatically different.

The masthead of Brown's paper noted that The Northern Publishing Co. was producing the paper and it listed Norman Brown, E. E. Bramble, and Alvin DeJulio as owners. I learned soon after that the real financial backing for my new competitor came from A. E. "Cap" Lathrop, the Fairbanks millionaire who opposed my campaign for statehood. Cap also opposed the introduction of airmail service into Alaska. He opposed the building of the Alcan highway. He opposed the idea of moving the state capital. In general, it seemed to me he opposed just about every progres-sive idea that might change his comfortable status quo. In Fairbanks it was sometimes said that he didn't want to change anything because he had it rigged so that you couldn't spend a quarter without Cap getting a nickel of it for himself.

I never considered the new weekly as serious competition, nor was I particularly alarmed when two years later Brown bought an old press and decided to go daily. Lathrop now started telling friends he was going to drive Atwood out of town with Brown's paper. I was too liberal for him and besides he was on the outs politically with my father-in-law, E. A. Rasmuson, leader of the moderate wing of the Republican Party.

True to Lathrop's philosophy, the new paper became a conduit for editorials opposing every progressive thing we stood for. On the days it had no downbeat editorial, Brown would fill the lead editorial space with Drew Pearson's column serviced out of Washington. This crackpot formula did not exactly compel people to switch papers, and Brown could not match our aggressive news reporting.

The population in Anchorage doubled with the buildup of military forces as Alaska's strategic importance in the Cold War grew. We needed a new press to keep up, but I found a long waiting line at the printing press plants. Fortunately, I was able to buy a fairly modern used press from the paper in Lincoln, Neb. I bought four units, shipped up two, and stored the other two in Seattle for future expansion. Then when offset printing became the in thing, I junked our letterpress and never used the two units stored in Seattle. I was one of the first to switch to offset with a state of the art Goss press on May 12, 1969. Many papers in the Lower 48 used to send pressmen up to study our operation.

Meanwhile, Brown's paper struggled. He could not afford new equipment, and only the income from his commercial printing plant kept his daily afloat. I have no doubt it would have gone under had it not happened that at that particular period a free-spirited Chicago debutante decided to flee to Alaska to escape from the trauma of her recent divorce from one of the wealthiest men in the nation.

Katherine Woodruff Field, then 37, came to Alaska in 1965. Soon after graduating from Smith, the elite East Coast women's college, she had married Marshall Field IV, heir to a department store fortune and the publisher of the Chicago Sun-Times. After her marriage of 13 years broke up in 1963, she packed her three young children into her new Pontiac station wagon and drove the rutted Alaska Highway to Anchorage where two college classmates already lived. She sought a fresh start away from the social high life of Chicago, which she said she never liked.

Kay, attractive and always impeccably dressed, showed up at Brown's paper and asked for a job. He had the good sense to hire her, at $2 an hour, first clipping news items for the library but soon reporting news stories. A year later, she returned to Chicago and married Larry Fanning, a close friend who had been a flamboyant editor in San Francisco and on the Chicago Sun-Times and Chicago Daily News.

(Fanning's friendship with the rich publisher's wife used to be a subject of gossip at newspaper conventions.)

Kay brought Larry back to Alaska and now they sought a fresh start together. They came to me and asked to buy the Anchorage Times. I told them it was not for sale, but suggested that the Fairbanks News-Miner seemed ripe for purchase. They said they did not want to live in Fairbanks. The next thing I know is that Brown announced he was retiring and selling his paper to Larry and Kay Fanning.

The Fannings bought the Anchorage Daily News in 1967. The shop was a wreck. By now, the original press was so old they couldn't buy parts for it. Whenever a part wore out, the local machine shop would have to build one, custom-made, saddling the new owners with expensive maintenance. Furthermore, Brown sold them the Daily News without the commercial printing shop, the operation which enabled the daily to meet its payrolls.

The Fannings did put out a much livelier paper. The Daily News editorial policy took a 180-degree turn, from Lathrop negativism to Fanning liberalism, and they hired several sharp liberal reporters. The Fannings spent their savings covering the deficits in the hope that new subscribers and advertisers would soon support the improved product. However, they badly misjudged Alaska readers. The paper's avant-garde stories on abortion, birth control methods, and minority issues might have played big in Chicago, but they made most Alaskans uncomfortable and wonder about relevance.

At one point, Kay told me that Larry couldn't sleep worrying about whether the press would hold up. I offered to help relieve his anxiety. We became an ally in the paper's survival. At times I would send my mechanics over to fix their linotypes. One day when their press broke down, I called and told Fanning to change the outmoded size of his newspaper page and we would print the paper. He did and we put the paper out for him. I never sent him a bill and he was grateful.

In 1970, Congress passed the Newspaper Preservation Act, which exempted papers from anti-trust prosecution if a paper showed it would go out of business unless it combined operations with a willing competitor. Larry Fanning was naive as a businessman, as editors often tend to be, but he sensed he could save the failing News if he could get such an agreement with the healthy Anchorage Times.

Larry invited me to lunch to talk about a joint operation. I was willing to listen. We did have a plant with a modern press and since we were an afternoon paper, that press sat idle at night. We could have easily published the slim press run of the morning Daily News, but Larry never got down to brass tacks to make a deal. Larry was a member of a breed that drowned themselves in martinis at lunch. We had several luncheon talks, but he would end up too drunk to follow up on specifics.

In February 1971, a short time after we talked, Larry died unexpectedly. He was only 57. People said he looked in fine form at a dinner party the night before, and I never knew he had a heart problem. He had run the paper four years but couldn't make it profitable. When his widow, Kay, took over, she found they were hopelessly in debt. With no financing institution likely to advance further funds, she turned desperately to Chicago for help.

Somehow, Kay convinced the trustees of the Marshall Field Estate to use funds held in trust for her young son, Ted. This was a little irregular since her son was still a minor, but she got an infusion that kept the paper alive. However, she knew she had to do something fast to stem the bleeding.

Kay next came to me. She said she was on the verge of bankruptcy and the only thing that could possibly save her paper would be a joint operating agreement with my paper under the Newspaper Preservation Act. The Times would take over the printing, advertising, and circulation needs of the Daily News and put out the Sunday paper. Editorial staffs would operate independently as before.

It is obvious now, with hindsight, that I should have said "No" and let her go bankrupt. In fact, my trusted right hand man, managing editor Bill Tobin, who had vast experience with the Associated Press, urged me to do just that. The News would have died and we would have had a clear field in Anchorage. But Kay Fanning was not an evil competitor, the likes of Cap Lathrop (who by now had been killed in an accident). She was a sincere idealist, a dedicated Christian Scientist, and I believed she honestly wanted to do what was right for the people of Alaska. Furthermore, we were always friends, and I believed in the Alaska principle that you help out your friends when they are in trouble.

In 1974, after much paperwork involving my accountants and her advisers, who included a trustee of her son's Marshall Field estate, we began publishing the Daily News in our plant under a detailed contract. In line with our agreement, Kay's paper had to generate enough money to pay the costs of producing it. The contract provided that within five years revenues would build up enough to meet that goal, but until that point was reached, Kay and her Chicago backers had to cover the shortages.

Things seemed to be going according to plan until the Internal Revenue Service stepped in. Kay had freely admitted that she had tapped the Field family resources to underwrite her losses, but I don't recall her ever discussing why she was cut off. According to a Marshall Field syndicate executive's explanation to me, the IRS challenged the propriety of investing funds from the son's trust into a venture that returned no profits. The IRS subsequently ruled that siphoning the money out of the trust to keep the paper afloat was more like supporting an expensive hobby rather than a business, and losses would no longer be tax deductible. Thereupon, the trustees notified Kay it would be inappropriate to contin-

NEWSPAPER WAR | 251

ue.

Cut off from the Field family funds, Kay's deficit in our contract grew to about $750,00 by the end of two years. We kept putting the heat on her to cover it, but for all intents her paper was bankrupt by the end of 1976. Ironically, this was the very year that the News won a Pulitzer Prize for its series on Jesse Carr, the Teamster Union boss who had become the most powerful figure in Alaska.

The circulation of the News, which at its height amounted to about a third of ours, dropped from 11,800 to 7,800 during the two years under the joint operating agreement. Many in town sensed Kay's distress. A group of volunteers organized as The Committee for Two Newspapers and even started a subscription drive to try to boost the circulation, which it needed to increase advertising.

That was morale boosting but made no dent in the losses. In desperation, Kay hired a big gun law firm, Flint and MacKay of Los Angeles, to try to change our agreement. They started lobbying me for modification of the contract so the deficit would be subsidized by Times profits. I told them it was unfair to my family to use my money to support Kay's losses and insisted that we stick to the regular terms. In fact, I felt I could show we were on schedule in building up the revenues in line with the five-year projections.

On Feb.9, 1977, the two parties held a summit meeting at the Anchorage Westward Hotel. Kay marched in with her lawyer, Philip M. Battaglia of the Los Angeles firm, and one guy from the Marshall Field trustees. I had an accountant and my own lawyer there. As noon approached, her lawyer stood up and delivered an ultimatum: We had a year to modify the contract—relinquish control of the joint operations to a third party, cut the Daily News in on part of the Times profits or face a $16.5 million lawsuit for breach of contract and violation of anti-trust laws.

I was incensed and felt betrayed. Neither giving up control nor sharing our profits was acceptable. We came back from lunch and said "no." At 3 p.m. they walked into federal district court and filed their $16.5 million lawsuit, charging unfair competition, breach of contract, and mismanagement of the Times in handling the joint operating agreement. They had it all planned before the meeting. The summit had been a farce.

Once Kay went to court, some of her popular appeal in town eroded. Frank Reed, the respected banker who co-chaired The Committee for Two Newspapers, resigned a few days after the suit was filed. Meanwhile, relations between Kay and me strained further as she persisted in using the courts as a forum to blaspheme me in uncharacteristic language. She tried to make me look like a big guy tramping on the helpless, little widow, a ruthless businessman who promoted the Times ahead of the News.

I countered with a suit charging Kay had been delinquent on her contract and asked that the Daily News pay $300,000 immediately due for services. Our joint contract had no provision for arbitration, but Judge James Fitzgerald refused to enforce the contract. Instead, he ordered arbitration in the joint operating disputes. The next thing I knew we were involved in lengthy and costly arbitration hearings, before an arbiter who was no more anxious to make a decision than the judge was.

For the next year, it was pretty much like a cold war between the two papers. The News stories about the litigation usually depicted the Times and its publisher as some sort of a powerful monster trampling on the young widow who was trying to carry on her husband's business. Additionally, Kay Fanning through her Marshall Field connections whipped up the interest of the East Coast press to carry stories very much like those in the local issues of the Anchorage News.

There was the time CBS television network news sent a team to Anchorage to "do an update" on the "newspaper war." Barbara Howar was the celebrity assigned to anchor the program.

I assumed this was to be another one of those whitewash jobs, wherein the News would be made the good guy and the Times and me the bad guy. In an effort to moderate some of the things they might say, I had a long lunch with the CBS producer, a young lady from New York, the day before the team was scheduled to interview me in my office. I had hoped to plant some seeds in her head that might suggest that the Times and Atwood were not all that bad, after all. After the luncheon I had no feeling that I had accomplished a thing.

When the CBS crew arrived I found I had nine people climbing around my office, each with a different mission. I had no idea such a small operation could be divided up so many ways to make it complex if not totally unmanageable. There were the cameramen, the light men, the sound men and others.

It took them about an hour to get ready for the interview. In that hour I was introduced to Barbara Howar and had a pleasant visit. She was a delightful personality and had many interesting things to talk about. We had many friends in common and got along well. During a lull, she recollected that during her first marriage her daughter grew up playing with a neighbor child whose mother's maiden name was Atwood and asked if she could be any relation to me. We quickly discovered that she was talking about my daughter, Marilyn. For the next few minutes she delighted me with accounts of how she enjoyed my daughter and granddaughter on P Street in Washington, D.C.

In another lull, Barbara ventured the thought that she didn't like my daughter's husband. I agreed with her heartily. My daughter's marriage ended in a terrible divorce experience.

By the time the CBS crew was ready for the interview, Barbara and I had bonded on many things. We felt very good about each other. She was seated facing me before the cameras. She had a tiny note pad covered with questions to ask me. As she began asking them, I could see they were trick questions designed to put me in a bad light. I gave her straight answers for each question as she asked it. The interview had hardly more than started when she stood up. So I stood up. Then Barbara said, while the cameras were still rolling, "I can't make a villain out of you." And she threw her arms around me in a big hug.

That was the end of the interview. Indeed, it was the end of the CBS report. Barbara and her crew, including the hardboiled producer from New York, headed home. They had spent days in Anchorage photographing the two newspaper plants and scenes around the city. None of it ever saw the light of day. Barbara had thrown their show and destroyed their mission.

I always say it was the most successful television interview I ever had. Thanks to Barbara Howar.

There were constant tensions during the years of litigation. There was the time Sheila Toomey, a reporter for the News, asked me for an appointment for her to do an interview with me in regard to the "newspaper war." She said she had an assignment from a prominent trade journal on the East Coast to do the story. I told her I didn't think she could do an impartial job on it and tried to put her off, but she cajoled me and sweet-talked me with promises that this time she would be strictly impartial and all that sort of thing.

When she arrived in my office I seated her opposite me at my desk and I planted on the desk between us a tape recorder, which I activated to start recording as I talked. While the recorder put it all on tape, I repeated to Sheila what I had told her before: that I thought she couldn't do a fair job in reporting this story, that she had no intention of doing it, and I even questioned whether she had an assignment from any publication to do this interview. The tape took down whatever reply she made and I told her this tape would be kept as evidence of what I really said in comparison with whatever she wrote.

We had a very formal interview. Her questions were quite different from what they usually are. When it was over, she took her notebooks and left. I never heard of that interview again. As far as I can determine she never wrote the story and there had never been an assignment for her to do it.

I spent a year or more before the arbitrator, and spent a million or more in lawyer fees and exhibits, yet at the end of the year we had accomplished precisely nothing toward ending the litigation. I told my lawyer that instead of spending another year and another million spinning wheels before an arbiter, let's settle out of court. I would pay anything under a million on a settlement that would terminate the contract, get the News out of my plant, out of my hair, and gone forever. Kay Fanning settled for $750,000. She agreed to vacate my plant within six months.

In the next several months, she kept the paper alive by public appeals for funds and using influential contacts. One of the latter was Robert Redford, the actor. Redford had come to Anchorage in 1976 to premiere the Watergate movie, "All the President's Men," in which he starred. Kay threw a large reception for him, attended by many Alaska dignitaries, including Governor Hammond who later took him fishing.

Now, in her moment of need, she cashed in on his friendship. As she told an American Society of Newspaper Editors convention, Redford "did help find some people who were willing to make some investment in the paper." I understood that it was Redford who stirred up McClatchy's interest in coming to Alaska.

One motivating factor for Redford was probably his interest in stopping development in Alaska. He was opposed to the oil and pipeline projects that were under way and was one of the leaders of the national conservation coalitions that were organized to try to save Alaska. The Anchorage Times supported wise management and development of natural resources. The News, which was always on the verge of bankruptcy, was opposed. He would no doubt be delighted to help Kay with her newspaper whenever he could.

Oil began flowing out of Prudhoe Bay in immense quantities in 1978. The Anchorage population swelled as the oil companies moved in and brought thousands of their most elite work force to become citizens of the city. Contractors and service people followed. The potential for growth and profits made Alaska's booming, biggest city a prize for any of the enterprising newspaper chains that were gobbling up independent papers during this era.

The story goes that Kay Fanning went to Sacramento to convince Charles K. McClatchy, head of the California-based newspaper chain, on the potential of Anchorage. Knowing the way syndicates scientifically evaluate promising markets, I doubt whether it took much convincing. In 1979, McClatchy bought 80 percent ownership of the Daily News while retaining Kay as publisher, a symbolic gesture that is supposed to show commitment to local autonomy.

Kay left the paper in the summer of 1983 to accept what turned out to be an ill-fated stint as editor of the Christian Science Monitor in Boston. But there was no doubt that the home office in California was calling the business shots well before she left. They expanded their circulation areas through the Matanuska Valley and started delivering the paper free. Then they did the same on the Kenai Peninsula, sending out trucks 100 miles away.

It was said that McClatchy put in $60 million to cover his operating deficits. He eventually built a new plant, which cost around $30 million by the time it was finished. They doubled the news staff, hired away many my good people, and spent money on advertising promotions that I could never afford. They signed contracts to take just about every syndicate service—columns, comics, features— that was available, not intending to publish them but to prevent my paper from getting them. Costs did not seem to matter. They kept throwing money into the newspaper operation year after year. As long as the Times existed they always operated at a loss.

I saw our circulation edge steadily narrowing under this onslaught. Yet, despite this, I kept getting feelers from newspaper chains wanting to buy the Times. The circulation of the Daily News finally topped ours, 46,165 to 45,089 by 1983. It wasn't that we were shrinking. McClatchy was gaining by "buying" expensive circulation in scattered areas beyond the Anchorage urban area. Nevertheless, once you are no longer the dominant paper, national advertisers go with the leader.

I decided it was time to sell to someone who had more millions of dollars than McClatchy had and could better deal with that kind of free-spending competitor. In 1985, I went to Gannett Newspaper headquarters to see Douglas McCorkindale, their expansion point man. He earlier had inquired about buying the Times and this was still a period when Gannett was buying heavily and becoming the largest newspaper chain in the country.

McCorkindale seemed very interested. We were talking in terms of $40 million as a starter. He tried to push things along, but I told him I had to check with Evangeline at home before committing anything. It happened that our daughter, Elaine, the assistant publisher of the Times, had just been elected the first woman president of the Anchorage Chamber of Commerce. If we sold the paper that year, she would no longer be a newspaper publisher and it might be embarrassing to be an "unemployed" chamber president.

I called McCorkindale and told him I had to delay a decision, but promised to be back. By the time Elaine's term was ending in 1986, the environment at Gannett had changed drastically. It had just laid out $300 million to acquire the Louisville Courier-Journal. But an even greater financial strain confronted Gannett. It was an expensive litigation with the U.S. Justice Department over a joint operation venture between its recently acquired Detroit News and the Knight-Ridder-owned Detroit Free Press. McCorkindale said Gannett would have to delay its decision on the Anchorage property.

The year 1986 was a real downer. Late that October, an armed crackpot came looking for me, shot up the office, and nearly killed Elaine and me. He walked in from the street and terrorized the circulation and classified department employees at their desks, tossing clutches of ignited firecrackers around the offices. The firecrackers sounded like machine gun fire as they detonated. He touched off smoke bombs and threw them into places where newspapers ignited and set the building on fire. The acrid smoke of the bombs filled the hallways and made breathing impossible.

Naturally, the employees had to flee for their lives through the alley door. The gunman went upstairs looking for me. My secretary came in to my office and carefully closed and locked the door behind her. Her action of closing the door was the first tip I had that something untoward was happening. She said to me, in a serious low voice, "He's got a gun and he's looking for you. You stay here."

I looked through the door adjoining to Elaine's office and saw her standing behind her desk talking back to the gunman. He had asked her to step out of her office and she responded, "What's the matter with you, are you crazy?" Whereupon he let loose a barrage of bullets.

I was in there with Elaine, like a flash. I crowded the gunman so he couldn't maneuver with his weapon. He fired it constantly. It was semi-automatic. I held the barrel down so the bullets went into the floor. The gun was strapped over the man's shoulder so I couldn't disarm him.

I beat him unmercifully with my one free hand. The two of us careened around the office, upsetting everything in our path, including computers, printers and such. Elaine ignored my order for her to leave and proved to be just as effective a street fighter as she was an assistant publisher.

The gunman, who didn't dare take his hand off the rifle's trigger for fear Elaine would take possession, suddenly held a handgun in his one free hand. He couldn't move, lying at a 45-degree angle across an office sideboard with Elaine and me on top. He could wave that handgun out of my reach, but he couldn't aim it without bending his elbow. And if he bent his elbow I could grab the gun.

My eyes were about eight inches from his throughout this melee. I used the weight of my body to hold him down and motionless. Elaine added her weight to hold him down and prevent him from aiming his rifle. My one hand held a glob of his hair that I used as a handle to turn his face toward me so I could beat his face and jaw repeatedly with the other hand, which became a bloody fist.

"Where is everyone?" I asked as I tried to hold this struggling character pinned to the sideboard. Finally, our secretaries summoned Dan Burns, a young, handsome pressman who was built like an athlete. He came in with a knife, cut the guy's shoulder strap, and took away the rifle. Jim Rose, the firm's comptroller, then wrested the pistol from the man's hand. That relieved the tension but we didn't move until the cops came, which seemed a long time later.

Police finally seized the attacker. He was Donald Lee Ramsey, age 41, a taxi cab driver. They found he carried 160 rounds of ammunition, a knife in one boot top and another handgun in the other. He also carried enough food and water for three days, and a garrot. He said his grievance against the Times was that we had refused to run a full-page ad on the grounds that it libeled U.S. Sen. Frank Murkowski. Ramsey told police he intended to hold me hostage for three days to make the Times print the ad. He didn't say what he planned to do with me after that.

I survived the scuffle with only bruises to my face and hands. I was now almost 80 years old. While I still felt strong enough to subdue gunmen, I felt my battle with McClatchy slipping away. My problems compounded the next year when I suffered the grievous loss of Evangeline, my loyal wife and confidante. She died suddenly of pancreatic cancer.

I was also troubled by the feeling that the loyalty of the Times staff, which had been a constant strength to me, seemed to be dissipating. The business office was split in two factions. We couldn't plan administratively. While many talented people still worked in the newsroom, I noted that some smoked pot or lived together without benefit of marriage. Was my shock in learning about these deplorable life habits a sign that I was out of it? Out of step with contemporary Alaska?

I could see me running out of money and losing control of my own paper. Circulation for the afternoon Times kept slipping, and I started believing years of warnings that modern readers wanted their paper delivered in the mornings. I now turned to Alaska to look for a buyer. When word got out, lots of people came and talked to me. Many looked like the Mafia sent them. Most couldn't explain what they would do if I sold them the paper. I always heard that McClatchy had a $10 million standing offer to buy the Times through a straw purchaser.

Then Bill Allen paid me a visit. In the spring and summer of 1989, Allen, chairman of Veco International, had made about a $75 million profit cleaning up the Exxon oil spill in Prince William Sound. He said he wanted to put his profits back into Alaska and asked me to sell him the Times.

I had reservations about selling it to someone so closely connected to the oil industry. We talked it over and he came up with a Hellenthal survey that asked in essence: "Would it make any difference to you if someone related to an oil company owned a newspaper in Anchorage?" The answer was 75 percent "No."

That impressed me. I sold the paper to Allen on Nov. 21, 1989, in a neat clean deal. He paid cash and did every thing he promised to do. He doubled the staff, bought new computers, and blew many millions by converting the Times into a morning paper in order to go head-to-head with McClatchy's morning Daily News.

Allen made substantial circulation gains, but he could not cope with reader habits. While many Alaskans openly professed to hate the liberal News, I believe they were too used to cussing it to give it up. So the Times did gain readers, but the News didn't lose. And neither made money. Frustrated after two years, Allen went to McClatchy and offered to buy the News. They convinced him he would end up better by selling them the Times, which he did on June 2, 1992.

The Times is dead, the casualty of a newspaper war. I fought its battles for 54 years. At first it was a fight to meet the weekly payrolls. Then it was the long hard series of conflicts to help Alaska emerge as a state and our little frontier town grow into Alaska's biggest city, which enabled us to become Alaska's biggest paper. Finally, I had to deal with the attack from a well-heeled predator from California committed to spending millions to wrest away fruits of the progress we helped cultivate, and which, ironically, its progenitor often opposed.

I can't fault Bill Allen for giving up the battle. He did everything with the paper that he promised to do. Like many independent owners in these times, he simply could not overcome the changes in reader habits that accelerate the national trend towards one-newspaper cities in which the wealthy chains win out because they have the deeper pockets.

It was said later that the McClatchy chain had spent $160 million to gain its foothold in Anchorage. And it had more millions available if needed to win the war.

Special headline for Celebration of City editor Elaine Atwood's birthday.

Elaine and Bob Atwood emerge from the Times building after successfully subduing a gunman that tried to kill Bob Atwood. Photo by Anchorage Times/October 21, 1986

CHAPTER EIGHTEEN

— CHAPTER NINETEEN —

Between Us

*"We have followed Alaska's course from wilderness to frontier to modern state.
Thus, on its silver anniversary we congratulate the Great Land
that has become a great state."*

—from "The Making of America: Alaska" in the National Geographic, March 1984.

It has been more than 60 years since the Alaska Railroad train huffed and puffed to its little wooden depot and deposited Evangeline and me in our new hometown, Anchorage, Alaska. The town was an isolated but spirited handful of 2,200 people living in an attractive, saucer-shaped townsite at ocean side, surrounded by magnificent mountains.

The town was like a tiny island of people in a sea of wilderness that stretched to the horizon no matter which way you looked. There was no road into or out of the town. The people had no such thing as long-distance telephone service. No air mail. No access to the radio programs so popular in the Lower 48. Anchorage was too far away. Isolation was dominant.

The truth was that Alaska was so far away it was beyond the periphery of national interest or concern. The United States bought it from the Czar of Russia in 1867 and, after some second thoughts in Congress, finally paid for it. In the first century of ownership the national interest was focused mostly on ways to administer it with minimum cost to the federal treasury.

In that first century one thing of world note happened. That was the gold rush at the turn of the century. It created brief excitement and brought in thousands of stampeders but they left as soon as the dust settled, most of them no richer than when they came.

In 1935, when Evangeline and I arrived, Anchorage was already 20 years old yet was the youngest city in the territory. Its only economic reason to exist was to provide services and support for the railroad, which like almost everything in Alaska was owned and controlled from Washington, D.C.

Evangeline was instantly accepted into the inner circles of our small

"BETWEEN US | 261

town society. After all, she was the "Crown Princess" of the town's banker. I was accepted warmly by my father-in-law's closest friends, but I felt a degree of skepticism on the part of others.

I got the impression they were looking down their noses at this brash youngster from the East who had the nerve to marry into the banker's family and now thinks he can run "our newspaper." Among those with a political bent I was suspected of scheming how to polish my father-in-law's political apple. He was the Republican National Committeeman for Alaska. And, of course, there were others who saw me as an opportunist who had married into money.

We enjoyed our new friends and the introduction to the mysteries of the Alaska lifestyle. Yet we were constantly appraising the values and potentials in our new life. How long should we enjoy this adventure and when should we return to the careers we had left?

Many things figured in our decision, not the least of which was an incident early on during the cocktail hour at a dinner at the home of Judge and Mrs. Thomas C. Price. She was one of the ruling arbiters in Anchorage society. We were surrounded by the "upper crust."

A hush fell over the room for a short moment. The elderly Judge Price, who had been physically impaired by strokes and was limited in body movement, was caught with an unfinished sentence dangling in midair. That hush was just long enough for all of us to hear him say, "Well, I came to Alaska to grow up with the country but I grew too damned fast."

When we got home that evening you can bet we talked a lot about whether Alaska was going to grow, and how fast. We agreed we didn't want to be another Judge Price.

This was still 1935 and Alaska was a vast piece of real estate virtually empty of people. The population had only passed the 60,000 mark in 1930. Evangeline and I could find no basis for optimism that the pace of development was changing. We decided we could spent five years of our lives enjoying Alaska and then return to our Outside careers.

That five years was fun. Chancellor Hitler and Admiral Tojo started their sweeps in Europe and Asia. The United States quickly became aware of the need of a military program in Alaska that would deny an enemy the use of this strategic place as a staging area for launching air attacks on the industrial centers of our nation.

The discovery of these strategic values in 1939 altered the course of Alaska's history. A billion-dollar crash program of military construction brought thousands of new people to the territory. Never again would this part of the world be forgotten or forlorn.

As I write this, six decades later, Anchorage is Alaska's dynamic metropolis with skyscraper hotels and office buildings, the home of a throbbing population of 250,000 people. Yet, wilderness still enchants us. Less than a half hour away, you can reach snow-capped mountain ranges, multiple glaciers, and fertile salmon streams as well as ancient Native villages, old gold mines and the nation's second largest national forest, where bear, moose and Dall sheep thrive.

Meanwhile, the state of Alaska has become a full-fledged member of this great nation's family of states. It is the richest state in natural resources, the country's largest supplier of domestic crude oil. It is also a mecca for millions of tourists from America, Europe and Asia who come in increasing numbers each year to see the highest mountains in North America, the Aurora Borealis that emblazons our skies on long winter nights, the world's most spectacular glaciers and other scenic wonders unmatched on the continent.

The state at this writing has a permanent population that tops 600,000, lifting it from its rank as the smallest in the U.S. Indeed, it is near the top of the list of states for educational attainment of its people and for per capita income.

How did this remarkable turnaround occur in such a short period of history?

Previous chapters have told of the events and changes in national needs that progressively made the Territory of Alaska the nation's baby state and soon the richest among all the states. From our rinky-dink beginning, the Anchorage Times also grew. It became the state's largest newspaper and the most outspoken champion of progress during this era.

Authors and poets have sometimes categorized Alaskans dramatically as colorful, swashbuckling characters who courageously braved the hardships and vicissitudes of the rugged frontier to make the Alaska of today. That is not what I observed. Credit for the state's successes was earned by the courageous people who staked their lives here despite warnings that this was not a fit place to live. But their method of taming the wilderness was the opposite of swashbuckling independence and bravado.

Most Alaskans emigrated at least 2,000 miles to get to this their chosen land. Their assets were strong hopes, determined ambition backed up by very little, if any, cash money. But they were young and ambitious in a land with no fences. Evangeline and I quickly learned that simply by being here we automatically became one of them.

As I say, it was automatic. No conscious decision was necessary. We could feel the great development potential that lay in the diversity of minerals hidden in our mountain ranges and our gorgeous river valleys. To us young folk it seemed that the older folk, who ran the country, were too casual toward the exciting future we thought was inevitable. We knew that the industrial centers of our great nation would some day need the natural resources that were hidden in Alaska and would bring the capital funds and know-how north to do it.

Independent men? The fact is that living in this land of long winter

BETWEEN US | 263

nights with extended periods of pipe-freezing weather made dependent men, dependent upon each other for backup and support. Survival in a vast wilderness with a sparse population requires interdependence, not independence.

When Alaskans needed a shoulder put to the wheel, everybody put his shoulder to the wheel and all pushed in the same direction. We trusted one another. In fact, there were few locked doors.

There was a fellow who came to Anchorage and bought Herb Brown's cottage for $1,700. It was a house that had been built by the Alaska Engineering Commission 15 years before when the Alaska Railroad was constructed. The buyer was surprised to have no key delivered with his title. When he asked Brown what he did with the key, Brown said he never had one and he thought it silly to even ask such a question.

The spirit of interdependence made each Alaskan "his brother's keeper," especially in times of trouble. It automatically became a "rule of the road" as roads were built and local drivers could venture away from town and out into the wilderness: no driver passed without stopping to help another motorist who appeared to be in trouble.

The first such road went to Palmer. It was built as a single lane gravel track, and inasmuch as the Alaska Road Commission, the federal road building agency, had no rock crushing facility, the road was topped off with mine-run gravel, which included rocks sometimes as large as bowling balls. Driving was hard on automobiles and passengers.

The Palmer road was built to support the farm colony development in the Matanuska Valley. It tied into the primitive road system that had been built in the valley for the new farmers. Anchorage residents discovered that, if they braved the hazards of the new road, they had access to much of the valley, which meant they could visit their new neighbors and also enjoy fishing and hunting in that area.

The Good Samaritan rule of the road often was vital to life and limb in those early days. There was the time a sedan with six passengers was immobilized far away from civilization, in the mountains near Hatcher Pass. A rock had knocked the petcock off the crankcase and dumped the oil. The engine couldn't run long without oil in the crankcase. A long cold night was ahead. Another carload of tourists, upon stopping to help, undertook to tow the disabled car 12 to 15 miles down the twisting mountain road to Wasilla for repairs. This was no easy trip for the towline was a bit of clothesline only six feet long.

The road was dark, dusty, rough, dirty and tortuous. The rear car constantly had to keep the rope taut for fear of ramming into the head car. Likewise, the head car hesitated to apply the brakes for fear of being rammed. By some miracle, they made it safely to Wasilla.

It being Sunday, the Wasilla garage was closed. When reached, the garage owner not only left the warm confines of his house to assist but

264 | CHAPTER NINETEEN

also used his Alaskan ingenuity to fix the car. He repaired the crankcase but was stumped when he discovered he had no gasket to use when he put the crankcase back on the engine.

He cut a gasket out of an old cardboard shirt box. He figured that would be good enough to get the car back to Anchorage. Actually, that car ran on bumpy Anchorage streets for 12 more years with that shirt box gasket never being replaced.

Anchorage was young and some benefits accrued from that municipal youthfulness. The town had not yet cultivated special interest groups that dominated daily affairs. Many of the businesses were still owned and operated by the people who established them. There were no well-defined cliques as are found in older communities.

I often commented that living in Anchorage was like living in a test tube. Our population was so closely knit that one could trace changes that would come with the addition of a new ingredient. As editor, I had no need for public surveys to find out what my readers wanted. I was surrounded by them and they told me, sometimes more than I wanted to know.

I note that today's newspaper publishers, looking for answers to declining circulation, debate whether they might be able to increase their relevance to readers by venturing into "civic journalism," which is also known as "public journalism." This is where editors and reporters not only cover the news but also take an active role in community affairs.

"As a practical matter, can a paper objectively report on a burning community issue when the editor sits on the commission that is promoting a particular point of view?" one prominent editor asked at a recent newspaper convention.

I can't help but be a bit amused by this. The leaders in our profession are debating as though this concept is a new style of newspapering. Yet I practiced this kind of journalism during the entire 54 years that I ran the Anchorage Times. And am proud of it.

Maybe it was a frontier mentality, but Anchorage citizens insisted that their editor put his energy (and often his money) where his pen was. When I proposed editorially that we connect Lake Hood and Lake Spenard to create a longer water runway for our floatplanes, they made me chairman of the committee to accomplish it.

When I criticized the chamber of commerce for its lack of aggressiveness, they elected me president (twice). When I editorially suggested the city needed a planning commission, the mayor created one and appointed me chairman.

By becoming involved, I got the feel of the town and often a beat on the news. Besides heading the Chamber, I was at various times either on or chairman of most of the civic committees of the town. I was an elder in the Presbyterian Church, sang in the choir for 18 years, and headed countless charity drives and building campaigns. I served on advisory boards of the Salvation Army, YMCA, USO and a long list of art, cultural, spiritual, recreational and even scientific groups. And I found no conflict with my interest in publishing unbiased news reports.

Evangeline outdid me. She organized the Parent-Teacher Association, Alaska Federation of Women's Clubs and the League of Women Voters, serving as the first president of each. She organized the Alaska World Affairs Council and served as its unpaid executive director for six years. She helped bring the opera to town, encouraged theater and worked hard to establish the Anchorage Museum of History and Art, probably the city's greatest tourist attraction today.

After a while, I found ways to lead discussion groups so that some member would express the idea I wanted mentioned. And when it was mentioned I jumped on it vigorously, saying things like "you certainly have a good idea there." As the discussion progressed, it was " his" idea and he was proud to have credit for it. And I, with my newspaper, could see that he got the credit. But I rarely could say "no'" when a really major issue affecting the welfare of Alaska was on the line, such as my decision in 1949 to become chairman of the Alaska Statehood Commission, which led the 10-year battle to get Alaska accepted into the union.

Many hit-and-run journalists who came into town for an instant analysis of Alaska would go back to New York or wherever and write with great disdain about my personal involvement in public issues. Ralph Nader and other special pleaders often painted me as a powerful Anchorage newspaper tycoon who dictated the terms of Alaska's development and would strongly suggest I was getting rich from projects my paper supported.

They were correct, but not for the greedy motives they tried to tag on me. I got richer as the people of Anchorage got richer as the town grew and prospered. Ours was the first paper to come out for statehood and I personally worked hard for it, paying my own expenses to and from Washington. Did I personally gain from it? Of course I did. Statehood was a big economic victory for all of Alaska. It broke the federal shackles and permitted Alaskans, rather than absentee owners, to control the economic and political destiny of our state.

It also has been hard for some writers to accept the way I shared in Alaska's first major oil strike, the discovery at Swanson River in 1957. As a newspaper, we were in the forefront in encouraging oil exploration long before Alaska was a state. Then I actually put my money where my editorial voice was when Locke Jacobs, a very visible oil lease speculator, convinced me and a dozen other businessmen to invest in the Swanson River oil well leases (as well as in many locations that produced only dry wells).

We were gambling along with thousands of other people that great pools of oil lay somewhere beneath Alaska's surface. We simply lucked out when Swanson River produced. Yet, even 40 years later, supposedly professional journalists cannot accept the facts. They still write stories hinting but never documenting that I and others struck oil because of insider information leaked to me by (take your choice) a high Interior Department official, an oil company geologist, a Bureau of Land Management higher-up, or some other unidentified but decidedly evil seer.

Attempts to revise history seem to be a national sport. I note that as generations die and memories fade, some contemporary Alaskans can't resist putting their own spin on history. Especially in recounting the facts relating to the effort of Alaskans to have their territory become a state.

I have described how the early idea of statehood was continually discouraged by politicians as well as business leaders, local chambers of commerce, and particularly the fish packers. It is pretty well documented that Governor Gruening was the first public official to publicly advocate statehood. He was a Democrat and rallied his party to become early supporters.

Despite this history, some Republicans state that they and their party were the unsung heroes of statehood. They contend that they stopped a bad statehood bill on the verge of passage in Congress and revised it to provide for a more generous land grant.

This is a blatant attempt to revise history. Perhaps a handful of individual Republicans had input into the content of the legislation, but the official party leaders never showed any interest when we needed help. The facts are that Congress, over the years, had several bills with land provisions that were found to be stingy. Each one failed to pass. And each year, a new bill with a more generous land formula was introduced. The Democrats controlled every Congress at this time, and the writing of each bill was in the hands of Democrats.

As far as I can recollect never did the Alaska Republican Party favor statehood without strings attached. Yet I have heard Republicans claim in local speeches that Sen. Robert Taft of Ohio, a power center among Republicans in Washington, and a Republican senator from Kansas visited Alaska in their effort to help win statehood. Both of those gentlemen were outspoken opponents of statehood and never turned a hand to help the Alaska cause, except possibly to get on the bandwagon and vote for the final bill.

I am also uncomfortable about the claims of statehood support regularly made by former governor Wally Hickel. He keeps referring to his considerable contributions in Alaska's fight for statehood during territorial days. My recollection is that he was a foremost early opponent of statehood, as were most of his Republican Party colleagues who worked with the salmon canning interests to preserve their comfortable status quo. I believe a review of the news stories of the statehood fight will show that Hickel hopped on the bandwagon only after the movement gained steam.

I also wince at the way some of the state's prominent political leaders magnify their achievements in writing about the success of Alaska after statehood. Writers regularly credit former governor Jay Hammond for the success of the Permanent Fund. He gladly accepts this distinction and even reinforces it in his book, "Bush Rat Governor." True, Hammond presided in Juneau when Alaskans voted in 1976 for an amendment to the constitution that created the fund. However, his was but one of several voices, including the Anchorage Times, that urged voters to approve the amendment that set up a system of putting oil revenues into a savings account out of reach of politicians.

On the other hand, hardly anyone knows that the person who deserves more credit than any one for the success of the fund is Elmer E. Rasmuson, the Anchorage banker who served as the first chairman of the fund's board of trustees. Almost single-handedly, Rasmuson sought the soundest investment techniques for Alaska. He traveled from New York to California at his own expense to interview the nation's most respected foundation money mangers. Based on those findings, he insisted at the outset on inflation-proofing the fund. Thus, Alaska's nest egg, now exceeding $16 billion, was spared the disaster experienced by Alberta, which neglected to inflation-proof its oil boom savings fund, a case Rasmuson personally investigated.

I believe history also has been deficient in keeping alive the contributions of many other truer heroes of Alaska's statehood success. Bill Egan, Alaska's first governor and a great person, fought hard for statehood but his health failed upon taking office and he could not follow through during that crucial period of Alaska's transition from territorial government. The newborn state was a ship without a rudder. It might well have foundered at the outset, as so many opponents were predicting, had not several inconspicuous Alaskans stepped in to establish the framework for a modern and stable new state government.

John Rader, then chair of the House majority caucus, and Tom Stewart, chair of the Senate Judiciary Committee, drafted most of the legislation establishing the executive branch. They conferred daily with Egan in the hospital, where they presented documents for him to approve and sign. These two lawyers also worked closely with the Judicial Council in setting up the state court system. They searched out the qualified candidates and greatly influenced the governor in appointing good judges to sit on the state's first courts, thus enabling the state to launch its court system with an air of unimpeachable integrity. Doing much research for them, also out of the limelight, were two other competent lawyers, Gary Thurlow, a Harvard Law grad who was Egan's assistant, and John Hellenthal, whose father had been a noted territorial judge.

Just as largely unsung people helped set the state on a stable course, the same became true for the Municipality of Anchorage after the merger of the borough and city. In 1969, when oil money began to flow, Max

Hodel, who ran the Alaska Sales & Service auto dealership, took on the unpaid job of organizing a massive community study that mapped the future development of Anchorage. Known as Operation Breakthrough, this 30-member steering committee targeted and recommended solutions for 25 major problems, ranging from such basics as education and air and water pollution to such rarely addressed societal issues as alcoholism and minority group relations. That report provided a guide for the renaissance of the 1980s when Anchorage became the nation's fastest growing city and it remains a useful document today.

Much has been written about how royalties from the oil companies enrich this state. But I doubt that many in this generation know how the civic contributions of people brought here by the oil firms have also enriched our quality of life. In particular, the work of Frank Turpin, an Exxon executive sent here in 1978 to run the Alyeska Pipeline Co., stands out.

Turpin joined the Anchorage Chamber of Commerce at the time Bob Penney, the president, was asking members what the chamber should be doing to stem the outflow of people who come here to do business but leave soon after. We were losing too many good people through the rotating door.

"Bob, the chamber is just reacting to problems. It ought to be initiating things," Turpin recalls telling Penney. He committed the common mistake. The next thing Turpin knew Penney assigned him to head a task force to find out how the chamber should be initiating solutions before problems occur.

Turpin went at it with all of the tenaciousness of a man looking for new oil. With no budget to work with, he visited the leading businesses in Anchorage, including the oil companies, and asked that each lend him a good employee for six weeks to work on the study. The result: a report titled "Anchors Aweigh, Anchorage" and in it a ringing conclusion that improving the quality of life in Anchorage would be the best way to encourage permanent residents. With it, Turpin presented a comprehensive plan for beautifying the city with more parks, bike trails, and flowers.

One of the members of Turpin's task force happened to be Tony Knowles, a Yale graduate who operated a downtown restaurant. Knowles subsequently was elected mayor. It was no coincidence that he ran on a city beautification platform. He not only implemented many of the recommendations in Turpin's report, but his reputation as the mayor who made Anchorage the city of parks, flowers and cultural amenities still served him well in his successful bid for governor in 1994.

It was amazing what citizens can accomplish when they are committed to improving the place they live. They can also make politicians in office look very good. Another who discovered this was George Sullivan, the first mayor of the Municipality of Anchorage.

I regarded Sullivan as a deadbeat and a showoff in the mid-1960s when he served as mayor of the city before unification. We had a good city manager and the mayor's office then was a ceremonial position. Nevertheless, on taking office, Sullivan resigned his job as manager of the Consolidated Freightways trucking firm and opened a mayor's office in City Hall and three years later the city council voted him a salary. We regularly editorially blistered Sullivan and council over his encampment.

When borough and city merged into the Municipality of Anchorage in 1975, the people rejected the city manager form of government and voted for a strong mayor. Sullivan beat out Jack Roderick, an attorney-journalist who had been mayor of the Anchorage borough. That is when Sullivan's life took off. He immediately grasped the problems of the fast-growing municipality and began to implement the recommendations produced in the study by the aforementioned citizen army under Max Hodel. Many good things happened. When Sullivan retired as mayor after serving 14 years, I was so impressed by his leadership that I tried to convince him to run for governor. I even promised him support of the paper, something I never did before or since. He gracefully declined and chose to step back and accept retirement from public life.

I concede that those who say the Times was too hard on Sullivan during those early days are correct. Editors have to make judgment calls every day of publication. We make mistakes. However, I make no apologies for what some consider the greatest shortcoming of my years at the Times—my support of development of this state when risks of changing the environment were at issue. I have taken much heat over the years from environmentalists, especially the brainwashed breed just out of college. They have never been taught that responsible development is not only good business but is also compatible with sustaining a healthy environment.

I was their bogeyman in the great green debate over effects of building the Trans-Alaska Pipeline in the 1970s. We stood alone, among the major Alaska newspapers, in attacking the costly pipeline delays resulting from the heavy environmental lobbying on Congress. And while the Fairbanks News-Miner for one began editorializing after pipeline construction that Alaska needs "no more progress," we disagreed. We kept urging companies that feed off the oil industry to establish offices here and encourage their workers to become citizens of Alaska.

Were we wrong? The environmental record of the Trans-Alaska pipeline is exceptional. It has become a model for permafrost construction that is studied by other countries and is a tourist attraction. Judging by their increased numbers, caribou love it. Cruise ships that visit Valdez offer a side trip to see the pipeline.

Meanwhile, firms that do business with the oil industry have settled here. Along with the personnel maintained in Anchorage by the major oil companies, these auxiliary work forces help stabilize the population, making our businesses and cultural centers less dependent on the shifting military population and the transients who come up in the summer.

I have suffered my share of setbacks (the failure to get the capital moved still hurts) and personal pain. The death of my Evangeline in 1987 robbed me of a much-needed stabilizer and co-pilot during these recent years when I had to make important decisions about the fate of the Times. The death of my older daughter, Marilyn, in 1994 has further depleted our little family. That leaves my remaining daughter, Elaine, to carry forth the Atwood commitment to Alaska after I am gone.

Yet, no setback or sadness can overtake the comfort I have in knowing that the biggest battle of my life—the campaign for statehood—has made Alaska a better place to live and an important contributor to the strength of the United States. Statehood has done for the nation just about everything we Alaskans promised it would do. Consider this abbreviated list:

••Alaska, which had never been important in the national economy, is now the number one state in oil production, providing about 25 percent of the nation's needs. And it contains the last of the nation's unexplored, high potential oil fields.

••Alaska has provided stable, loyal outposts for strategic military facilities that served well in the Cold War and remain an integral part of the nation's defense system.

••Alaska is the home of 85 percent of all the land in national wildlife refuges in our nation, providing the few remaining sanctuaries in the world where wild animals roam free and people can still find wilderness without man's footprints.

••Besides enriching the gross national product, this young, sparsely settled state has provided men with important leadership roles in federal government. Sen. Ted Stevens with 28 years in office has become the second most powerful man on the Senate Appropriations Committee, through which all federal money must flow. His colleague, Sen. Frank Murkowski, 16 years in office, is chairman of the Senate's Energy and Natural Resources Committee. Our one congressman, Don Young, has 24 years in office and heads the House Resources Committee. Since the 1994 election, these two Alaska congressmen have held the most powerful positions in overseeing all environmental legislation that comes before Congress. Alaska has also produced a Secretary of Interior (Hickel) and a U.S. ambassador to Brazil (Tony Motley).

I do not believe Alaskans receive the credit due them for the responsible way we have accepted the mantle of statehood. The national media still focuses on our bear attacks, wolf snarings, and quirky happenings in the wilds. Somehow we still are not regarded as equal partners and the Lower 48 attitude is that our destiny is to remain locked up as a giant park for people to visit and a place where the nation's last healthy packs of wild wolves can roam free (however marauding they might become).

And how has the federal government treated us since statehood? Implicit in the compact we signed jointly is the understanding that the Statehood Act could not be amended by a unilateral action of either party. Yet, consider these unilateral actions taken by the federal government to the detriment of Alaska citizens since that compact was signed:

••Congress passed a law forbidding Alaska from exporting North Slope crude oil to its natural and nearby markets, the countries on the growing Pacific Rim. Since oil must go to domestic markets, Alaska is further penalized because the archaic Jones Act mandates it can be shipped only on the rusting, expensive U.S. merchant marine fleet, which the act protects. The loss to the state alone since 1977 has averaged between $171 million and $283 million per year and it costs the federal treasury between $1.2 billion and $1.8 billion depending on how price effects are calculated. (Even the nation's liberal president, Bill Clinton, finally recognized the unfairness and in 1996 signed legislation lifting the export ban—but not the despised Jones Act.)

••In 1980, Congress passed the Alaska National Interest Lands Conservation Act that dedicated more than 100 million acres of Alaska land to federal conservation systems such as national parks and preserves, wildlife refuges, national forests, wilderness areas and wild and scenic rivers. This effectively abrogated terms of the statehood compact in that it all but prevents Alaskans from oil and mineral development in those areas, a lockup that cost the state estimated revenues of some $29 billion so far.

••In expanding the boundaries of the Arctic National Wildlife Range under the 1980 act, Congress designated a 1.5 million strip near the coast of the Arctic Ocean (about 8 percent of the range's total acreage) for further study of its wildlife and its oil and gas resources. Despite the nation's growing dependency on foreign oil (about 50 percent today compared to 30 percent 10 years ago), Congress refuses to permit even a limited exploration to determine the potential of the coastal plain—perhaps the greatest reason why Alaskans feel that the federal government is not respecting its commitment to help the state develop its resources.

Undoing this lingering national misunderstanding, or ignorance, of the rights of Alaskans who built this great state is our biggest challenge today. During his recent term as governor, Hickel went to the courts to try to force the issue. His several suits against the federal government claiming many billions of dollars in damages were belittled by constitutional historians and lost the first round in the courts. However, Governor Knowles has continued the legal battle, undoubtedly hoping that a new court and new rulings will take a dimmer view of federal powers and give state's rights a fairer hearing.

I would much rather see an enlightened nation elect an enlightened congress and presidential administration that would face up to the damage that unilateral federal intervention has done to the rights of Alaskans. But today's society seems to demand that lawyers and judges settle our disputes. If the adversarial course is the only way to go, I stand ready to testify from the viewpoint of one who was there at the beginning that Alaska has lived up to its commitment in the statehood compact and that, unfortunately, the federal government has not.

I have great faith that the American people still have the spirit to correct blatant injustices. As more and more people visit this state to admire its natural wonders, it is my hope that they will learn more about us. They will see that Alaskans are not ice-bound oddballs, that we share the same ambitions to get ahead in life, and that we have a great respect for preserving our natural treasures as we seek to become economically self-sufficient. It is my hope that increased public understanding, rather than costly and prolonged litigation, will persuade Congress to lift those federal shackles that still single out Alaskans and prevent us from enjoying full rights of citizenship in the United States.

As I take stock of my years here, I realize that the hard work and struggles along the way have been outweighed by the fun and joy. Never did I anticipate when I arrived so long ago that Alaska would become my love. Nor did I expect to find so many caring people pulling together against often forbidding natural and political elements. Most people know our natural wonders are great. I hope these personal reflections will add a dimension of knowledge about the brave, diverse people who made this state great.

The Atwood family. From Left: Bob's younger daughter, Sara Elaine; Bob Atwood; Bob's wife Evangeline and his older daughter Marilyn.

274 | CHAPTER NINETEEN

Epilogue

After the death of Bob Atwood on Dec. 10, 1997, the task of completing the story of his life fell to his younger daughter, Sara Elaine Atwood.

Bob's wife, Evangeline, died in November 1987, and his older daughter, Marilyn, passed away in October 1994. Elaine, as the family's only survivor, had the multiple tasks of managing her father's estate, assuming the chairmanship of the Atwood Foundation, and as time permitted doing the final editing of this book.

She was no novice, of course, in the field of editing and publishing. Beginning in 1964, she was a writer and editor for The Anchorage Times. In the later years of her father's leadership of the newspaper, she served as assistant publisher and was directly involved in all Times editorial, personnel and business operations.

During the years her father spent at his computer keyboard writing his story of Alaska, she was his constant advisor and editor. And a demanding editor she was, too — no easy task, considering her father's own credentials as a much-honored publisher, editor and writer.

Despite being in declining health for the past five years of her life, she devoted considerable time to work on her father's book — in the end, going through it line-by-line in the process of the final editing. She also personally handled the massive task of assembling Steve McCutcheon's marvelous photos which she and her father had selected to illustrate this book. Unfortunately, she did not live to see the book in print.

Elaine Atwood died at her Anchorage home, the Marilaine, on Jan. 30, 2003, just two weeks before she would have observed her 63rd birthday.

— W.J.T.